NO KING BUT CHRIST

The story of Donald Cargill

Maurice Grant

EVANGELICAL PRESS
12 Wooler Street, Darlington, Co. Durham, DL1 1RQ, England.
© Evangelical Press

First published 1988

British Library Cataloguing in Publication Data
Grant, Maurice
No King but Christ: the story of Donald Cargill
I. Title
285'.2'0924

ISBN 0-85234-255-1

Typeset by Outset Graphics, Hartlepool.
Printed in Great Britain by The Bath Press, Avon.

I have followed holiness, I have taught truth, and I have been most in the main things.

Donald Cargill,
Last Testimony, 1681

For the winter storms did not hinder him; for he preached to the people when it was raining, snowing, hailing on his head and bare hands; it being ordinary for him still in preaching and praying to hold them up to heaven, where his conversation was.

Testimony of Robert Hamilton of Preston

Contents

Preface

When he published his biography of Richard Cameron in 1896 Professor John Herkless remarked that he had found the 'lion of the Covenant' to be a lion in his den. He could hardly get at him: the materials for a biography were so scanty that the author grew alarmed, wondering how to make his quota of bricks with so little straw. If that was the case with Richard Cameron, it is still more so with Donald Cargill. Even in 1714, when the first edition of the *Cloud of Witnesses* was published, the compilers were obliged to admit that while a true and full relation of his life was 'very necessary' there were not in their hands 'such well-attested narrations thereof as might furnish them with an exact and full history thereof'. At this greater distance in time, without the benefit of contemporary recollection, the task is undeniably still more daunting. But in some respects it is easier: the public records of the period have been extensively indexed and codified; many records, formerly in private hands, have become available for public inspection; and the painstaking researches of genealogists have brought to light many hitherto unrecorded facts. As a result it is possible to throw some rays of light on parts of Cargill's life which were formerly shrouded in obscurity. The image, certainly, is still dimmed in outline and parts of it will doubtless never be clarified completely; but enough is revealed to enable a consistent and credible picture to emerge.

Some of the traditions that have grown up around the men and women who suffered for their faith in seventeenth-century Scotland have tended to represent them as adherents of a movement which was diverse in some way from the main current of Scottish Presbyterianism. Cargill is well enough known as one of the principal figures of the period, but it is around him particularly that many of these misconceptions have tended to concentrate. Too often he has been depicted, even by not unfriendly hands, as something of an austere dogmatist, clinging obstinately to a fanatical creed which brought himself and his followers into needless conflict with the authorities. It has been part of my purpose to show that, on the contrary, the principles for which Cargill contended lay at the very heart of the Scottish reformed tradition, and that the actions which he took were of the highest importance in preserving the historic testimony of the Scottish church. The result is, I hope, to place Cargill's position in a truer historical perspective and to dispel some of the misunderstandings which have gathered around his life and character.

It only remains for me to acknowledge the help I have received in the preparation of this work. My thanks are particularly due to the Librarian of New College Library, Edinburgh, for permission to quote from Dr Robert B. Tweed's valuable unpublished thesis on Cargill's family background and formative influences. I am also indebted to Dr David Lachman who read the manuscript and made valuable suggestions; to the staffs of the University Libraries of Edinburgh, Glasgow and St Andrews, the National Library of Scotland and H.M. Register House, Edinburgh, for their ready co-operation in my researches, and to Miss Anna Campbell for her assistance with typing.

Maurice Grant
EDINBURGH
September 1988

1.
The early years

The lands of Cargill, on the borders of Perth and Angus, are first mentioned in Scottish history about the middle of the twelfth century. Many centuries earlier, the area around Cargill, at the foothills of the Grampians, had marked the northernmost limits of the advance of the Roman legions under Agricola and, according to one tradition, the lands took their name from one of the forts built by the Romans to hold their line of advance against the northern tribes. Situated as it was in the fertile plain of Strathmore, watered by the Tay and the Isla, Cargill was a very desirable spot for a landholding; and under the feudal system operated by Malcolm Canmore and his successors it was granted as a barony as early as the end of the twelfth century. The first recorded use of the name as a surname occurs in the middle of the thirteenth century, when one 'Peter of Kergill' witnessed a charter during the episcopate of Geoffrey, Bishop of Dunkeld (1236-1249). Some years later, in 1260, a 'Walter of Kergyl' is recorded as a witness to a land transaction at Perth. This provides clear evidence that the name of the lands had been adopted by the proprietor, or feudal tenant, as was often the case, and through time the name passed to his family and descendants.

The association of the lands of Cargill with the Cargill family seems, however, to have ended before the end of the thirteenth century, when they were apparently exchanged for the lands of Lasington in the north-east of the Cargill barony. These lands were in turn exchanged some two centuries later for the lands of Kinloch in the same area. With the disposal of the latter in the mid-sixteenth century, the association of the Cargill line with their original homeland came to a close. By then, however, the Cargills had extended their influence far beyond their original area: collateral branches had established themselves in Angus, Aberdeen and other parts of the country, and in the neighbouring Perthshire parishes they had become particularly numerous.

By this time the social and political life of the country was undergoing rapid change. Old values and traditions, adhered to for centuries, were being cast aside; and the country was entering on the period of religious and political ferment which was to culminate in the triumph of the Protestant Reformation. The counties of Perth and Angus were among the foremost in the struggle, and some of their leading families played a prominent part in the tumultuous events which led to the final success of the Reformation in 1560. The destruction of the monasteries at Perth in May 1559, following John Knox's famous sermon there, was one of the most notable of these events, and the towns of Perth, Dundee, Brechin and Arbroath were settled with Protestant ministers as early as September of that year. It is fairly clear therefore that the part of the country where the Cargills were most numerous, and their influence most prominent, was one of the first to feel the impact of the Reformation and to participate in its effects.

It is not altogether surprising, then, to find that on 21 May 1574, at the Palace of Holyroodhouse in Edinburgh, there was issued a warrant in the name of the boy king James VI, appointing a young man by the name of Donald Cargill as 'reader' to the vacant parish of Rattray.[1] Donald Cargill was almost certainly a native of either the parish of Rattray or the parish of Blairgowrie, and the social position which he apparently enjoyed suggests that he could well have been a son of John Cargill of Kinloch, the last member of the Cargills of Lasington and Kinloch, and so a direct descendant of the original Cargill line. The office to which he was appointed was a temporary expedient adopted by the newly-formed Church of Scotland until an adequate number of ordained ministers could be settled to the parishes: in this early period of its existence the church found it convenient to employ the services of young men of good character and education to read the Scriptures to the people and, if found fit for the work, to exercise a preaching ministry. Such a man was young Donald Cargill, born perhaps about 1550, and obviously the recipient of a good education, probably at the University of Aberdeen or St Andrews. The young man successfully passed his qualifications for the readership, and was duly admitted to the office. His appointment carried with it the tenancy of the vacant 'vicarage' of Rattray, and he accordingly assumed the title of 'vicar' soon after his settlement in the parish. This office he continued to hold for the remaining forty-nine years of his life, serving for the first seventeen years on his own, and remaining on, apparently as a preaching assistant, after the settlement of an ordained minister in 1591.

Shortly after his settlement in the parish Donald Cargill married, and in time he became the father of two sons and two daughters. But times were difficult and, probably to help him support his wife and growing family, he decided to supplement his modest income as reader by practising the skills in law he had learned as a student. In April 1583, nine years after being appointed to the readership, he was admitted as a 'notary public', or local solicitor,[2] and he continued to practise his legal profession concurrently with his preaching ministry for the rest of his life. As preacher and notary Donald Cargill's place in the parish was clearly of the first importance, and the advancement of the reformed faith among his parishioners, and particularly in his immediate family, was obviously due in no small measure to the weight of his influence.

Donald Cargill's elder son John, who was born about 1582, followed in his father's footsteps. About 1607 or 1608, at the age of twenty-five, he too was admitted as a 'notary public', and when he married in 1614, by which time he had been ordained an elder in his father's church, he set up in business on his own account as a lawyer. His brother Lawrence, the youngest member of the family, was not born until about 1600, and so was little more than a boy by the time his elder brother had embarked on his profession. Lawrence stayed on for some years with his father, helping him with his legal work, and on occasion also helping his brother. Eventually, in 1623, after a lifetime of service to the parish, Donald died.

Lawrence seems to have continued living in the family home
for a further three years, until in 1626 he too married and set
up a home of his own. His bride, Marjory Blair, was a first
cousin on his mother's side, a daughter of Patrick Blair, of
Ardblair in the parish of Blairgowrie. They settled in the
small landholding of Nether Cloquhat, near Bridge of Cally,
which Lawrence had bought in May 1626 as a future home for
himself and his wife. It was apparently here, some time in the
following year, that their eldest son Donald, the subject of
this biography, was born.[3] He was the first of five children,
two sons and three daughters, who were eventually to be born
to Lawrence and Marjory Cargill. Not for long, however,
were the family to remain in their first home at Nether
Cloquhat. About 1632 Lawrence's brother John died, not
much past middle life, and two years later, when Donald was
six or seven years of age, Lawrence sold Nether Cloquhat and
returned with his young family to Rattray, where he took a
tenancy of the small estate of Bonnytown. There he set up in
business as a notary in succession to his father and brother,
and for the remaining twenty-three years of his life continued
to pursue an apparently successful practice.[4]

It is likely that old Donald Cargill had provided his two sons
with a good education, and Lawrence was determined that his
own sons should enjoy the same advantage. One of the most
noted schools of the time was the Grammar School at Aberdeen, where Lawrence may well have been educated himself.
In any event it seems fairly clear that he had the means to
realize his wish, and that it was to Aberdeen that he sent his
eldest son Donald, probably about the year 1637, when he
was nine or ten years of age. It is reasonable to assume that
Lawrence Cargill was hoping to train his son in the legal profession to succeed him in the practice, but, as subsequent
events were to show, he also cherished for him a deeper ambition which he could not yet reveal. Lawrence had grown up
surrounded by strong religious influences, and his father's
long service in the parish had brought him into close contact
with the work of the ministry. It was a calling which, though
Lawrence had not followed it himself, he deeply cherished for
his son. He had brought him up in the same home environment and surrounded by the same influences which he himself

had known in his boyhood.[5] But Lawrence well knew that the
ministry was not a mere profession, in the same sense as the
law, and he had no intention of pressing his son into it until he
knew him to be spiritually qualified for the work in hand.

Young Donald's arrival in Aberdeen coincided with the
outburst of national feeling which had greeted the king's
attempt to impose the new Service Book and Canons on the
church, and which culminated in the signing of the National
Covenant in Edinburgh in February 1638. The country was in
a ferment of agitation and Aberdeen shared in the general
upheaval. The city had never been noted for its sympathies
with the Presbyterian cause and initially its attitude to the
Covenant was no more than lukewarm. But internal influences and external pressures gradually combined to change
that position. Some of the more influential of the city magistrates were firm Covenanters, and when the Marquis of
Montrose, in his early zeal for the Covenant, arrived in the
city in March 1639 he found little opposition. The Covenant
was duly signed by the local population and Aberdeen took its
stand behind the national effort to preserve the liberties of the
church. The aims of the Covenant were strongly advocated by
two prominent local ministers, Andrew Cant and John Row,
both of whom exercised a powerful influence. In the years
that followed, Aberdeen suffered severely in the civil disorders which accompanied the struggle between king and
Parliament, most notably in September 1644, when Montrose, now fighting for the king, took the city by storm and
gave it over to be plundered by his troops.

Cargill could not fail to be influenced by these events. His
home background had strongly predisposed him in favour of
the cause of the Covenant, and it seems clear that the impressions he gained at Aberdeen served to reinforce that influence. His cousin Patrick, with whom he seems to have lodged,
was a merchant in the city, and appears to have been a prominent supporter of the Covenanting cause. He would also, in
all probability, have come under the same influences at
school, where the sons of many of the local protagonists of the
Covenant would have been his classroom companions. He
probably also heard the preaching of Cant and Row and
perhaps also William Robertson, another fervent supporter

of the Covenant, who ministered at St Clement's Chapel
throughout this period.[6]

The most profound influence on Cargill's life at this time
may, however, have come from an unexpected source which
was to play a still more prominent part in his development in
the years ahead. Samuel Rutherford, formerly minister of
Anwoth in Galloway, had been banished from his parish for
nonconformity, and had arrived in exile in Aberdeen in 1636.
While there, he may have had some little liberty to preach privately, and it would not have been surprising if he had
gathered around him a band of sympathizers for the same
cause. If Donald Cargill was among that group — and it is not
fanciful to suppose that he was — it would have marked for
him the start of an association that was to have the most profound influence upon him in later life.

By 1643, when he was fifteen or sixteen years of age,
Donald had completed his schooling. The next logical step
was university, and so towards the end of that year he seems
to have turned his steps towards the University of Aberdeen,
where he embarked on a course of philosophy. Whether he
had any indication of his future calling at this time is not clear,
but in any event it is doubtful whether he enjoyed much freedom to study, for by this time the civil disorders in the country
had reached their height. These culminated in the capture
and sacking of the city by Montrose in September 1644, following which the cause of the Covenant went into a temporary decline. For Cargill the change of circumstances must
have been particularly discouraging, quite apart from the dis-
ruption which it caused to his university course, and he
appears to have decided, probably towards the end of 1644, to
leave Aberdeen and to continue his education at St Andrews.
It is likely that there he hoped to find not only peace and quiet
to pursue his studies, but also an atmosphere more generally
to his liking, since St Andrews had been largely insulated
from the civil disorders of the time and was noted as a main
centre of support for the Covenant. At all events he is on
record as having matriculated in the second year philosophy
class at St Salvator's College early in 1645.[7] The remainder of
his course was apparently uneventful, and he seems to have
graduated in the summer of 1647. He then appears to have

St. Salvators College
St. Andrews - Fife

returned to his family home in Rattray, probably with the intention of gaining further practical experience in his father's profession in preparation for succeeding him in the notary's chair.

But events were destined to move differently. It is fairly clear that the strong religious impressions of Donald's home background had been quickened by his experiences at school and university, and particularly no doubt by his contacts with Rutherford and the others of his company whom he had met. These were soon to issue in a climax. The background to the great spiritual crisis of his life is not altogether clear, but it seems that shortly after completing his university course, probably in that same summer of 1647, Donald accompanied his father on a visit to family relatives in the Bothwell district of Clydesdale, not far from Glasgow. Who these relatives were is not now known, and it is futile to speculate,[8] but it was while he was there, apparently later that same summer, that his spiritual crisis reached its height. The religious impressions of his early life, reinforced by those he had gathered at Aberdeen and St Andrews, were suddenly borne home to his conscience with a fearful power. He felt utterly crushed; his spirit was overwhelmed with a sense of the justice and awful holiness of God and of his own worthlessness and wretchedness. Nowhere could he find relief. His was not the temperament which could seek solace from confiding its sorrows to others: he chose to bear the burden alone.

At last, grief gave way to despair. A wretch such as he was not fit to live: he deserved only to be in hell. He would do away with himself rather than continue to live in such a condition. Opportunity readily offered. And so, one day, as he recounted later, he went down to the edge of the Clyde, and stood poised on the verge. But his purpose was frustrated; for each time that he prepared to throw himself into the river he was disturbed by someone passing on the road above. So far was he from regarding this as the voice of Providence, that he became even more determined to achieve his purpose. If he could not drown himself, he would take his life in some other way.

The countryside around Bothwell had long been known for coal-mining operations, and the landscape was strewn with

St. Andrews - Fife

the relics of abandoned mineworkings and unprotected
shafts. He decided he would throw himself into one of these,
and at last put an end to his wretched life. And so, very early
one morning, he set out for the chosen spot. He reached the
edge of the pit. Deliberately he prepared himself. He shed his
outer clothing, for it was new and would be of use to someone
else. He stood poised on the brink. And then, just as he prepared for the final leap, there came to him a voice, clear and
unmistakable: 'Son, be of good cheer, thy sins are forgiven
thee.' To Cargill it was none other than the voice of God and,
as he himself was to tell later, it came with such life and power
as at once to put an end to all his fears and doubts, and he
could no more resist it than he could the light of a sunbeam
darted upon his eye. He was filled immediately with not only
an inward peace, but with an unshakeable assurance of his
salvation that was to remain with him to the end of his life. 'I
bless the Lord,' he was to say years later, 'that these thirty
years and more I have been at peace with God, and was never
shaken loose of it.'

Cargill evidently concluded that he had been prepared in a
very special way for a very special work; for by being able to
'lay aside as assured' his own salvation, as he himself liked to
put it, he was able to devote himself the more completely to
the salvation of others, and to the honour of the cause and
interest of Christ. It is impossible to gain a proper understanding of his character, or the actions he took in later life,
without taking account of this early experience. It gave direction and purpose to his entire life and, while he remained by
nature diffident and self-depreciating, he was able from this
time onwards to act with determination and conviction in the
things which to him now mattered most of all.

To no one could the effects of Donald Cargill's momentous
experience have been so evident — or so deeply gratifying —
as to his father. His prayers for his son had been answered
beyond all his expectations, and now at last he could reveal to
him his long-cherished ambition. As soon as his son's fitness
for the work had become clear to him, Lawrence began to
urge him, with a kindly but pressing insistence, to dedicate
himself to the duty of the ministry. But at first he had little
success; for while young Donald was now receptive to the

things of the Spirit his natural temperament was averse to his father's desire and he shrank from the thought of the responsibilities being pressed upon him. He was conscious too, as much as ever anyone was, of the tremendous solemnity of the ministerial calling and of the danger of 'running unsent', and he pleaded with his father that he was unfitted for the work. But his father was not to be denied; and so Donald yielded so far as to devote one day to prayer and meditation to seek God's will. At the end of it he was no longer in any doubt. As he had meditated there had come to him, with telling power, the words from Ezekiel 3:1: 'Son of man, eat this roll, and go speak unto the house of Israel.' It was God's commission to the prophet and it was Cargill's call to the ministry. It was a call that came from God himself, an irresistible call that had to be obeyed at whatever cost. Many years later he was to say, 'The Master must be obeyed, his commands must be done . . . as we should never run uncalled, so we should never sit when our Master commands us to run . . . when the Master speaks, the servant ought to be at command.' For Cargill the Master had spoken; and from that moment the servant was at his command.

There now lay before him a period of some four years' divinity study as a preliminary to licence for the ministry. There was no doubt about where he would go to receive his training: St Mary's College, St Andrews, where Samuel Rutherford was now Professor of Divinity, and later principal, was the obvious choice. Accordingly Cargill went there, probably in the early months of 1648. It was a move which at once brought him into direct contact with the major influence on his early life. Rutherford, then at the height of his powers, had recently returned to St Andrews after a four-year absence in England, where he had been one of the Scottish Commissioners to the Westminster Assembly. While there he had published a series of works on practical theology and church and civil government which, together with earlier works on similar themes, had marked him out as a scholar and divine of outstanding ability and earned for him a national and even international reputation.

Rutherford's position was strictly that of the Reformers, and in the field of church government he followed in the

Samuel Rutherford

direct succession of Andrew Melville, who held the office of principal of St Mary's College at the beginning of the century. It was Melville who declared, in a memorable interview with King James VI, 'Sir, there are two kings and two kingdoms in Scotland; there is King James the head of this Common-wealth, and there is King Jesus the King of the Church, whose subject King James VI is, and of whose kingdom he is not a king, nor a lord, nor a head, but a member.' This principle of the spiritual independence of the church, which lay at the very heart of Scottish Presbyterianism, had been defended by Melville, often at great personal cost, against the encroach-ments of the king and nobles, and in Rutherford it found an equally vigorous protagonist. In his theological and practical works, which display an erudition seldom excelled, Ruther-ford applied all his massive powers to assert the sovereignty of the church in her own sphere and the distinctive but com-plementary responsibilities of church and state. It is certain that Rutherford asserted this principle no less vigorously in his lectures to his students. For him, indeed, it was of the very essence of revealed religion; it was a reflection of the sovereignty of God, on which reformed theology had placed such leading emphasis. Christ's headship of the church had been determined by God the Father and revealed in his Word, and to disregard or deviate from that standard was to question the divine authority itself. Viewed in that light, the Presbyterian system was a logical extension of reformed doc-trine; the ecclesiastical structure developed by Melville was a natural development of the work of Knox and his fellow Reformers.[9]

Both in doctrine and in practice then, the teaching in Rutherford's classroom was the classical teaching of the Scot-tish Reformation. In his application of these great truths Rutherford could draw on resources not only of intellect but of deep spiritual experience. It was this blend of the intellec-tual and the spiritual, the doctrinal and the devotional, that made his influence so profound and that left an enduring impression on his students. As an aid to his teaching he had skilfully adapted to his use the scholastic method of argument and debate then so much in vogue in the schools and univer-sities, and with which his students were well familiar from their academic training. In the propositions and syllogisms of this formal system Rutherford strove to convey the profound spiritual truths which he taught, harnessing the methods of the schoolmen to the service of the divinity class. For Cargill in particular this form of teaching was calculated to have a special appeal. It was something he could relate to his past experience and which he could readily absorb. In Rutherford's lectures he could find an echo of his previous training in philosophy, and a sympathy with his own logical cast of thought. Both by his manner and method then, no less than by his personality and influence, Rutherford contrived to imprint his teaching with a particular emphasis upon Cargill's mind. There are sound grounds for concluding that Rutherford's influence was the decisive factor in Cargill's early spiritual development, and the impact of that influence can be traced in many of his actions and utterances in later life. For Cargill the opportunity to give practical expression to Rutherford's teaching was to come in full measure in later years — not indeed in the academic environment which may have been his preference, but in conditions far more testing and in circumstances infinitely more difficult.

During his stay at St Andrews Donald Cargill had the opportunity to make the acquaintance of other young men of his age who were studying for the ministry and who were to be settled as ministers in later life. With one of these, Robert M'Ward, who acted as Rutherford's secretary at the Westminster Assembly, he established a friendship which was to continue for many years and to witness many changes of fortune. Another young man, James Blair, who was a son of the noted Robert Blair, minister of St Andrews, was a fellow-student at both St Salvator's and St Mary's College. With a third, Alexander Jamieson, later minister of Govan in Glasgow, Cargill formed a friendship that again was to last beyond their student days and to endure through difficult times ahead. These friendships, however deep they may have been, were clearly not so important for his future as the influence of Rutherford, but they meant that during his time in the divinity class Cargill enjoyed the fellowship of like-minded companions whose society could not but reinforce the influence of his teacher.

Donald Cargill seems to have completed his divinity course early in 1652. His movements over the following three years are somewhat uncertain, but the available evidence suggests that on completion of his studies at St Mary's College he returned once more to Rattray, where his parents were still living, and applied to his local presbytery — the Presbytery of Dunkeld — for licence to the ministry. For this he needed to produce a testimonial from his teachers at St Andrews, which seems to have been readily granted, and also to undergo a series of 'trials' or exercises, which it was customary for the presbyteries to prescribe. These consisted of a homily or discourse on a text prescribed by the presbytery, a discourse in Latin on a chosen head of divinity, a popular sermon, a lecture or exposition on a chapter of Scripture, a critical interpretation and application of a prescribed passage, an examination in the original languages and questions on ecclesiastical history and on church government and discipline. The trials normally extended over a period of six months and provided a stern test of the applicant's preaching and intellectual abilities. Cargill apparently acquitted himself to the presbytery's satisfaction and probably received his licence towards the end of 1652. He then appears to have returned once more to St Andrews, for his name is found associated with the St Andrews Presbytery at intervals between April 1653 and March 1655. He could not have been a full member of the presbytery, since he was not yet an ordained minister, but he appears to have attended several of their meetings around this time and he took a regular part in their devotional exercises. The inference appears to be that he had assumed duties of some kind which involved his residence within the bounds of the St Andrews Presbytery, and that while there he had placed himself under the presbytery's jurisdiction as an 'expectant', or probationer, in order to further his preparation for the ministry and also, no doubt, in the hope that when called to a charge in the area he would have the presbytery's recommendation to support him.[10]

While there is no documentary evidence to indicate the nature of Cargill's business in St Andrews, the mere fact of his return, so soon after receiving licence to preach, suggests that he was hoping to renew some acquaintance made in the area

during his university days and possibly to establish it on a
more permanent basis. It was a well-known custom for young
men training for the ministry, both at this time and later, to
take on appointments as private tutors or chaplains to
families of the local nobility and to occupy themselves in this
way during the long university vacations. If Cargill had taken
on such an appointment — and it is very possible that he had
— later events strongly suggest that the family with whom he
had associated himself were the Beatons or Bethunes of
Blebo, a country estate some five miles to the west of the university town. The Laird of Blebo, Andrew Beaton, was a
noted Covenanter, an elder in his local congregation, and a
member of the St Andrews Presbytery. It is entirely credible
then that Cargill, having shared the fellowship and friendship
of the Beatons during his divinity training, and perhaps
earlier, should now have returned to resume his duties as
their chaplain, while at the same time preparing himself in
association with the St Andrews Presbytery for the wider
work of the ministry.

Sadly, Cargill's association with the Beatons, which was
obviously intimate and close, was soon to be clouded by
tragedy. In June 1653 Andrew Beaton died, leaving a widow
and a family of six children. Cargill, who must have felt the
loss keenly, appears to have stayed on at Blebo for some considerable time thereafter, combining his work as tutor and
chaplain to the Beaton family with a preaching ministry in
various charges in the St Andrews Presbytery. Having placed
himself under the presbytery's jurisdiction he was obliged to
confine his preaching — except with their consent — within
their own bounds, so that the opportunities open to him were
fairly limited. There were moreover a considerable number
of other 'expectants' within the presbytery, so that the competition for vacant charges at this time was relatively keen.

In the neighbouring Presbytery of Cupar, on the other
hand, the situation appears to have been rather different.
There, the parish of Strathmiglo, some ten miles to the west
of Cupar, had fallen vacant on the death of its minister, John
Murray, in October 1653. It was customary to give priority to
the claims of probationers to fill vacant charges, but the
Cupar Presbytery were apparently unable to call on any suit-

able probationers from within their own bounds. They therefore petitioned the St Andrews Presbytery, in December 1653, to send three of their probationers, whom they named, to preach at Strathmiglo with a view to a call. Among these three was Donald Cargill.

Having submitted himself to the authority of the presbytery, Cargill was morally obliged to follow their direction, and when they acceded to the Cupar Presbytery's request he went and preached at Strathmiglo on a day in early January 1654. His two colleagues preached there at around the same time. At the beginning of February the Strathmiglo elders reported to the presbytery that they had heard all three probationers with satisfaction, but that a few of their number wanted a wider choice before committing themselves to a call. The presbytery eventually granted the request, though not before being warned by one of their members that divisive elements were at work in the congregation and were attempting to frustrate a settlement. Invitations were sent to two further probationers, one from Perth and one from Edinburgh, to preach in the parish. One of the two preached in early April, but because of local opposition the other was not able to preach until late August, by which time the divisions in the congregation had become clearly marked. All parties now agreed, however, that the election of a minister should no longer be delayed, and it was duly arranged to take place after the morning service on 10 September.

On the due date, after public intimation, the Strathmiglo session convened. The names of the five probationers who had preached were brought forward and a vote taken. Of the twelve elders present, eight voted for Cargill and four for one of the other candidates, with none voting for the remaining three. The session's decision, however, on a majority vote, reflected the divided opinion of the congregation as a whole and, following the afternoon service, when the congregation were given an opportunity to dissent, three influential members, led by Lord Balfour of Burleigh, the principal local 'heritor' or landowner, lodged a formal protest against Cargill's election and asked for it to be presented to the presbytery. This effectively halted proceedings for the time being. In the meantime, until the presbytery met, Burleigh and his supporters were at pains to gather signatures among the parishioners in support of the dissent.

The presbytery's first reaction, after consulting the provincial synod for advice, was to convene a meeting of all the parties at Strathmiglo on 27 October, to try to achieve a settlement. A suggestion that a compromise candidate be adopted, in place of the two voted upon, failed to find favour with Cargill's supporters in the majority of the session, who insisted on their previous choice. The presbytery decided that the only way out of the impasse was to take a census of the congregation, for and against, and to decide the issue on the basis of the result. By the beginning of December the lists of assenters and dissenters were in the presbytery's hands and, after allowing a request by Burleigh that several dissenters who had not yet signed be permitted to do so, the presbytery appointed four of their number to scrutinize the lists and report the result to the next meeting. On 14 December, after due examination, the four ministers reported the dissenters to be in the majority. This, however, was by no means the end of the matter. Three of the elders, supporters of Cargill, put in a paper to the presbytery accusing Burleigh and his supporters of improper tactics and alleging that persons under church discipline had been allowed to subscribe the dissent. However, the elders declined to put their names to the paper and the presbytery were themselves divided on whether they should be ordered to do so. It was at this juncture, with matters becoming increasingly acrimonious and confused, that a development took place which changed the situation completely and solved the presbytery's difficulties for them in a quite unexpected way.[11]

It seems clear that, whatever the objections to Cargill's settlement may have been, they were not grounded on anything in his personal character or conduct, but rather reflected a deep division at this time in the life of the church as a whole. Since 1648, despite much spiritual advance, the peace of the church had been rent by a series of internal disputes. These had centred basically round the question of whether persons who had taken part in the ill-fated 'Engagement' in support of Charles I, or who were otherwise considered unsympathetic to the aims of the Covenants, should be given places of trust

in the army and judicatories of the country. The 'Resolutioners' as the moderate or liberal party were called, favoured
such a policy; the 'Protesters', who were in a minority after
1651, maintained that only those loyal to the Covenants
should be entrusted with such positions. Cargill's old teacher,
Rutherford, was the recognized leader of the Protesters and
naturally became the focus of the other side's opposition. As
principal of St Mary's College Rutherford was considered to
be in a position to influence his students, and any of them suspected of sharing his sympathies could expect little favour at
the hands of the opposite party. It is by no means improbable
that the Resolutioner majorities on the St Andrews and
Cupar Presbyteries, having identified Cargill as a supporter
of Rutherford, had used their influence to oppose his settlement within their bounds, and the contemporary evidence
would seem to support this view.[12] If so, it was the first of the
persecutions Cargill was to suffer at the hands of his fellow-
ministers, and by no means the last.

The dispute was producing similar unhappy effects in other
parts of the country. In Glasgow, where a majority of the
synod and presbytery were on Rutherford's side, particular
difficulty was being experienced in settling the vacant Barony
parish, which had been without a minister since the death of
its previous incumbent, the erudite and eccentric Zachary
Boyd, early in 1653.[13] Internal disagreements in the congregation had prevented unanimity in the choice of a successor
and the matter had been placed in the presbytery's hands. But
two influential members of the presbytery, Hugh Blair and
George Young, were fervent Resolutioners, and were suspected of conniving with the Town Council of Glasgow,
whose consent was needed to the settlement, to exclude any
minister who espoused the Protesters' cause. Eventually the
provincial synod, perturbed at the continuing delay,
appointed a special committee in October 1654 to work with
the presbytery to secure a settlement to the Barony and other
vacant charges. Several local probationers had apparently
already preached at the Barony and been rejected, and the
committee seem to have felt themselves obliged to look
further afield for a suitable candidate. How their choice was
determined cannot now be proved, but it is reasonable to

assume that they were guided partly by reports from sympathizers and partly perhaps by the personal recommen-
dations of some of their own number. At all events their
choice eventually fell on the disputed candidate for
Strathmiglo, Donald Cargill.

That Cargill should have been chosen, out of an undoubted
variety of possible candidates, was certainly a tribute to his
preaching reputation, which had evidently reached the Glasgow ministers; and if, as was likely, there was felt to be an el-
ement of victimization about his treatment at Strathmiglo, this
obviously counted further in his favour. Cargill, for his part,
could well have regarded the Glasgow ministers' intervention
as a special dispensation of Providence on his behalf. In his
present environment he had found little to encourage him; his
hopes of finding a charge had not been realized, and in the
divided state of the church his relations with the majority on
the St Andrews Presbytery were becoming distinctly
unhappy. He duly accepted the invitation, and early in 1655
went to preach at the Barony for a trial period. By doing so he
was effectively deserting his candidature for Strathmiglo, and
his departure for Glasgow was reported to the Cupar Presbytery on 22 February. Some weeks later, when Cargill's position had become clear beyond any doubt, the presbytery were
at last able to agree with the Strathmiglo parishioners that the
call to him should be regarded as at an end.

Notwithstanding his natural diffidence, which never completely deserted him, Cargill could well have set off for Glasgow with some reasonable hopes of success. He had been
given some cause for encouragement; the invitation bore all
the signs of divine guidance; and the prospect of fellowship
with ministers who shared his views and feelings so closely
was no doubt particularly inviting. It was then all the more
disappointing to him to find that the character of the congregation fell far below his expectations. They seemed to take
lightly the preaching of the Word and they appeared uncon-
cerned at the solemnity of his message. To a man who felt so
deeply the solemn responsibilities of the ministerial calling,
this was all intensely discouraging. Something of his old
doubts and fears returned. How could he preach when the
people were so unresponsive? Though he had arranged to

preach again the following Thursday, he determined not to stay. 'They are a rebellious people,' was his answer to the ministers who besought him to remain. In vain did the ministers urge him that if they had not known the people to be 'rebellious', they would not have asked him to preach to them. He was on the point of departure, with his horse ready, and bidding farewell to some few friends who had come to take leave of him at the house of James Durham, minister of the Inner High Kirk, when a woman in the company, Isobel Boyd, said to him suddenly with great earnestness, 'Sir, you have promised to preach on Thursday; and have you appointed a meal to a poor starving people, and will you go away and not give it? The curse of God will go with you.' The rebuke was devastating, but effective. Cargill, his resistance at last overcome, sat down in a chair, sighed deeply, and said to her with feeling, 'Then, Isobel Boyd, pray much for me.' In her rebuke he had heard the voice of the Master himself, reproving his faint-heartedness, pointing him to the path of duty and obedience. It was only one of many victories he had to win over his own spirit; there were to be numerous similar conflicts ahead of him.

With Cargill's own resistance ended, the other obstacles to his settlement speedily fell away. He received an apparently unanimous call from the people, and the Resolutioners in the presbytery, for some unknown reason, refrained from their usual opposition, though Cargill's views must have been well enough known to them. The town council, too, voiced no objection to his settlement. So unexpected was this turn of events that several of his contemporaries were convinced of a special intervention of Providence. Even the refusal of the St Andrews Presbytery to grant him a testimonial — a final token of their disfavour — did not impair his prospects.[14] If Cargill had needed any further evidence, it was not long forthcoming; for when he applied to the presbytery for ordination, the first text from which they asked him to preach was the very verse in Ezekiel which had come to him with such power in first determining him to enter the ministry. There was now no doubt or difficulty left. Towards the end of March 1655, amid much general satisfaction, he was successfully settled in the Barony, where, according to a contemporary, 'He continued to exercise his ministry with great success, to the unspeakable satisfaction of his own parish, and of all the godly who heard and knew him.'[15]

2.
The Barony of Glasgow

Donald Cargill began his ministry in Glasgow in a period of spiritual prosperity for the Church of Scotland. Some 100 years earlier, at the time of the Reformation, a spiritual revolution had taken place in the country and the effects of that momentous event still lingered. But through time the structure of the Reformation church had been eroded by the Stuart monarchy, who saw in the imposition of an episcopal system a means of curbing the independence of the church and bringing it effectively into subservience to the state. Such a system suited the autocratic conception of monarchy held by James I and his son Charles, who regarded themselves as holding the crown by divine right and consequently entitled to exercise authority over both state and church. James was sufficiently shrewd to introduce his plans by degrees, but the more heavy-handed methods of his son provoked a popular revolution which culminated in the signing of the National Covenant in February 1638. This pledged the people of Scotland to defend the reformed religion and to resist all encroachments on its purity.

Later that year the General Assembly of the Church in Glasgow, which continued to sit in defiance of an order by the king's commissioner, overthrew the episcopal innovations and restored the Presbyterian government of the church.

Five years later the Parliament and Church of Scotland joined with the Parliament of England in signing the Solemn League and Covenant, the basic object of which was to secure the establishment of a Presbyterian system of church government in the whole of Britain and, as an immediate practical

step, the help of the Scottish Parliament and people in the
struggle of the English Parliament against the king, in which
both sides had had recourse to arms.

While the cause of the Parliament, with Scottish assistance,
initially triumphed, the rise of the Independents under
Cromwell and the subsequent domination of both king and
Parliament by the army dispelled any prospect of the Solemn
League's long-term aims being achieved, and Scottish support
for Charles II, who was crowned King of Scotland at Scone in
January 1651, led to two disastrous collisions with the army of
the Protector which left Scotland at Cromwell's mercy and
sent the young king into exile. For nine years, from 1651 to
1660, Cromwell's military government ruled Scotland with an
iron hand.

The Scottish church was, however, allowed a generous
measure of freedom to rule its own affairs; the only restriction
was a prohibition on meetings of the General Assembly,
which Cromwell regarded more as a hot-bed of political agitation than a forum for ecclesiastical debate. And indeed the
suspension of the Assembly may well have been partly
responsible for the degree of spiritual prosperity which the
church enjoyed during this period, for it helped to muffle the
often bitter disputes between 'Resolutioner' and 'Protester'
which were to linger on throughout the Commonwealth
period and to be a source of friction within the church until
the Restoration.

Meanwhile, the spiritual condition of the church continued
to flourish. It was a time of powerful preaching and of memorable ministries. In Glasgow, Cargill had as his colleagues
James Durham, in the Inner High Kirk, and in the Outer
High Kirk, first Andrew Gray and then his former fellow-
student Robert M'Ward. These ministers all preached in the
same building which housed Cargill's congregation, and his
fellowship with them must have been intimate and close. It
would be natural to conclude therefore that the early years of
his ministry in Glasgow were happy ones. But while that may
have been so in one sense, at the same time they were years
clouded with deep personal tragedy. For at this time Cargill
was called upon to endure such a series of domestic difficulties and afflictions as must have tried his faith to the utmost

and impressed him with a sense of the inscrutable workings of God's providence.

Since settling in Glasgow Cargill had evidently continued to keep in close touch with Andrew Beaton's widow, Margaret Brown, and her family, and the news he was now receiving gave him cause for growing concern. On Andrew Beaton's death two years earlier the estate had passed to his eldest son Andrew, then about twelve years of age. Andrew was not, of course, old enough to claim the inheritance, and so the administration of the estate passed to a cousin of his father's, Robert Beaton of Bandone, who acted as tutor or legal guardian on his behalf. It seems that relations between him and his cousin's widow became strained, possibly owing to disagreements over the management of the estate, and as a result Lady Blebo, as she was known, was left without adequate means and was forced to incur heavy debts. The news of this situation grieved Cargill deeply. He obviously regarded himself as under an obligation to Lady Blebo for her own and her husband's kindnesses to him in earlier days and her present changed circumstances moved him to pity. It is likely too that, other, more personal, feelings stirred his mind and prompted him to action.

Towards the end of 1655, almost certainly on Cargill's initiative or at least with his encouragement, Lady Blebo and her family moved to Glasgow. From his own resources Cargill arranged for the rent of a house for her and her servants from Sir Archibald Johnston of Warriston, the former Lord Clerk Register, into which she moved in November of that year. He also saw to the arrangements for the education and maintenance of her six children, which Robert Beaton was obliged to pay under the terms of an earlier agreement.[1] Cargill was determined that despite her reduced circumstances Lady Blebo should continue to live in a manner befitting her station and he spared no trouble or expense to ensure that she was properly provided for. The bond of friendship between them grew steadily stronger as the months passed and soon ripened into a deep affection. On 10 April 1656, just over a year after the start of his ministry, Cargill and Lady Blebo were married.[2]

For Cargill it was a step which immediately involved him in

many difficulties. He became responsible for all Lady Blebo's
outstanding debts, which were numerous, for the wages and
maintenance of her servants and for a host of other commitments. All these he discharged to the best of his ability,
though it imposed a severe strain on his resources. His stipend
from the town council of Glasgow had not yet been placed on
a regular basis and he was dependent on interim payments
until a firm arrangement could be made. As a result he was
soon in acute financial difficulty, with no immediate prospect
of relief. But he now had, for the first time, the comforts of a
settled home, and this he clearly treasured above all the
material inconveniences. His life up to now had been a rather
lonely one, partly from choice and partly from circumstance,
but he may have hoped that now he would be able to enjoy the
normal comforts of domestic life and have the companionship
of a like-minded wife to support him in his work among the
people.

But it was not to be. On 12 August 1656, only four months
and two days after their marriage, Lady Blebo died. What
caused her death, or whether the intense pressures surrounding her had a hand in it, cannot be known for certain. To
Cargill, however, the blow was a shattering one. Apart from
the deep personal grief which it caused him, it left him in an
even worse financial position than before; for since the marriage had lasted for less than a year and a day and was without
issue, he had no claim on his wife's personal estate, which
went to Robert Beaton as legatee on the children's behalf.[3]
He was left, however, to pay the expenses of the funeral,
which was conducted with appropriate state and ceremony,
and to pay still more outstanding debts. The funeral expenses
alone came to £190 and there were servants' fees of £86.
These were additional to the debts he had discharged on his
marriage, which had amounted to some £450. Lady Blebo's
estate amounted in all to £1298 and Cargill naturally expected
that his expenses would be reimbursed to him from the
estate.[4] He was therefore surprised and hurt when Beaton
refused, apparently taking the view that Cargill had brought
his difficulties upon himself. Cargill pleaded with Beaton for
the money, pointing out the extraordinary outlays he had
incurred, but Beaton remained inflexible. At last, reduced

almost to penury, Cargill was forced to summon Beaton before the commissioners of justice at Edinburgh, where on 30 July 1657 he obtained decree against him for most of the outstanding expenses. It was a step that he must have taken with great reluctance, and only through extreme force of circumstances, and the open quarrel with his deceased wife's relatives must have been extremely distasteful to him. It does not, however, appear to have soured permanently his relations with the Beatons, who were ready to come to his defence in later years and to do him good service, and the attitude of Robert Beaton appears to have been untypical of his wife's relatives generally. Of the six children two were to die young: Elizabeth, the youngest, seems to have died not long after her mother and Andrew, the eldest and heir to his father, died within a few years afterwards.

For Cargill it had been a distressing and trying experience. Typically, he never appears to have referred to it in later life and few of his friends in later years seem to have been aware of the trial he had undergone. Though he was still under thirty years of age, he never remarried: he seems to have accepted it as the will of God that in the special work to which he was being called he was to be denied those ties of domestic affection which in other circumstances would have been a source of comfort and support to him. Friends he had, and loyal ones, who stood by him to the end, but only for those four brief months in 1656 did he enjoy the happiness of home and family for which he had sacrificed so much.

Other sorrows crowded in upon him. Towards the end of 1657 his father Lawrence died, apparently before reaching the age of sixty. Around the same time he lost two of his closest colleagues in the ministry in Glasgow. Andrew Gray, a young man of outstanding gifts and abilities, died in 1656 at the age of twenty-two, and James Durham, an intellectual giant and the author of a remarkable range of theological literature, died in 1658 at the age of thirty-six. Cargill obviously felt all these losses keenly. They cast a cloud over the early years of his ministry in the Barony and he became an increasingly lonely figure. But they do not appear to have affected his pastoral work and he continued to exercise a successful ministry in the parish. In September 1658, after protracted

negotiations, he at last reached agreement with the town
council on the payment of his stipend, which was fixed at the
generous sum of 1300 merks[5] a year, payable in two equal
instalments at Whitsun and Martinmas.[6] He now had some
relief from his financial pressures and could look forward to a
regular income so long as he remained in the charge.

3.
The contemporary setting

By 1660, when Cargill had been ministering in the Barony for some five years, the political state of the country was undergoing rapid change. The death of Cromwell in 1658 had foreshadowed the end of the military dictatorship and amid the civil chaos which ensued the calls for the return of the king became general. On 29 May 1660, after an exile of nine years, Charles II was restored to his father's throne. Nowhere was there greater enthusiasm for his return than in Scotland, where in January 1651 he had been crowned and had solemnly sworn to maintain and defend the Covenants. He had gone further: in a declaration at Dunfermline in August 1650, he had humbly acknowledged his own sins and the sins of his father in opposing the Covenants and the work of reformation. He had declared that 'He will have no enemies but the enemies of the Covenant, and that he will have no friends but the friends of the Covenant,' and he had solemnly asserted that he had 'not sworn and subscribed to these Covenants, and entered into the oath of God with his people, upon any sinister intention and crooked design for obtaining his own ends, but so far as human weakness will permit, in the truth and sincerity of his heart, and that he is firmly resolved in the Lord's strength to adhere thereto and to prosecute to the utmost of his power all the ends thereof in his station and calling, really, constantly and sincerely all the days of his life'.

Events were to show the degree of 'truth and sincerity' in Charles's words. The declaration had been made when he was an exile from his own land, desperately seeking support from any source to regain his throne, and his avowal of the Coven-

ants, as events proved, was no more than a device to attract
the support of the Scottish Presbyterians to his cause. At that
time the Protesters held the majority in the church, and the
king's acceptance of the Covenants was of course a vital pre-
requisite to their support. But for the king the experience had
been a humiliation: he felt that the weakness of his position
had been exploited and that the declaration had been
extracted from him under duress. He had been affronted by
the direct and pointed way he had been spoken to about his
personal life, and he found the Protesters' criticisms of his
father particularly to his distaste. He had harboured a grudge
against the Scottish Presbyterians in general, and the Protesters in particular, ever since, and he only awaited his opportunity to make his displeasure felt. Ever loyal to the memory of
his father and grandfather, he shared their conception of
monarchy: absolutism in church and state. Presbyterianism,
with its insistence upon the headship of Christ and the
spiritual independence of the church, was obviously incom-
patible with those claims. To Charles, as to his forebears, it
was a challenge to the divine right which he asserted and the
absolute supremacy which he claimed, and he seems to have
become convinced at a fairly early stage that nothing short of
its complete overthrow would serve his purpose. His sense of
personal resentment gave a keener edge to his determination.
He would vindicate his father's memory by succeeding where
his father had failed, and he would replace the Presbyterian
system with a system of church government subservient to the
Crown. He lacked no number of willing helpers to put his
ambitions into practice. A sizeable proportion of the nobility
had chafed under the stern discipline of the Presbyterians and
were eager to throw off the yoke: others had been
impoverished by the Civil War and the Cromwellian occu-
pation which followed and were only too ready to put
personal gain before the claims of conscience.

But the king's chief instrument in the overthrow of the
Scottish church was to come from within the church itself. In
February 1660, James Sharp, the Presbyterian minister of
Crail, had been sent by some leading Scottish ministers to
London to negotiate the future settlement of church govern-
ment in Scotland after the Restoration. Sharp had later spent

some time with Charles in Holland and after the king's return he was deeply involved in the plans being made in London for the future of the Scottish church. He was ostensibly an agent for the 'Resolutioners', who had hoped to gain some advantage to themselves in the settlement of the church under Charles, but the outcome of his work was to betray both Resolutioners and Protesters alike. Sharp had realized from the outset how the king's mind was working and he set out to accommodate himself to the king's policy in every detail. At the same time as he was sending back reports to Scotland of his hopes of a promising settlement for the church, he was deep in complicity with Charles's ministers over the overthrow of Presbyterianism and the re-establishment of episcopacy. A typical example of his duplicity was the letter which, at his instigation, Charles sent to the Presbytery of Edinburgh in August 1660. This promised 'to protect and preserve the government of the Church of Scotland, as it is settled by law, without violation', the inference being, as indeed it was meant to be taken, that the Presbyterian system would be maintained. As events were to show, however, the 'law' was not to be the law as it then existed, settling Presbyterianism; it was to be the law as rewritten by Charles and his parliaments, with the active connivance of Sharp, reimposing episcopacy. By the time the church in Scotland discovered the real effect of Sharp's intrigues, the pass had been sold; Sharp was to gain honour and preferment for himself, but a lasting name for infamy among his fellow-countrymen.[1]

The new order was not long in making its influence felt. Within six weeks of the king's restoration the Marquis of Argyll, who had been the leader of the Scottish Presbyterians and the foremost Scottish statesman of his time, was seized in London and imprisoned. A month later a number of ministers who were engaged in drawing up a supplication to the king were arrested in Edinburgh. One of them was James Guthrie, the Protester minister of Stirling, who had been one of Sharp's principal opponents in the Protester/Resolutioner controversy, and against whom Sharp had a particular grudge.

In the spring of the following year Argyll and Guthrie were brought to trial in Edinburgh, on charges of complicity with

Cromwell, and both were found guilty and executed. Sir Archibald Johnston of Warriston, who had been clerk to the 1638 Assembly and was later one of the Scottish commissioners to the Westminster Assembly of Divines, was to be another victim. He succeeded in escaping to the Continent after the issue of an order for his arrest, but was later captured and executed. By striking at these three eminent figures in church and state the new regime had given sufficient earnest of its intentions: it was now to reinforce this initial onslaught with a systematic and deliberate attack on the foundations of the church itself.

Charles's first Scottish Parliament met on 1 January 1661. Its members were carefully chosen to reflect the king's wishes and they well knew what was expected of them. Their first act, significantly, contained an oath of allegiance to the king, to be taken by all members of Parliament, acknowledging the king as 'only supreme governor of this kingdom, over all persons, and in all causes'. The wording of the act was deliberately ambiguous, since the Parliament did not, for reasons of policy, wish to advance too far at one step, but it made it sufficiently clear what their ultimate intentions were. They went on to pass acts asserting the king's prerogative in appointing officers, making peace and war, convening meetings and making bonds and leagues, declaring that any such bonds or leagues made without the consent of the sovereign were illegal. This, quite clearly, was a veiled attack on the Covenants, though the time was not yet considered ripe for a direct assault. The Parliament felt confident enough, however, to ordain that the Solemn League and Covenant of 1643 was not obligatory and to forbid the king's subjects to renew it or swear to it 'as they will be answerable at their highest peril'. The Oath of Allegiance, extended to include these further acts, was ordered to be taken by all persons holding positions of public trust, who were thereby required to acknowledge the king's absolute prerogative in all the matters legislated for in the acts. Having prepared the way, the Parliament now advanced to bolder measures. At one stroke they rescinded all the parliaments held since 1640, thus effectively repealing all the acts in favour of Presbyterian church government and the Covenants, at the same time declaring that all the troubles of 'these twenty-three years' (since the signing of the National Covenant in 1638) had been upon 'the specious but common pretext of reformation, the common cloak of all rebellions'. This done, a further act was passed declaring the king's intention 'to maintain the true reformed Protestant religion, in its purity of doctrine and worship, as it was established in this kingdom during the reigns of his royal father and grandfather of blessed memory', and, significantly, 'in such a frame as shall be most suitable to monarchical government'. These were, of course, clear indications of the reintroduction of episcopacy, for which the way had now been well and truly prepared. Before adjourning, the Parliament had one more act of homage to pay to the king: they ordained that 29 May, the date of his Restoration, should be observed 'this present year and in all time coming' as a solemn anniversary thanksgiving, to be employed in 'public prayers, preaching, thanksgiving and praises to God for so transcendent mercies', and recommending all ministers, magistrates and others in positions of authority to ensure that the day was duly kept and observed.

Parliament had set the pattern for the future government of the Scottish church; it was left to the Privy Council, the executive instrument of the king in Scotland, to put it into effect. Having been invested with a sovereign prerogative 'over all persons and in all causes', Charles could now, through the Privy Council, issue decrees and proclamations on his own authority, merely using Parliament to endorse his decisions. Accordingly, on 14 August 1661, he addressed a letter to the Council declaring his 'firm resolution' to interpose his royal authority for restoring to the Church of Scotland its 'right government by bishops as it now stands settled by law' and instructing the Council to take all appropriate steps to put this policy into effect. The true meaning of the letter of the previous year to the Presbytery of Edinburgh was now clear, and Sharp's perfidy was plain for all to see. The council wasted no time in giving effect to the king's instructions. On 6 September the restoration of the bishops was announced by public proclamation. On 12 December the ordination of ministers without the bishops' consent was prohibited, and on 9 January 1662, in response to another directive from the

king, all church courts — synods, presbyteries and kirk
sessions — were forbidden to meet without the king's authority. The bishops themselves were consecrated on 7 May following and took their seats in the second session of Parliament which opened the following day.

The Parliament's first act was to confirm the restoration of
the bishops and to repeal all acts giving the church jurisdiction
over its own affairs: henceforward no power would be
allowed within the church 'other than that which acknowledged a dependence upon and subordination to the
sovereign power of the king, as supreme, and which is to be
regulated and authorized, in the exercise thereof, by the
archbishops and bishops who are to put order to all ecclesiastical matters and causes, and to be accountable to His Majesty
for their administrations'. Here indeed was the new order
writ large — a system of church government entirely in the
hands of the bishops, who were answerable to no one but the
king; complete deprivation of the church of the right to regulate its own affairs, and the abrogation of all the laws confirming Presbyterian church government.

It was but a step from this to declare, as the Parliament proceeded to do, that the National Covenant of 1638 and the
Solemn League and Covenant of 1643 were unlawful oaths,
imposing no obligation upon anyone who had taken them. To
reinforce still further the power of the bishops, all ministers
who had been ordained since 1649 were required to seek collation from the bishops by 20 September in order to continue
in their charges, and all 'private meetings or conventicles in
houses under the pretence of religious exercise' were forbidden. And, as if to deal the finishing stroke to the Covenants
and all that they stood for, the Parliament ordered that all
persons in positions of public trust should be required to
swear a declaration that the Covenants were unlawful, that
they had been imposed against the fundamental laws of the
kingdom and that all the meetings and assemblies held in connection with them were unlawful and seditious.

By 9 September 1662, when the Parliament rose, the
Presbyterian government of the church had been destroyed,
the Covenants, which enshrined the principles of the Scottish
Reformation, were discredited and disowned, and the gov-

ernment of the Church of Scotland, as by law established, was firmly in the hands of the king.

4.
The darkness falls

To Donald Cargill, in his charge in the Barony, this turn of events came as a severe blow. A young man, and a young minister, in his first charge, he had already won his way into the hearts and affections of his people, many of whom were to stand by his side throughout the difficult times ahead. The prospects of a long and successful ministry among them had seemed bright. Instead, only a relatively short time after the personal tragedy of his wife's death, he suffered fresh grief over the distressed condition of the church.

The calamity was not altogether unexpected, for at about the time of the Restoration, or just shortly before, Cargill had attended a general meeting of ministers where the shape of coming events had been graphically predicted. Robert M'Ward appears to have had a particularly strong premonition of the coming disaster, for he had prayed earnestly that God, 'in mercy, love and pity, would seal, spirit and fit a remnant to stand steadfast, whatever and from whatsoever airt [direction] the winds might blow: and that there might be a succession of faithful witnesses raised up to follow the Lord fully in life and death'.

M'Ward himself, as events turned out, was to be an early victim. In February 1661 he preached a sermon in the Tron Church in Glasgow in which he took as his subject the public and national defections of the time. The first Parliament of the new reign was only a month old, but already its intentions were becoming abundantly clear. 'For my part,' said M'Ward, 'as a poor member of the Church of Scotland, and an unworthy minister in it, I do this day call you who are the people of God to witness, that I humbly offer my dissent from all acts which are or which shall be passed against the Covenants and the work of Reformation in Scotland: and I protest that I am desirous to be free of the guilt thereof, and pray that God may put it upon record in heaven.' It was a mild enough protest, but it evoked a severe response. M'Ward was arrested, brought to Edinburgh and imprisoned. It was June before he was brought to trial, and in the meantime Argyll and Guthrie had been executed. M'Ward expected a similar fate, but instead he received sentence of banishment. He chose to settle in Holland, where he was to play a very important part in the life of the Scottish church over the next twenty years, welcoming those who were banished, gaining the sympathy and support of the Dutch churches, and conducting an extensive correspondence with the church at home. On 1 January 1662 his old presbytery showed their appreciation of his services by drawing up a testimonial in which they paid warm tribute to his character and ministry. Cargill, who at this time was moderator of the presbytery, was the first to append his signature, and the document was sent to M'Ward in the land of his exile as a token of his brethren's continuing regard and affection.[1]

M'Ward's departure left Donald Cargill bereft of yet another faithful friend. He continued to exercise his ministry at the Barony, though the shadows were by now beginning to lengthen around him. He had not yet declared his mind publicly, though it must have been clear, at least to his own congregation, where his sympathies lay and what his position would be when the time for decision came. He did not observe the first anniversary of the king's restoration in 1661, but since the act ordaining its observance had been passed only two weeks previously, and as many other ministers had also ignored the occasion, either deliberately or through lack of knowledge, his omission was apparently allowed to pass unnoticed.

The following year, however, there was to be no room for doubt. In 1662 29 May fell on a Thursday, the day that Cargill was accustomed to give a weekly sermon. By now the new regime's attack on the church was far advanced: the acts supporting the Reformation establishment and the Covenants had been rescinded, and only the previous day the Parliament had passed the act restoring episcopacy. Cargill had three possible courses open to him: to cancel his preaching day altogether and to say nothing, to preach as usual and not to mention the occasion, or to preach and at the same time to give his testimony against the new order. The temptation to be silent, or to evade the issue, must have been strong, and it was an occasion which demanded strength and courage. From what is known of Cargill's practice on other occasions where he had a particular difficulty to face, or a work of particular importance to do, he must have spent much time in prayer, and as a result he became totally and completely convinced of the rightness of the action he was to take.

The fateful day came, the people assembled, in far greater numbers than usual, no doubt aware that some sensational event was afoot. On entering the pulpit, Cargill immediately declared his position: 'We are not come here,' he said, 'to keep this day upon the account for which others keep it. We thought once to have blessed the day wherein the king came home again, but now we think we shall have reason to curse it. And if any of you come here in order to the solemnizing of this day we desire you to remove.'[2] Whether any of his congregation complied with his charge is not recorded; it is more than likely that the seriousness of his words and the earnestness of his manner compelled them to stay. 'For me,' he went on, 'I desire to be found in the way of my duty, being our ordinary day, otherwise I would not have preached a word on that account.' And he went on in similar strain, using strong arguments from Scripture to reinforce his words.[3]

Cargill well knew what the consequences of his action would be. He had seen what had happened to M'Ward, and he knew that by speaking out as he had done he had effectively ended his ministry at the Barony. Among his hearers were those who would report his words to the authorities, and there were apparently some in his audience who were anxious to bring him to justice themselves. In the outcry that followed his sermon he was obliged to forego his preaching ministry for a time and to live in concealment for his own safety. But he had many loyal friends to rally round him and he had no lack of refuges to which to turn. Many of his congregation welcomed him to their homes and he continued to preach from house to house as he had opportunity. It was an early experience of the kind of life with which he was to become much more acquainted in later years. His financial resources too were again under strain, for the town council, in a reaction to his sermon, withheld payment of the half-year's instalment of stipend which was due to him at the Whitsun term, though they were later to relent and rescind this decision.[4]

After some weeks, however, there was a temporary respite. Either because of some influence brought to bear on his behalf, as on a later occasion, or because the authorities did not want to bring more proceedings against individual ministers until their plans for the future of the church had fully unfolded, the pressures upon him relaxed; he was able for a while to return to his own church and even to officiate at a communion service. But the relief was to be short-lived. On 1 October the Privy Council, in what became known as the Act of Glasgow, ordered all ministers who had not received collation from the bishops to remove from their parishes by 1 November and not to reside within the bounds of their respective presbyteries, and forbade their parishioners to hear them preach or to acknowledge them as their ministers, under penalty of being punished as frequenters of private conventicles. As a result of this act some 400 ministers, representing a third of the total ministry of the church, were ejected from their charges. A subsequent act of 23 December extended the time-limit for compliance to 1 February 1663, but this apparent concession was accompanied by a threat of more rigorous measures against those ministers who did not comply. Ministers who continued to preach, either in public or private, or who kept meetings in families other than their own, were to be punished as seditious persons; and any persons who did not attend their own parish churches, now occupied by the nominees of the bishops, were made liable to heavy fines. It meant that the attack on the church, which had begun the year before with the acts of Parliament everting the Presbyterian order, had now extended to affect the lives of every minister and individual member who remained loyal to Reformation principles. From now on the Church of Scotland was in the furnace, a furnace which was to grow ever hotter as

the years passed and was to test to the utmost the faith and
endurance of those who remained loyal to that principle
which had become the distinctive testimony of the Scottish
church: the right of Christ, and of Christ alone, to bear the
rule in his own house.

Even before the Act of Glasgow was passed, the Privy
Council had been active in prosecuting individual ministers
who had either spoken out directly against the new order in
the church or who had refused to apply for collation from the
bishops. Several ministers in the Presbytery of Edinburgh
were forcibly ejected from their charges on the very day that
the act was passed. The act itself was the signal for a mass
ejection of ministers which would leave many of the congregations pastorless until replacements of a very different kind
were found for them by the bishops. The scope of the act was
sufficiently wide to cover all ministers who had refused to
acknowledge the episcopal system, but there were some
whose conduct was considered to merit particular notice and
of whom an example had to be made. Hardly surprisingly,
one of these was Donald Cargill. On the same day as the Act
of Glasgow was passed, 1 October 1662, the Council issued a
proclamation in the following terms: 'Information being
given, that Mr Donald Cargill, minister of the Barony Church
at Glasgow, has not only disobeyed the Acts of Parliament for
keeping an anniversary for His Majesty's happy Restoration,
and for obtaining a lawful presentation and collation from the
Archbishop of Glasgow before 20th September last, but also
that his conduct has been most seditious, and that he has
deserted the flock to their great prejudice by the want of the
ordinances, therefore the Lords of Council declare the
foresaid church to be now vacant and at the disposal of the
lawful patron, and for avoiding of the inconveniences that
may follow by his residing at Glasgow or places near adjacent,
they command and charge the said Mr Donald Cargill not to
reside in any place on the south side of the river of Tay, and
to cause transport his family and what belongs to him out of
the town of Glasgow before the 1st November next, with
certification that, if he be found to contravene and to be seen
on this side of Tay he shall be apprehended, and imprisoned
and proceeded against as a seditious person: and ordains that

these presents be intimated to him personally at his dwelling-house and at the Mercat Cross of Glasgow and parish church where he lives, that he pretend not ignorance.'

By his 'having deserted the flock' the Council were apparently referring to Cargill's action in leaving his church to escape the consequences of his sermon. As for 'the want of the ordinances', he had continued to exercise his ministry as best he could after his forced separation from his congregation and, as events were to show, many of his people valued his ministry so highly that they were prepared to risk the increasingly severe penalties for private meetings rather than lose the benefit of it. Many of them were to stand loyally by him for the rest of his life, and wherever he went he kept in regular contact with his old parish. As late as March 1681, after almost twenty years of separation from them, he is to be found writing 'to his parish of the Barony Kirk of Glasgow' expressing his great indebtedness for all their kindness to him: 'How to requite my obligations,' he says, 'I know not; to return all is impossible.' The bond between pastor and people was not, then, to be broken by the arbitrary command of the Council: it was to continue, and to grow stronger and firmer, as the years went by. Surely nothing can testify more clearly to the success of Cargill's seven years' ministry and to the impact he made upon his people than this evidence of the affection and esteem in which he was held, and which was to be a source of continuing comfort and support in the difficult times which lay before him.

For the moment, however, the banishment order had to be obeyed. No sooner, indeed, had it been passed than the authorities sent a party of soldiers to the Barony to enforce it. Cargill himself narrowly evaded them by leaving the church by one door as they entered by the other, and the soldiers contented themselves with taking away the church keys. But the seriousness of his position, if he defied the order, was sufficiently plain; and so he determined that, rather than court needless danger, his proper course was to obey. The north of the Tay was a customary place of banishment in those days and it had no bearing on the fact that it happened to be Cargill's native region. This fact did, of course, have obvious advantages for him, and it appears that by the date demanded he left Glasgow and took up residence once again in Rattray. For the next ten years he was to live in relative obscurity, and very little is known of his life during this period. It is clear, however, from legal documents and other sources that he was often away from his native parish for long periods, and he is heard of at various times at Perth, Dundee, Alyth, Coupar Angus and elsewhere. It seems likely therefore that though he was nominally resident at Rattray he was in the habit of constantly moving about, and this suggests that there may have been small groups of friends and sympathizers in these places with whom he stayed and to whom he preached privately. There is no record, however, of his having preached in public during this period, nor does he seem to have taken any part in the public affairs of church or state.

After Cargill's banishment the measures against the non-conforming ministers and their followers became still more severe. By an act of Parliament on 10 July 1663, which became known as the 'Bishops' dragnet', the Privy Council were authorized to prosecute the nonconforming ministers with the full rigour of the law, 'as seditious persons and contemptuous of the royal authority', and also to punish by fines and 'such other corporal punishment as they shall think fit' all persons absenting themselves from the parish churches. The Council, as always, were quick to act: on 13 August they ordered the ministers to 'remove themselves, their families, and goods belonging to them, within twenty days after publication hereof, out of these respective parishes where they were incumbents, and not to reside within twenty miles of the same, nor within six miles of Edinburgh or any cathedral church, or three miles of any burgh royal within this kingdom, under penalty of being proceeded against with that strictness that is due to so great contempts of His Majesty's authority over church and state'. This measure, known as the 'Scots Mile Act', led to great hardship: it meant that the ministers, some of whom now had to move home for the third time within a year, were denied the benefit of living with friends or relatives in the burghs and were compelled to take up residence in rural areas, many of them remote from centres of education and employment for their families. At the same time the measures against non-attenders at the churches were put into full force: agents were employed to inform on persons contravening the act, and in some parts of the country, notably the south-west, detachments of troops were introduced to ensure that the law was enforced. These troops inflicted great hardship on the people and led to intense resentment.

It was just such a situation, in the area of the country around Dumfries, that led in November 1666 to the first serious challenge to the government, when a company of ill-armed but resolute men, goaded beyond endurance by the depredations of the soldiers, took prisoner the commander of the troops in the area, Sir James Turner, and marched north through Ayrshire and Lanarkshire towards Edinburgh. The small force gathered strength as it went and there were hopes of assistance from the capital, but these were in vain, and as the company turned homewards they were attacked and routed on the slopes of the Pentlands by government forces under General Dalyell. The 'Pentland Rising', as it came to be called, was the first harvest of the government's policy of imposing on the country a system alien to its religious traditions and against the deepest convictions of many of its people, and it was the precursor to far greater trouble in the years ahead. To try to discourage future revolts, the government exacted a bitter revenge: many of the leaders of the rising, and some, such as Hugh McKail, who were only marginally connected with it, were tortured and executed, and others sent as slaves to the plantations. But the spirit of the people was not broken and their determination to resist the oppressions of the government remained firm.

5.
In the wilderness

While Cargill's public work may have been at a standstill he found himself involved, almost immediately on his return to Rattray, in a series of personal and family business activities which were to take up much of his time over the next ten years. Although many of the details of these remain obscure, there is enough evidence to show that the practical concerns of his immediate family and relations were a matter of deep importance to him, and he did not hesitate to involve himself actively in their affairs where he saw their interests at risk. It is clear from the record of these transactions that Cargill possessed a sound business sense and an expert knowledge of the law, which he did not hesitate to place at the disposal of his family when the circumstances called for it, often at considerable disadvantage to himself.

On his father's death in 1657 Cargill had inherited from him a quarter share of the small estate of Wester Banchrie, where his father had spent the last three years of his life. It was apparently there, towards the end of 1662, that Cargill chose to settle on his return to his native parish. Though he was now denied the opportunity of exercising a public ministry, he could find consolation in the company and fellowship of the many friends and relatives who resided around him and who were in sympathy with his position. His brother James was in the old family home of Bonnytown. His first cousin on his mother's side, Thomas Lundie, was the parish minister and a confirmed adherent of the Presbyterian cause. His uncle, George Drummond, husband of his father's sister Grissell, and his first cousin on his father's side, Donald Cargill of Hatton, were both elders in Rattray Kirk. It was in the fellowship of men such as these that Cargill no doubt spent much of his time in these first months following his banishment.

It must soon have become evident to him, however, that in the circle of his immediate relatives there were cares and anxieties which cast a cloud over the happiness of their fellowship. The long years of civil strife and disorder had spelt disaster for many of the smaller landholders, and Cargill's relatives were no exception. His brother James, who had inherited his father's estate of Bonnytown, was finding increasing difficulty in paying his annual rents. His cousin Donald was in an even more serious position. Thirty years earlier he had inherited from his father the estate of Hatton, the lesser estate of Easter Drimmie, an eighth portion of Kirktoun of Rattray, which had been left by his grandfather, and the small estate of Kirklands. As time went on and external circumstances grew more difficult, he found the management of these estates increasingly burdensome and was forced to borrow heavily. By 1663 both the Hatton and Easter Drimmie estates were burdened with heavy debts, and the two small estates had been 'wadset', or mortgaged to the sitting tenants. His position soon became critical. Creditors were pressing urgently for payment, and he was in imminent risk of being 'put to the horn', or publicly outlawed as a defaulting debtor.

It was at this juncture that Cargill came into the picture. He could not fail, through contact with his family and friends, to learn of his cousin's financial position, and in any case it was probably well enough known in the parish. Two considerations seem to have weighed with him: firstly, sympathy for his cousin and his wife and his duty to them as his relatives; and, secondly and not less important, concern for the public interest of the church and the cause which his cousin represented. While therefore the actions that Cargill decided upon were taken in the immediate context of a family business affair, they were almost certainly motivated by the same kind of considerations which influenced his public work and ministry, both before this time and after.

Cargill seems to have prepared his plans carefully and, although he acted jointly with his cousin in many of the transactions that followed, he was clearly the prime mover throughout. In July 1665 the first step to resolve the crisis was taken. By two mutual contracts, between Cargill on the one hand and his cousin and his wife on the other, Cargill had transferred to him the whole of his cousin's estates, including, of course, the burdens which went with them.[1] The immediate effect of this move was to avert pressure from his cousin and to transfer responsibility to Cargill for settling with his cousin's creditors. He set about this task with determination. In December 1665 he paid off the debt of 3,000 merks on the Hatton and Easter Drimmie estates and freed them from the burden which his cousin had contracted some years earlier.[2] The Hatton estate Cargill kept for his own use, but to meet the outstanding debts it was necessary to sell all the remaining property. The Easter Drimmie estate was sold jointly by Cargill and his cousin in June 1667,[3] and in the next and following years the estate of Kirklands and the eighth portion of Kirktoun were sold on a similar basis to the existing mortgagees.[4] About the same time Cargill sold his own estate of Wester Banchrie and obtained a new charter for Hatton in his own name from the feudal superior.[5] As a result of these transactions his cousin apparently succeeded in meeting the demands of his creditors and so avoided the actions for recovery which had threatened him: and he was able to make an honourable departure from the parish for his new home in Perth, being granted a testimonial by the Rattray Kirk Session.[6]

Cargill had succeeded in his objective, but at great cost to himself. Even before his purchase of the Hatton property he had been obliged to borrow money from friends, and as his commitments increased he was forced to borrow still more heavily. In the six years from 1665 to 1671 he granted bonds to creditors for at least 4,500 merks, equivalent to 3,000 pounds Scots or £250 sterling, some three and a half times his yearly salary in Glasgow.[7] He seems to have been able to repay most of this money, and it is likely that some of the debt was written off completely. On at least three occasions, however, his creditors grew impatient and issued writs for payment against him. In 1671, and again in 1676 and 1678, he was subjected to having writs affixed to the door of his house at

Hatton by a court messenger, and to having his debts publicly proclaimed at the Mercat Cross of Perth.[8] He was apparently able to avoid more serious consequences, perhaps as a result of the intervention of friends, but these incidents must have caused him considerable pain and embarrassment. For not the first time in his life he had lost materially through his consideration for others, allowing himself to come close to impoverishment rather than see his friends suffer hardship.[9]

Cargill's legal affairs involved him from time to time in visits to Edinburgh, where his various transactions were recorded and registered in the Books of Council and Session. He appears to have assumed that this necessary business did not constitute a breach of his confinement, and there are grounds for supposing that he had been given some official assurances on this score. Eventually, however, a formal complaint was made against him to the Privy Council, and the Council felt compelled to act. On 23 December 1668 they issued the following proclamation: 'The Lords of His Majesty's Privy Council, considering that Mr Donald Cargill, late minister at Glasgow, was by an Act of Council of the date at Glasgow, the 1st October 1662, commanded and charged not to reside in any place on the south side of the water of Tay, and to transport his family and what belonged to him out of the town of Glasgow against 1st November thereafter, with certification if he should be found to contravene or to be seen on this side of Tay he should be apprehended, imprisoned and proceeded against as a seditious person, and the said Lords being informed that the said Mr Donald Cargill has, without any licence or warrant, broken the said confinement and has repaired to the City of Edinburgh and other places at his pleasure in high and proud contempt of authority, do ordain letters to be direct to Messengers at Arms to charge the said Mr Donald Cargill by open proclamation at the Market Crosses of Edinburgh and Forfar,[10] in respect he has no constant residence, to compear before the Council the seventh day of January next to answer for breaking his said confinement and contempt of authority, under the pain of rebellion, with certification that letters shall be direct to denounce him *simpliciter.*'

The form of this proclamation was more severe than its

intent: there was by this time a general spirit of clemency in the air, and the Council were anxious to avoid severe measures. Cargill's wife's relatives, the Beatons of Blebo, apparently intervened to some purpose on his behalf, and when he answered the summons and appeared before the Council he was merely ordered to return to his place of banishment.[11] This was the precursor to a more general act of clemency. On 7 June 1669, after some negotiations between certain of the Presbyterian ministers and the Earl of Tweeddale, who was a member of the Privy Council, the king authorized the Council to allow such of the ministers 'as have lived peaceably and orderly in the places where they have resided' to return and preach in their former charges, or to such others as the Council might approve, without the necessity to obtain collation from the bishops or to attend church courts under their jurisdiction.

On 27 July the Council gave effect to the king's letters in two acts which became known as the First Indulgence. Some forty-two ministers took advantage of the liberty thus given to them to resume preaching. The bishops, who were not apparently consulted, took strong exception to the Indulgence as a weakening of their authority, and they resented the fact that it had been promulgated without their consent. But while ostensibly the Presbyterian ministers were granted a measure of liberty, in reality they were kept firmly under the control of the king. Ministers who did not attend the presbyteries, now under the jurisdiction of the bishops, were confined to their parishes; and all the ministers who benefited from the Indulgence were forbidden to admit persons from neighbouring parishes to their communions, or to baptize or marry their children. The Indulgence thus ran counter to the principle of spiritual independence which lay at the heart of the Presbyterian system. It was natural that some ministers should seek relief from oppression and confinement by accepting it, but their compliance came to be regarded by others, under equal constraint, as a denial of the headship of Christ and a complicity with the enemies of the church. The Indulgence thus came to be a subject of strong contention and the cause of many bitter controversies among those who until now had been of one mind and one heart.

Cargill was not among those who accepted the Indulgence, and he was later to oppose it bitterly. But he did not declare his mind on the subject until after the Second Indulgence was granted some years afterwards, and in the meantime he felt able, without compromising his position, to take advantage of the general climate of relief which it brought. Perhaps encouraged by the Beatons, on 1 September 1669 he put in a petition to the Council that his confinement be taken off and that he be permitted to go about his lawful affairs. The petition was granted, subject to a condition that he must not on any occasion reside in Glasgow, and that he repair to or reside in Edinburgh only for the purpose of attending to legal business and with the consent of the courts. It was a much-needed relief, for it enabled him to resume contact with his friends in the south without the fear of persecution, and particularly to minister once again to the members of his old congregation in Glasgow, where he was still remembered with warm affection. This he apparently did not regard as a breach of the Council's order, which merely enjoined him not to 'reside' in the city; it is probable that to keep strictly within the terms of the order he stayed with friends in the neighbourhood, and kept in touch with his old congregation from there. He seems to have been more or less permanently resident around Glasgow from about 1670; at all events he is not recorded as having been at Rattray any later than December 1671. He did not, however, break his ties completely with his native parish: he retained possession of the Hatton estate for the rest of his life, though from the records remaining it is clear that it was much more of a liability to him than an asset. At one stage in his later years he apparently considered selling it, but this he was prevented from doing by an arrestment placed upon the property for his outstanding debts. It seems plain that these were contracted, or at least aggravated, by non-payment of rent by his tenants, and Hatton was to remain under debt so long as he held it.

His long exile over, Cargill soon found himself in congenial surroundings once again. For some two years after his return he seems to have enjoyed a surprising measure of freedom; he was able to go in and out among his people, preaching privately in houses and publicly on the sabbath in prearranged meeting-places in the city. Indeed, so generous was the liberty afforded him that he found himself able to minister to his people much as he had done when he was settled in his charge. Not knowing how long the opportunity was to last, he took full advantage of it while he could. He found lodging in the house of Margaret Craig, a widow, where he was to stay for some years, and there he started a series of twice-daily expositions, preaching morning and evening to all who came to hear him. He adopted a plan of working progressively through Scripture, and eventually had made his way through the greater part of the Bible.

While resuming these pastoral duties Cargill also found opportunity to establish contact with several of his former ministerial colleagues in Glasgow who, like himself, had not accepted the Indulgence. With them he formed a 'field presbytery' of nonconforming ministers which met regularly for some years and seems to have enjoyed a surprising freedom from interference, though its existence must have been known to the church authorities. This body, not the only one of its kind in Scotland at the time, was not only able to act as a debating forum but to exercise the functions of a church court, even to the extent of taking students on trial and licensing them for the ministry. One of the students to receive licence from this presbytery, early in 1673, was James Wodrow, father of the church historian, whose certificate of licence was signed by Cargill and several of his fellow ministers.

But while the Indulgence brought in its train a short-lived relaxation of the persecution, the omens for the future were not bright. On 16 November 1669, only some four months after the granting of the Indulgence, Parliament passed an act which went further than any other in asserting the king's supremacy over the church. The act, which was to become known as the 'Act Explanatory' was, as the name implies, intended to explain and construe the Act of Supremacy passed by the first Parliament in 1661, which, so far as ecclesiastical matters were concerned, had been left deliberately ambiguous.

The new act left no room for any doubt. It asserted 'That His Majesty hath the supreme authority and supremacy over all persons and in all causes ecclesiastical within this kingdom; and that by virtue thereof, the ordering and disposal of the external government and policy of the church doth properly belong to His Majesty and his successors as an inherent right to the Crown; and that His Majesty and his successors may settle, enact and emit such constitutions, acts and orders, concerning the administration of the external government of the church, and the persons employed in the same, and concerning all ecclesiastical meetings, and matters to be proposed and determined therein, as they in their royal wisdom shall think fit; which acts, orders and constitutions are to be observed and obeyed by all His Majesty's subjects.'

Nothing could be more comprehensive; nothing could mark out more plainly the absolute supremacy which the king now claimed over the church and over every aspect of its government. Here was the very negation of the Presbyterian system on which the reformed Church of Scotland had been built; here, to the Presbyterian, was the Crown, absolute, dictatorial, arrogating to itself that complete control over the body of Christ to which only Christ, the Head, had the lawful right. The words in the act 'as an inherent right to the Crown' were particularly significant, since they plainly meant that to disown the king's authority in ecclesiastical matters was to disown him as king, and thereby to be guilty of treason: they linked the ecclesiastical power inextricably with the civil, so that to deny the one was to deny the other.

In this lay the seeds of the persecution which, before long, was to reach its full height. Many a loyal Presbyterian could not bring himself to say the apparently innocuous words, 'God save the king', since to do so would be to acknowledge the king in the comprehensive extent of his power, ecclesiastical as well as civil, and to acquiesce in all the measures he had introduced in the exercise of that power, including the disowning of the Covenants and the overturning of the work of reformation. To many, including Donald Cargill, refusal to bow to the claims of the royal authority as asserted in this act was to be the decisive test of loyalty to Christ, and to carry with it the issues of life and death.

6.
In the high places of the field

The arbitrary step of the Explanatory Act was soon followed by another. In his letter to the Council authorizing the Indulgence, the king had made it clear that since provision was now being made 'for the wants of such as are, and will be peaceable', all ministers who continued to preach without authority and to keep conventicles would be severely punished. The Act of Indulgence itself did not specify any measures against conventicles, and it was left to the Parliament of the following year to give full expression to the king's will.

The frequency and persistence of these field-meetings had been a source of mounting irritation to the government, who saw them as a direct challenge to their authority. In the early days, following the ejection of the ministers, they had been relatively few and infrequent, and mainly concentrated in the south-west. The incursions of the soldiers under Sir James Turner had severely restricted these meetings, and the much greater severity of the measures brought in after Pentland had effectively put an end to them in that part of the country. But a year or so later, in the wake of a notable spiritual revival in Northumberland, they had begun again in the east and south-east, and by 1669 had spread as far north as Fife and Stirling-shire. A wave of spiritual fervour was beginning to sweep through the country, and the popularity of the field-meetings increased with it. A greater discernment was making itself felt among the people, and the nominees of the bishops could no longer satisfy their spiritual needs. In the field-meetings, among the ejected ministers, they could find that satisfaction for their souls which was lacking in their own parish churches. The drift from the churches gathered pace; some of the ejected ministers could number their congregations in thousands, while the churches stood almost empty.

From the government's point of view the situation demanded drastic action, and this was not long in coming. On 13 August 1670 Parliament passed an act declaring that preachers at field conventicles were to be punished with death and the confiscation of their goods: preachers in houses, other than their own, were to be imprisoned and, if they failed to promise not to repeat the offence, they were to be banished from the country. Those present at conventicles, whether in houses or in the fields, were to be heavily fined, and rewards and indemnities were offered to any who arrested a field preacher or who happened to kill him or any of his hearers in attempting to do so. It was a draconian measure, intended to drive the people back to the despised nominees of the bishops, and like all measures aimed at dragooning the conscience, it failed in its purpose. Attendances at field-meetings swelled to still greater proportions, and many of the hearers, now under threat of their lives, started to carry arms to defend themselves. Far from securing conformity, the act only succeeded in forcing a confrontation, which sooner or later was bound to break out into bloodshed. It was the precursor of many similar measures which were to be introduced over the next eighteen years, and which were to impose an ever-increasing weight of persecution on the field-preachers and their hearers.

One effect of the 1670 act was to bring a growing number of people before the Privy Council on charges of attending conventicles, and it was not long before the Council themselves began to feel the burden of enforcing the act. The numbers of the field-meetings, and of those attending them, showed no signs of diminishing, and the Council were obliged to spend a great part of their time in levying fines and in following up complaints and information. This coincided with pressures from another source, for the country was now becoming involved in a protracted war with Holland, and it was no time for the government to be embroiled in civil distractions at home. In England, a toleration to dissenters was granted early in 1672 for just this reason, and it was no surprise when later in the year a similar measure in the form of the Second Indulgence was published in Scotland. Again, this was strongly opposed by the bishops, but they were, as before, effectively overruled.

This Indulgence, which was more comprehensive than that of 1669, was aimed specifically at 'the disorders which have lately been by the frequent and numerous conventicles' and at remedying 'so great an evil in the greatest manner that could be thought on'. It specified about eighty ejected ministers and assigned them in groups of two, three or four to specific parishes, mainly in the west and south-west. Stringent rules were applied as to their behaviour: no minister could leave his allotted parish without licence from the bishop, or marry or baptize any outside his parish, and no persons from other parishes were to be admitted to communions. The Indulgence was accompanied by a warning to other ministers, not covered by the Indulgence, not to absent themselves from the churches of the parishes where they resided, under pain of imprisonment, nor to preach except at the invitation of the minister assigned to the parish by the Indulgence.

In the list of ministers mentioned in the Indulgence stood the name of Donald Cargill. That he should have been included is hardly matter for surprise, since he had not attracted the particular notice of the Council on the ground of keeping conventicles, and his behaviour since being granted his liberty three years earlier had apparently given the Council some reason to suppose that he could now be made to conform. He had been treated leniently by the Council on his earlier appearance; he had acknowledged their authority by petitioning them for freedom from his confinement; here now was his opportunity to redeem his indiscretion of ten years earlier and to enter once more on a settled charge. The parish chosen for him was Eaglesham in his old presbytery of Glasgow, where James Hamilton, who had accepted the First Indulgence, was already settled.

Others of Cargill's former colleagues in Glasgow had accepted the First Indulgence or were to accept the Second, and the pressures on him must have been strong. He well knew that to accept meant not only the opportunity to pursue his ministerial calling without the fear of persecution or intimidation; it offered security, a settled charge and a regular stipend. To refuse, on the other hand, would invite certain retribution, because the Indulgence was framed in obligatory terms, and disobedience to it would be regarded by the Council as an act of defiance. But Cargill's mind was clear. He could not resume his ministry on such terms: he could not yield to acknowledge the authority which his acceptance of the Indulgence would imply, an authority which claimed jurisdiction over Christ's church of which he alone was the Head; an authority which had destroyed the foundations of that church into which Cargill had been ordained as a minister, and which even now was oppressing and persecuting its members. Although Cargill well knew what the consequences of refusal would be, he did not hesitate. From now on there would be no prospect of resuming a settled ministry, no permanent congregation, no regular income; at best the opportunity to pursue his ministry privately, among small groups of people; at worst, if he chose to defy the authorities by preaching publicly, the prospect of bitter persecution. But having made his first choice he was not long in making his second. By now, the persecution against the field-meetings had intensified; heavy fines were being exacted, not only from those attending the meetings but from the owners of lands where they were held, and from others suspected of withholding information. On the very day after the Indulgence was granted Parliament had passed an act confirming in all its severity the earlier act against conventicles, and imposing even greater restrictions on those ministers who had not accepted the Indulgence and their hearers. It was a time for men to make plain where they stood. From now on Cargill would minister not to a country parish, nor to a city charge; he would minister to the people of God in Scotland wherever their lot might be cast, wherever there were those who remained loyal to the church and its Head, wherever there was a witness against the tyranny that sought to usurp the authority of Christ. It was a decision taken in full knowledge of the likely consequences and in full dependence on the God who had called him to his service.

Cargill did not embark on his work alone. As events

proved, there were many who felt as he did, and the
Indulgence, far from restricting the activities of the field-
preachers, served only to increase their numbers. Up to now,
the main burden of field-preaching had been borne by a relatively small group of ministers from the south-west, among
whom John Welsh, the former minister of Irongray, was the
most prominent. Welsh was ably assisted by three of his
ministerial colleagues from the same area — Gabriel Semple
of Kirkpatrick-Durham and Samuel Arnot of Tongland, both
of whom had been with Welsh in the Pentland Rising, and
John Blackader of Troqueer, an indefatigable field-preacher
from the earliest days. All four had preached regularly in
their own parishes after being ejected from their charges and
they had subsequently engaged in preaching tours in other
parts of the country. They were supported from time to time
by ministers from other areas, particularly by John Dickson
of Rutherglen, who had been among the first to preach in the
fields. Generally, however, there were few of the 400 ministers ejected in 1662 who had dared to preach publicly, or if
they did, who ventured beyond the bounds of their former
parishes.

In the wake of the Second Indulgence, however, this situation was to undergo a rapid change. The Indulgence itself,
like the previous one, had brought with it a general atmosphere of relaxation and relief, however unpromising the
omens might otherwise be. Other events about this time con-
spired to produce a similar effect. The government's attention was occupied by the continuing Dutch war, and there
were internal disagreements over the administration of
Scottish affairs between the king's comissioner, the Duke of
Lauderdale, and powerful elements among the nobility. In
March 1674, perhaps in response to pressure from his political
opponents, Lauderdale secured a general indemnity for all
offences committed before that date, including accession to
conventicles. This measure in particular had an important
psychological effect. In the words of a contemporary writer,
it was 'looked at by the common people of Scotland rather as
an encouragement for the time coming, than as a remission
for what was past'. The result was that 'From that day forward

the truth was, Scotland broke loose with conventicles of all
sorts, in houses, fields and vacant churches.'

The increasing enthusiasm of the ordinary people found a
ready response among the ranks of the ministry. Ministers
who had previously been silent, or who had been content to
preach privately in houses, now took their stand openly in the
fields. Those who had already been active were stirred to new
heights of activity. The 'field presbyteries' which had grown
up in various parts of the country were busy licensing young
ministers, eager to take their place beside their elders. Before
long, the number of field-preachers had risen to upwards of
forty. The authorities, distracted as they were in other directions, were content for a time to leave the field-meetings relatively undisturbed, and these consequently increased still
more in numbers and frequency.

While not curbing the field-meetings directly, however, the
government were well aware that the meetings were being
supported by these same ministers who had refused the recent
Indulgence, and they now took steps to call these men to
account. Of these ministers Cargill, of course, was one. As
early as the autumn of 1673 he and several other nonconforming ministers were cited to appear before the Privy Council to
answer for their default. When a similar order had been
issued to Cargill five years earlier he had obeyed it, but the
circumstances now were different. In that case it had been a
question of his personal confinement, over which he recognized the Council's jurisdiction; on this occasion it was a question of the terms on which he should exercise his ministry. He
therefore clearly felt that it was his duty to obey God rather
than men, and so refused the summons. At the same time he
was careful to make it plain that he was not acting in any spirit
of contumacy, or contempt of the Council's authority over his
person, for he joined with seven others of his non-complying
brethren in preparing a supplication to the Council in which
they fully vindicated their stand.

Framed in respectful but firm terms, the supplication gave
a 'sober and ingenious relation of the reasons which lie
weighty on our consciences and bind us up from compliance
with your lordships' commands in this matter'. The ministers

stressed that they were not acting through 'a contempt of or disrespect unto authority, which we always highly esteem in the Lord, as our consciences bear us witness, resolving through grace to submit to all things lawful'. They even went so far as to concede to the king a lawful right in ecclesiastical matters, though they were careful to define this as consisting merely in conferring on the church 'whatsoever is commanded by the God of heaven'. This was, of course, entirely consistent with the Presbyterian concept of the civil power as the external guardian and protector of the church, while not conceding to it any jurisdiction in the spiritual sphere. The king's power was therefore, in the words of the supplication, 'only cumulative [i.e., concurrent] and auxiliary to the church, not privative nor distinctive'. Compliance with the Indulgence, the supplication went on, would be equivalent to a submission to prelacy, 'a plant that our heavenly Father never planted', and would bind the supplicants to a principle contrary to their most deeply held beliefs. 'And so', they concluded, 'we most humbly beseech your lordships, that what favour it shall please His Majesty in his royal clemency to grant, may not be inconsistent with our known principles, to which we stand engaged by solemn covenants and oaths. In granting of which desires, as your lordships will undoubtedly make glad the hearts of many thousands of His Majesty's loyal subjects, so you will much encourage us your humble petitioners to continue serious supplicants at the throne of grace for establishing His Majesty's throne in righteousness, and for pouring out a spirit of righteous judgement on your lordships, that we may lead a peaceable and just life in all godliness and honesty.'

By adding his signature to this moderate and conciliatory document, Cargill was making it clear that he acknowledged the power of the state in its own sphere. Indeed he was never to challenge this principle, nor to refuse obedience to the civil power in matters within its proper control. His conflict with authority, which was to become increasingly acute from this point on, arose directly from that authority's claims to regulate the affairs of the church. That principle Cargill could not yield; but while he stood inflexibly in its defence he acted with due deference and respect to the authority of the state as a lawful power, concerned at the same time that it might be brought to see its divinely ordered function in relation to the church. It was in that spirit that he had added his name to the supplication.

Cargill and his fellow-ministers could hardly have expected, however, knowing the Council's complexion, that the supplication would have produced the desired result, and this may explain why the document appears never to have been formally presented. The Council's attitude to the non-conforming ministers was becoming all too plain, and the ministers may well have concluded that, however moderately they presented their case, any attempt to justify their conduct before the Council would be futile. That this was no false assumption was soon to be proved; for in June 1674, irritated by the continuing prevalence of the field-meetings, the Council resorted to severer measures. Rewards were offered for the capture of the leading field-preachers, and the armed forces were ordered to seize them wherever they could be found. Welsh, Semple and Arnot were singled out for particular notice: rewards of 2000 merks each were offered for their capture and 1000 merks for any of the others. At the same time the Council summoned all the non-complying ministers they knew of, including Cargill, to appear before them on 16 July to answer to charges of unauthorized preaching. Again the ministers failed to comply, and this time the Council, affronted by their continued disobedience, ordered them to be denounced publicly as rebels, and in contempt of public authority. The sentence was duly proclaimed at the market crosses of Haddington, Lanark, Cupar, Perth, Dunfermline, Stirling, Glasgow, Linlithgow and Edinburgh over a period from 25 to 30 July.

Even these measures proved unavailing: the field-meetings continued to multiply, the preachers being loyally protected by the people wherever they went. The Council's next move was aimed therefore not at the ministers directly, but at those who continued to give them sustenance and support. On 6 August 1675 a charge was issued to 'all and sundry His Majesty's lieges and subjects' ordering them 'not to reset, supply or intercommune with any of the foresaid rebels nor furnish them meat, drink, house, harbour, victual nor no other thing useful or comfortable to them, nor have intelligence with them by word, writ, message or any other manner of way, under the pain to be repute and esteemed art and part with them in all the crimes foresaid and pursued therefor with all rigour to the terror of others'.This process, known as 'letters of intercommuning', was intended to leave the field-preachers without even the most basic human comforts, and it marked the beginning of a new era of repression. Severer penalties were brought in for attendance at conventicles and the list of fines and imprisonments grew daily. Bonds were imposed on landowners, making them responsible for any nonconformity by their tenants. Troops were brought in to enforce the Council's orders and to suppress the field-meetings by force of arms. Under pretext of quelling a threatened rebellion, a horde of troops from the Highlands, strangers to the customs of civilization, and intent only on plunder and rapine, were let loose on the western shires. By every means at their disposal, the Council tried to force the people and the preachers into submission. But it was of no avail. The greater the oppression, the greater the resistance; the more the preaching of the Word was persecuted, the more it was valued; the more keenly a preacher was sought for, the more devotedly he was protected. For preachers and people alike it was a time of testing, and each showed a common loyalty to the other.

Up to the mid-1670s the main centre of field-preaching activity continued to be the east and south-east of the country, particularly Fife and the Lothians, where Welsh, Dickson, Blackader and others ministered regularly to congregations of thousands. By 1677, however, the emphasis was tending to move to the south-west and Galloway, which soon became the scene of some of the most remarkable instances of spiritual power. About this time Welsh and his colleagues started the practice of observing the sacrament of the Lord's Supper in the fields. These became particularly memorable occasions, with multitudes thronging from all quarters and remaining together for periods of up to three days. Of particular note was the communion held at Skeoch Hill in Welsh's own parish of Irongray, near Dumfries, on 2 June 1678; Blackader has left a graphic description of a similar occasion at East Nisbet in the Border country on 21 April of the same year.[1]

All this while, Cargill continued to minister to his old flock in Glasgow. Few details survive of his activities in this period, but it seems likely that after continuing his private house-meetings for some time he began to preach fairly regularly in the open fields. It is clear that he was not infrequently subject to harassment. Robert Law, another nonconforming minister of the time, records that in May 1675 the persecution of meetings in Glasgow, both in houses and in the fields, was so severe that the ministers then residing there were obliged to leave and seek refuge elsewhere. Again in June 1677 he records that 'There was great trouble to them that kept conventicles in and around Glasgow, by soldiers.'

On the other hand, however, there is clear evidence that in the midst of this persecution the field-meetings continued to flourish. The Archbishop of Glasgow, writing to Lauderdale on 15 August 1676, complained that conventicles in and around Glasgow had of late been so frequent and numerous that the soldiers were unable to control them and that within two weeks previously there had been two such meetings in the Barony (Cargill's old parish) and others in the parishes of Cambuslang, Mearns, Eastwood and Kilpatrick, each attended by upwards of 3000 persons.

Cargill was certainly involved in these and other meetings about this time, both in his own parish and elsewhere. On occasion, too, he seems to have ventured further afield, and there is some evidence to suggest that he joined Welsh and others in preaching tours in other parts of the country. On 4 and 11 June 1676 he is recorded as having preached at Dovan Moor, beside Kennoway in Fife, where his preaching colleague was the noted James Fraser of Brea. Again he is mentioned in a Privy Council minute of 21 June 1677 as having preached in various places in Fife, Perth and Stirlingshire with Welsh, Fraser and others. He also appears to have visited parts of Ayrshire, including the towns of Ayr and Prestwick, and to have paid at least one visit to the Border country, apparently at the invitation of Lady Douglas of Cavers, a noted friend of the persecuted preachers. It is likely that his movements about the country were somewhat more

extensive than these sparse records suggest, and that his visits
may have extended also to other parts, including possibly the
north of England. At the same time, however, it is clear that
by far the greater part of his ministry continued to be given to
Glasgow and Clydesdale, and it is with that area that his name
became particularly linked. He appears to have been
associated for most of this time with a relatively small, close-
knit group of ministers who regarded Glasgow as their particular care and who did not itinerate about the country in the
manner of Welsh, Dickson and Blackader, who were far
more generally known among the people. This no doubt
explains why, even as late as 1677, Cargill had not come to
particular notice among the forty or fifty ministers still
preaching in the fields, and why his standing among the
people as a whole certainly did not match that of Welsh and
his fellow-preachers.

Events, however, were soon to change this situation
dramatically and to bring Cargill into a position of prominence which he was destined never to lose. By the beginning
of 1678 Glasgow and Clydesdale were being influenced by the
spiritual revival which had so signally affected other parts of
the country, and the effects which it produced were proving
similar. Cargill soon found himself in the midst of a powerful
spiritual movement which brought crowds flocking to his
preaching. He did his best to adapt himself to the situation,
but the unwonted activity soon began to tell on him in a
particularly frustrating way. His voice, strained beyond
endurance by preaching to unusually large multitudes, broke
down completely, so that he could not make himself heard at
any distance. He was sorely discouraged; if the affliction continued it would mean an end to the work on which he had set
his heart. The people, denied the benefit of his preaching,
were obliged to invite other ministers to take his place, and
for a time — perhaps a considerable time — he was forced to
remain silent while others preached.

Eventually however, on the occasion of a visit by John
Blackader, Cargill, to the surprise of the people, ventured to
give a short address from Isaiah 44:3: 'I will pour water upon
him that is thirsty, and floods upon the dry ground.' His hearers were apprehensive, knowing the state of his voice, but as

soon as he had started there was a marvellous transformation. 'It pleased the Lord,' says a contemporary, 'to loose his tongue and restore his voice to that distinctness and clearness, that none could readily exceed him in that respect ever after; and not only his voice, but his spirit was so enlarged, and such a door of utterance given him, that Mr Blackader, succeeding him, said to the people, "Ye that have such preaching as this, have no need to invite strangers to preach to you. Make good use of your mercy."'

To those present, what they had witnessed was nothing other than a divine seal of approval on Cargill's ministry; and from that moment his place among the ministers of the 'suffering remnant' was assured. Great crowds flocked to hear him, some travelling many miles, and the calls on his time became frequent and pressing. From this time onwards he seems to have entered upon a particularly intense phase of activity in and around Glasgow.

By now the whole of the west and south-west had been transformed into one vast area of spiritual awakening. It was, in Patrick Walker's words, 'a day of the power of the gospel, to the conviction and conversion of many souls, which made some to call in question if there had been a greater, since the apostles ceased out of the world, in so short a time and in so little bounds of the earth, as in the south and west of Scotland for some years after the standard of the gospel was publicly set up in the fields'. Cargill, his preaching powers now at their zenith, was in the very centre of this great movement of the Spirit and he dedicated himself to it with memorable fervour. John Blackader, whose memoirs provide a valuable insight into the events of the period, recorded that in the summer of 1678, when he himself was lying ill in Glasgow, Cargill kept 'frequent great meetings at several places near about the town' with 'people flocking out in multitudes on all hands'. About this time he is said to have preached outside Glasgow on eighteen consecutive Sabbaths to crowds so huge that the singing of the psalms could be heard in several parts of the city. The very size of the multitudes deterred the authorities from intervening and Cargill found himself able to preach freely without interruption.

Cargill's early ministry in Glasgow, the personal sorrows

and hardships which he had undergone, the years of enforced silence, had all been part of his preparation for his great work. There were few of his contemporaries who could accompany the preaching of the Word with the same degree of human sympathy and the same insight into the character and conscience; he had been schooled in affliction, he had had to fight against faint-heartedness and despondency, and he could communicate his message with a tenderness and understanding that were born of deep personal experience. 'What comes not from my heart,' he said on one occasion, 'I have little hope will go to the heart of others.' It was this closeness of contact, this directness of approach from the heart of preacher to hearer, that was to make his ministry memorable in the recollection of all who heard him, and to give him a special place in his hearers' affections. 'Mr Donald', as he became affectionately known, was not only a much esteemed, but a much loved figure. 'A man greatly beloved indeed' is one hearer's affectionate remembrance of him, many years later, and in so saying he was clearly speaking for many who counted it a rich privilege to sit under Cargill's ministry, or to share his company.

The same writer gives a significant insight into the secret of Cargill's success when he records that 'From his youth he was much given to secret prayer, yea whole nights,' and it was clearly this closeness of fellowship with God, which he made part of his very way of life, that gave Cargill that sanctity of character which impressed so deeply those who came into close contact with him. Throughout his life, and increasingly as the years went on, he was so conscious of the presence of the God who had called him that at every crisis he was fully assured of the course he was to follow and the action he was to take. There were many duties, indeed, from which his natural inclinations shrank and which, left to himself, he could not have brought himself to do; but the assurance that he was acting under the direction of a divine power strengthened him in every time of trial and put his fears to flight. As a minister of God, bearing his authority and called to his service, it was not for him to feel afraid or despondent. 'Oh', he said on one occasion, 'it does not become a minister of the gospel to be moved with fear: he is to be holy, an overseer, watchman, leader, therefore it is unsuitable for him to be overcome with such things. Nay, Christ their Master often forbids them to fear, and foretells them what they are to meet with when about his work, and yet not to fear or succumb under either fears or favours. When a minister of the gospel is tender, and has the awe of God upon his spirit, and his glory before his eyes, he will not be much afraid. Being fitted of him, and our commission made manifest by him, we ought to go on acting in faith upon him, undertaking what he calls us to, against all infirmities within and oppositions without. Let us never stand then when God calls, for here is the promise sufficient to bear all charges: "Lo I am with you alway, even unto the end of the world." Here is fulness of comfort and consolation in this one promise, that he will be with us. Nothing should frighten us. Here is a sufficiency: "He will never leave us nor forsake us." It is true, ministers have not the promise of worldly ease, or of safety from trouble; but they have the promise of safety in troubles, and deliverance out of them. When ministers have great promises from God, they are not to look for exemption from trouble. That is not the promise to be accomplished to us while in time. Fighting and victory here, and the crown above. Let us then look unto him for determination in duty, and thus go on in the strength of God the Lord.' It was on these principles that Cargill acted, and in that assurance that he lived.

7.
The woeful Indulgence

Cargill's new prominence brought with it its own dangers. He was now much more closely sought after by the forces of authority, and he was forced to be increasingly circumspect in his movements. Early in 1679 the reward for the capture of any of the preachers named in the 'letters of intercommuning' was raised to 2000 merks, with higher rewards for the most prominent offenders.

By this time, Cargill was virtually living the life of a fugitive. Hunted by the soldiers, his movements watched by spies and informers, he had many remarkable escapes. On several occasions the house where he lodged was closely searched, but on each occasion he happened to be absent. To his friends, many of his deliverances seemed providential. He escaped more than once merely by walking unnoticed past the band of soldiers who had come in search of him; on another occasion, when closely pursued, he was kept in safety by a soldier's wife after fleeing into the first house he came to; and once he remained hidden behind a pile of books which the occupants of a house where he was preaching had hastily stacked up in a window around him.

Sometimes, indeed, he seemed to have a presentiment of danger. The story is told how, one day when he was about to mount his horse to go to preach, he suddenly said, 'I must not go yonder today,' and shortly afterwards, having been informed of his intended whereabouts, the enemy arrived in search of him at that very spot. Such incidents, in the words of a contemporary, go to prove 'that the secret of the Lord is with them that fear him', and it is difficult not to see in Cargill's life at this time an evidence of that closeness of communion with God which, for a few, has been known to bring even future events within the realm of the human understanding.

It was about this time that Cargill seems to have first made the acquaintance of a young man with whom he was to become closely associated at a future stage of his ministry. Richard Cameron, then about thirty years of age, was born in Falkland in Fife about the time that Cargill was studying at St Andrews, and he had followed in Cargill's footsteps by matriculating in the university in 1662 and graduating as Master of Arts three years later. For some time he had worked closely with the curate of his native parish, acting as precentor or leader of the praise, and also, for a while, as local schoolmaster. However, after hearing first the Presbyterian ministers who had accepted the Indulgences, and then the field-preachers, he had thrown in his lot unreservedly with the persecuted church. He became private chaplain to the family of Sir William Scott of Harden in the Border country, a man of Presbyterian sympathies, but Cameron's uncompromising views soon proved too much for his employer, and he was obliged to leave his service. After finding sanctuary for a time as chaplain to Lady Douglas of Cavers, well-known for her support for the nonconforming ministers, Cameron made the acquaintance of John Welsh, who formed a high opinion of his abilities and urged him to accept licence for the ministry. At first he refused, but urged by Welsh and other ministers he eventually assented, and was licensed some time in the spring of 1678.[1] He immediately began an uncompromising and forthright ministry.

The evangelical note was never far from Cameron's preaching, but for him it could not be kept separate from the purity of the church; if the church was to evangelize and strengthen its witness, it must first cleanse itself from the evils which had overtaken it. Foremost among these evils, in Cameron's opinion, was the Indulgence. He attacked it, and the ministers who had accepted it, with a vigour and force which soon marked him out from all his fellow-ministers. His zeal for the cause, coupled with a natural ardour of temperament, drove him on regardless of fear or favour, and the outspoken nature of his attacks began to give offence not only to those who had themselves benefited from the Indulgence but to others, including Welsh himself, who could not bring themselves to regard the Indulgence as necessarily evil. The most controversial feature of Cameron's preaching, and that for which he was held in the deepest disfavour, was his practice of dissuading his hearers from attending the preaching of those who had accepted the Indulgence. While he may not have been the first to proclaim this principle, he was certainly the most outspoken; and Welsh and Semple, who had jointly been responsible for licensing him, soon felt themselves obliged to place some curb on his activities.[2]

Something of a crisis was reached on 4 August 1678 at a communion in the fields at Maybole — said to have been the largest such meeting ever held — when Cameron and another young probationer, John Kid, organized a meeting of their own some distance away from the main meeting, and drew away many of the people from hearing Welsh and the other ministers.[3] On the 22nd of the same month, almost certainly at Welsh's instigation, Cameron found himself summoned before a meeting of ministers in Edinburgh to answer for his conduct. He duly obeyed the summons, but declined to accept any censure, or to refrain, even for a period, from preaching against the Indulgence. The ministers dismissed him with a warning, to which, however, he paid little heed. He soon found encouragement in another quarter, for John Brown of Wamphray, Robert M'Ward's fellow-exile in Holland, wrote him a letter expressing warm support for his uncompromising stand, and at the same time wrote to Welsh and some others disputing the Edinburgh meeting's claim to ecclesiastical jurisdiction. Brown's intervention caused considerable offence and brought himself and M'Ward into much disfavour. Cameron, however, strengthened by this accession of support, pressed on undaunted. In October and November he preached frequently in various places in Ayrshire and Galloway, amid considerable popular acclaim. His preaching soon became so objectionable to Welsh that on one occasion at Irongray he rebuked Cameron publicly for his 'impertinence', bringing not a little public resentment on himself as a result.

Eventually Welsh and Semple decided that it was time to

The Covenanters by W.H. Weatherhead

take a firmer stand. On 14 November, at Dunscore near Dumfries, they met with two other ministers as a 'presbytery', and summoned Cameron to appear before them to answer for his continued defiance. Cameron duly complied, but again refused to accept any censure, or to moderate his preaching in any way. The ministers, nonplussed, decided to write for advice to some of their brethren in Edinburgh, suggesting a general meeting to discuss the matter, and to confer with Cameron about his future conduct.

In the meantime Welsh and Semple met again on 26 December at Dundeugh in Galloway, with Samuel Arnot as 'moderator of presbytery'. Whether Cameron was summoned on this occasion is not certain, but in any event it appears that he did not attend. This may have been due to the influence of his friend Robert Hamilton, with whom he had now become closely associated, and who was to play a prominent part in some of the events which were to follow. Hamilton, a son of Sir Thomas Hamilton of Preston, was a young man of strong principle and character, firmly attached to the cause of the persecuted church and uncompromising in its defence. He supported, and practised, the principle of carrying defensive arms at field-meetings and was, like Cameron, particularly outspoken on the contentious subject of the Indulgence. Hamilton seems to have felt that the tyranny of the times called for more positive action on the part of those who adhered to the Presbyterian cause, and he is said to have tried, during the summer of 1678, to stir up some of the people in the west into an armed rising against the government. Whether this allegation is well-founded cannot conclusively be proved, but it is beyond doubt that Hamilton's activities about this time, coupled with Cameron's continuing condemnation of the Indulgence, gave offence to many of the older ministers, whether or not they had accepted the Indulgence, and led them into a general suspicion of the 'younger men' into whose hands the control of affairs seemed to be passing. Certainly Hamilton's popularity was not enhanced by his conduct at the Dunscore and Dundeugh meetings, where he appeared personally and denounced Welsh, Semple and the rest for their behaviour towards Cameron and their betrayal of Presbyterian principles.[4]

The issue of the Indulgence, which was regarded by many of the older ministers as a matter of particular delicacy and difficulty, and so not to be pressed unduly, had now been brought uncompromisingly into the open. Feelings on the subject ran high, and Cameron and Hamilton were accused of spreading dissension and disunity among the people and of causing disaffection towards ministers who did not share their radical opinions. However, Cargill did not join in the chorus of criticism and was obviously concerned to weigh the issues carefully before committing himself to a public view. On an issue of such importance it was inevitable that he should have to declare his mind sooner or later, but as always he acted with deliberation. To preach separation from those who were ordained ministers of the gospel was a fundamental step to take, and to Cargill, with his high conception of the ministerial office, it was a particularly daunting one. But on the other hand he had become convinced that the Indulgence, in its source and effects, was an evil of such magnitude that, cost him what it might, it was his duty to oppose it to the utmost. It was one thing, however, to hold a view personally and another to declare it openly in public, and for some time he seems to have hesitated. It was just at this juncture that he received a letter from his old friend Robert M'Ward in Holland which seems to have done much to set his doubts at rest. Rather surprisingly, Cargill and M'Ward do not seem to have exchanged letters before this time, though M'Ward was a regular correspondent of several of the other nonconforming ministers, including Blackader and Dickson. M'Ward had apparently been told of Cargill's disappointment at not having heard from him, and so he begins with an apology: 'It may be you are displeased with me, I have not written a line to you before this time: but if instead of another apology I should say if you had hinted by a line your desire of it I would not have been wanting in giving it some poor return.' He goes on in a gracious strain: 'Let me tell you, dear brother, I have not only been refreshed when I remembered and called to mind auld lang syne in reference to you, and how the Lord your God, even your own God, has kept you still, with him holding you by your right hand and upholding you in your integrity, but more particularly I am made to rejoice because of what I have heard of your usefulness to his people, your straightness in his work, while many are starting and staggering and stumbling as halting betwixt two ways.' He congratulates Cargill on the recovery of his voice: 'He has I hear given you a new voice that you are in case to be a mouth to thousands: blessed be the Giver, and blessed be he who has given it to you, to give yourself to him and for him to his people.'

The greater part of M'Ward's letter is taken up with the Indulgence ('this wretched Indulgence, one of the greatest plagues and snares that ever befell the Church of Scotland') and the calamities which he saw coming upon the church because of it. 'Oh the taking from this usurper, this stated enemy to Christ, is a guilt of such crimson dye that every man may meditate terror in the apprehension and fearful expectation of that vengeance wherewith it is like to be awaited . . . The great plea for the indulged is, many of them are godly men. I grant it, and I honour them as such; but alas, I must say this argument has been so managed and made use of as I fear not to say, neither care I if it be known to all Scotland that I said so, their godliness has been of greater prejudice to the cause and precious interest of Christ than all the ungodliness of the prelates and their underlings ever has been or could be. I think I am in no great mistake if I affirm the godliness of those engaged in that course should rather have imposed upon all the lovers of our Lord Jesus Christ and his interests a necessity of warring against the sin and snare wherein they are fallen, lest their example should have proved contagious to the church, and of mortal consequence to the cause.'

M'Ward goes on to express his sorrow about a report that had reached him that certain young ministers in Scotland had agreed not to mention the Indulgence in their preaching. He asks Cargill to verify the truth of this, and to give him 'a full and particular account of the condition of the poor remnant, of the carriage of ministers indulged and non-indulged, and of what success the gospel has'. He closes with words which must have brought his friend much comfort at a time when he sorely needed it: 'I must thank you (and I desire to rejoice in the forethought in what addition it will make to the crown of glory which the Chief Shepherd will of grace set upon your head at his coming) for your work and labour of love amongst that poor precious remnant in Glasgow: whereby I hear, and I hear it with joy, you are much endeared to their soul. O man greatly beloved, go on in the strength of the Lord: preach, witness and wrestle within sight of the garland and the glory to be revealed; give not way to despondency; say not at the sight of every emergent difficulty, "What is my strength, that I should hope?" Nay rather, think of what is his strength, his promised strength, who sends you not to this warfare on your own charges, and then go forward as strengthened with all might according to his glorious power, unto all patience and all longsuffering and joyfulness.'

M'Ward added a postscript which was of particular interest to Cargill in his present circumstances. In it he mentions that he is enclosing a copy of a paper by his fellow-exile, John Brown, on the question of hearing the conforming ministers. This, says M'Ward, had been discussed at length between Brown and himself, and they were now 'perfectly of the same mind' on the matter. Their conclusion, supported by reasoned argument and Scripture proof, was that those who had accepted the Indulgence should not be heard, and, adds M'Ward, he had taken the trouble to transcribe the whole of Brown's paper on the subject for Cargill's benefit.

M'Ward's letter was typical of several which he and Brown sent over to Scotland at this time, and they elaborated their arguments in a series of books and tracts which received a wide circulation. The best known of these was Brown's *History of the Indulgence,* an exhaustive and skilful treatment of the subject, in which he fully exposed its pernicious influence on the church. The writings of the exiles caused considerable controversy in the church at home and aggravated the resentment caused by their support of Cameron. For Cargill, however, they provided an eloquent expression of his own feelings: they convinced him that his thoughts on the matter were right; and the powerful arguments which they drew from Scripture confirmed him in the view that the Indulgence was an evil of the greatest possible consequence for the testimony and witness of the church.

Cargill had not been directly involved in the controversy surrounding Cameron, which had so far been relatively localized in nature. Events were, however, soon to bring the issue into a wider arena. Two other young probationers, John Kid and Thomas Hog, had been reported to the Edinburgh meeting the previous August for proclaiming similar opinions to those of Cameron. Kid, unlike Cameron, refused to attend when summoned, and Hog was to prove equally trouble-some.[5] Early in 1679 he preached in the vicinity of Glasgow and publicly urged separation from the ministers who had accepted the Indulgence. The result was the calling of a meet-ing of all the nonconforming Glasgow ministers at the Haggs, near Glasgow, to which Hog was summoned. Welsh and Sem-ple, now experienced in dealing with recalcitrants, attended the meeting. Hog was censured and ordered to submit himself to the authority of the ministers who had given him his licence. At the same time, to clear themselves of any misun-derstandings, the ministers decided to write an open letter to one of the ministers who had accepted the Indulgence, to be communicated to the rest, in which while affirming their unyielding opposition to the Indulgence they disclaimed any association with the separatist views of the young probationers.

Cargill was apparently present at the Haggs meeting, for he later had to defend himself against charges of having spread false reports of its conclusions. The controversy surrounding Hog had brought the issue of the Indulgence home to him more closely than ever before and it seems to have given him the final impetus he needed to declare his mind publicly. Preaching near Glasgow on 9 February, he forthrightly con-demned the Indulgence and supported the call for separation from the ministers who had accepted it. Inevitably, it was a step which instantly involved him in bitter controversy. Welsh, who was himself preaching about Glasgow at this time, was deeply offended and, according to one account, contradicted Cargill publicly. His attitude seems to have been typical of the ministers in general. It was one thing for these principles to be preached by a small group of young pro-bationers, who could be charged with rashness and over-enthusiasm, but quite another for them to be supported by a minister of Cargill's standing and repute. Not only so, but Cargill's undoubted popularity and influence with the people would lead many of them into following him and cause them to desert the ministry of those who opposed him. Worse still, it could lead to a division among the people as a whole, and to lack of unity in the face of the common enemy. All these arguments were no doubt pressed upon Cargill, but he was fully assured of the rightness of his step. In his considered view, ministers who had benefited from the Indulgence could not be distinguished from the favour they had accepted: fellowship with them was fellowship with what the Indulgence represented — with the denial of Christ's rights as Head of the church, with the subversion of the divine order of church government, with the usurping and blasphemous claims of the state. Of these consequences Cargill was now utterly certain, however great the pressures brought to bear upon him might be.

So far indeed was he from regretting the step he had taken that he joined openly with Cameron and others in giving further public testimony to his disputed views. Preaching with Cameron and another probationer, John King, on 24 April he broached the controversial subject again. He was only too keenly aware of the views of some, including several of his friends, that he had adopted too rigid a stand on the subject. He faced the issue squarely: 'There are some of you who will have us to recant what we have spoken in that matter: but it is strange if such a sudden change should come, when we have been of such a judgement for several years past. The Lord is witness, we desire not to discredit any of the ministers of Jesus Christ, yet we must say that the authority of men is pleaded and not reason, and zeal is shown to their reputation more than to the church. "Oh, but they are great holy men," say some. The Lord has that word by the apostle, in the second chapter of Galatians: "Whatever they were, it maketh no matter to me, for God accepteth no man's person." And of the Indulgence we will say this, that because it subjects the church of God to the magistrate in the regulating and the exercising of their offices so that they must come and go at his bidding, or likewise be silent or preach at his bidding, that is the subjecting the church and ministry to his usurped power, and the accepting of liberty on that ground is a homologating of his usurped power . . . We are sure that the church of God is injured and enslaved by this liberty and acceptance. It may be thought, it is not an acceptance but a submission. But there is more than a submission here; there is an acceptance of a favour. "They confine," say some, "but their persons." I answer, they have confined their ministry, and we may say that they themselves do more confine their ministry than their persons, for they have taken more liberty to themselves than to their ministry.'

Cargill well knew that in speaking out in this way he had laid himself open to bitter criticism. Those who had accepted the Indulgence, and those who sided with them, would be sure to represent him as acting in a self-righteous Pharisaical spirit, and they would not be slow to look for inconsistencies in his own conduct. After all, had he not himself given up his ministry in Glasgow at the instance of the Council? Cargill anticipated this charge and had his answer ready: 'It may be further said, we left our ministry upon their appointment. We acknowledge this before God, that it was our fault that we so soon relinquished our particular charge. But our yielding to their banishment was not a yielding of our ministry; for we exercised where we could; and it shows that we did not subject our ministry to men, that we hold on to preach upon hazard.' He was careful not to exclude himself from his general criticism, with perhaps a hint of the struggle that had taken place in his own mind on being offered the Indulgence: 'There is another second part that concerns us, to mourn for the concurrence we have had in desiring, concurring and countenancing at least: all have lusted after this in their hearts: not only did we think to make use of it, but in effect if we could have got a good bargain we would have sold the public liberty for a private benefit: for wherever the temptation came, almost there was a yielding. It may be said, "Let us see Scripture for it." We shall only mention two places, one is the fifth chapter of Galatians: "Stand fast therefore in the liberty wherewith Christ hath made us free," which is not a liberty from ceremonies only, but from all subjection to men in things that concern God. In a word, the people should by this lose their liberty of calling a minister to feed them; and upon the other hand the ministers should lose their power to send such and such men to such and such places. Another text is Galatians 2: "False brethren unawares crept in, who came in privily to spy out our liberty which we have in Christ Jesus, that they might bring us into bondage: to whom we gave place by subjection, no, not for an hour; that the truth of the gospel might continue with you." This is clear, the gospel would have died with the Indulgence, if all had closed with it. We must say, we ought not to give subjection in anything that belongs to the liberties of the church, and glory of Christ, no, not for an hour.'

The immediate effect of this sermon, and Cargill's open association with Cameron and the other probationers, was that three days later, on 27 April, he was called before a meeting of ministers at Glasgow, probably comprising the members of the 'field presbytery' with which he had been associated in earlier days. His fellow-ministers charged him with supporting separatism and keeping company with younger men who were ignorant of the principles and traditions of the church. Cargill replied, with some warmth, that he had found more of the life and power of godliness in these young men than in those who were most highly thought of in the public ministry of the time. Cameron, he declared, had done nothing but what worthy men in former times of the church's apostasy had done, such as Guthrie and Gillespie. And as for the charge of separatism, it was those who accepted the Indulgence who were the real separatists; though to vindicate himself he maintained that he had not preached separation from them as ministers, but only while they remained in the parishes to which they had been assigned by the Indulgence. Matters were not apparently pressed further at this time, but it must have been obvious to Cargill, as he parted from his fellow-ministers that evening, that the gulf between him and them was growing steadily wider, and the path before him was becoming an increasingly lonely one.

8.
The break at Bothwell

For several years, although the sternest measures were in force against attenders at field-meetings, direct conflict between them and the forces of authority was largely avoided. Many of the hearers, indeed, carried arms, and had done so since 1670, but their strength of numbers usually acted as a deterrent to any attackers, and the authorities were generally content to leave the meetings unmolested while sparing no opportunity to prosecute any whom they suspected of attending them. Throughout the 1670s this situation continued, so that even by 1679 there were some twenty or thirty ministers still preaching in the fields, and no significant decline in the number of their hearers. But the year 1679 was to bring a very radical change and to usher in an era of persecution on a scale hitherto unknown.

To some extent this situation resulted from the annoyance caused to the government by the activities of Robert Hamilton and his followers, who were by now acting as a kind of self-appointed armed bodyguard to Cameron in his preaching tours about the country. Hamilton had already been involved, as early as November 1677, in a violent incident at the home of his friend John Balfour of Kinloch, in Fife, when a party of soldiers who approached the house were fired upon and one of them was seriously wounded. How far Hamilton himself may have been responsible for incidents of this kind is not altogether clear, though it has been suggested in his defence that several of the actions for which he and his men were blamed about this time were the work of malcontents and other disaffected persons who had infiltrated his following and who did not share the high ideals which he and his friends professed. Be that as it may, it is clear that the activities of Hamilton and his men were regarded with increasing dismay by some of the older field-preachers and their adherents, since they seemed bound to lead to a confrontation with the government, and to provoke acts of reprisal.

As events were to show, these fears were not misplaced. On 11 March 1679 Robert Johnstone, the Town Major or Sheriff's Officer of Edinburgh, was lured to a house in the city under pretext of dispersing an unlawful meeting and was there set upon and wounded by a party of men, of whom Cameron's brother Michael was said to have been one. Less than three weeks later, on 30 March, a small party of soldiers who came within sight of a field-meeting at Cummerhead, near Lesmahagow, were opposed by Hamilton's men by armed force and some of them taken prisoner. Possibly the most serious of these incidents took place on 20 April at Loudon Hill in Ayrshire, when a government trooper was shot dead and another seriously wounded, in circumstances which could scarcely be described as a provocation.

These events brought about a marked deterioration in the atmosphere. Their immediate result was to impel the government to greater efforts against the field-meetings in general and to deploy more troops to suppress them. Cameron, for his part, appears to have become increasingly embarrassed by Hamilton's activities on his behalf, and he is said to have publicly expressed his regret for the Loudon Hill incident in particular.

The event, however, above all others which made 1679 a year of crisis was the violent death, on 3 May 1679, of James Sharp, Archbishop of St Andrews and Primate of Scotland. As a reward for his labours in settling the government of the church, Sharp had been given the honour of being made chief ecclesiastical dignitary in the country, and he had used his position to his own best advantage. He had pursued relentlessly those who had challenged or affronted the authority of the government; he had, as a member of the Privy Council, used his utmost endeavours against those who had defied its edicts; and he had even, for a time, been in

charge of a Court of High Commission which had been
formed specially to try offenders against the new ecclesiastical system. Sharp was regarded by the body of Presbyterians
in Scotland — even by those who did not take their principles
so far as to attend field-meetings — as a traitor to his church,
and he was charged by many with the blood of those who had
been tortured and executed after Pentland. The bitterness
against him was of that special deep-seated kind that is
reserved for the man who has sold his friends into the hand of
the enemy and then proceeded to enrich himself with the
spoils.

It was this hated figure whom a band of resolute men —
zealots rather than saints — found in their power on the road
to St Andrews on the morning of 3 May 1679. They had not,
indeed, been looking for him. His deliverance into their
hands was to all appearances quite fortuitous; they had been
looking merely for one of his agents, whom they had intended
to frighten but not to kill. But in Sharp's unexpected appearance they saw the finger of Providence and, having been given
this opportunity, as they saw it, of avenging the terrible
wrongs he had inflicted on the church, they proceeded, with
grim determination, to carry out what they felt to be their
divinely appointed task. It was a deed that was to bring severe
retribution, not principally on the agents themselves, most of
whom escaped, but upon the whole body of the Presbyterians. 'Was the archbishop's death murder?' became one of
the standard ensnaring questions put as a test of loyalty to
those who were brought before the Council, and for many a
day the suffering church was made to answer for an action
that it had not sanctioned, and in which none of its principal
members had had a part.

At the time of the archbishop's death, Cargill was in Glasgow. He probably foresaw the troubles this event would
cause, though later, when put to the question, he chose
neither to justify nor condemn it, but contented himself by
quoting the scriptural warrant for a private person to kill
where he had a call from God to do so, as in the cases of
Phinehas and Jael.[1] Cargill himself would before long be in
company with the perpetrators of the deed, though he may
not at the time have realized it, for on Thursday, 22 May he

preached at a fast-day service near Campsie where several of them were present. Since the events of 3 May they had been living as fugitives, sheltered here and there by friends, but they now made common cause with a more influential group under the leadership of Robert Hamilton, who was already known to some of them, and who seems to have seen in this new accession of strength an opportunity for the kind of public testimony which he had long advocated. In this resolution he was supported by the party who had now joined him and of whom he became the effective leader. But such was Hamilton's respect for Cargill's judgement that first of all the latter's opinion had to be sought; and so on Monday, 26 May, Hamilton, accompanied by David Hackston of Rathillet and John Balfour of Kinloch, both of whom had been present at the death of the archbishop, rode into Glasgow and talked the matter over with Cargill. Cargill assented to their proposal in principle, though it appears that the substance of the testimony or declaration was not discussed in any detail, and a draft of it had not yet been drawn up. This work fell mainly to Hamilton and Hackston, and Cargill, who remained behind in Glasgow when they returned to their quarters at Hamilton, took no active part in it.

Hamilton's intention was to make the public demonstration at the cross of Glasgow, but it was decided that the presence of the king's forces there, in strength, made this too hazardous a venture. The imminence of 29 May, the day of 'solemn anniversary thanksgiving' was, however, too good an opportunity to miss, and an alternative arrangement was soon decided upon. Accordingly, on Thursday, 29 May, Hamilton and some eighty armed men rode into the town of Rutherglen, put out the bonfires blazing in the king's honour and publicly burnt the detested acts of Parliament and Council. At the same time they published a declaration testifying against the tyranny and oppression of the 'cruel and perfidious adversaries', the Acts of Parliament overturning the Presbyterian government of the church, the act establishing the king's supremacy and 'all other sinful and unlawful acts emitted and executed by them'.[2]

This was a deliberate, calculated act of defiance, of a kind unknown since Pentland, and designed to have the maximum effect. The government were infuriated, particularly as the outrage had happened only a few miles from Glasgow, where their troops were stationed for the express purpose of keeping order. An immediate commission was given to John Graham of Claverhouse, who had already gained notoriety through his repressive activities in the south-west, to apprehend any who had taken part in the affair and to kill all whom he found in arms at conventicles.

Having made a preliminary sortie in which he took several prisoners, Claverhouse heard on 31 May that a large field-meeting was planned for the following day at Loudon Hill, near Newmilns, where he would have good hope of capturing some of the rebels. The prize was too good to miss, and although warned against it by others who knew the strength to which Hamilton's force had now grown, on the morning of 1 June Claverhouse accordingly set out for his objective. He had not far to seek, for news of the meeting had spread widely, and it had attracted not only those involved in the affair at Rutherglen but a substantial number of sympathizers from the surrounding shires. The meeting had not long started when Claverhouse arrived on the scene; but having got warning of his approach his intended victims had already sent away their womenfolk and children and had drawn them-selves up in battle order. They were an untrained little army, with no pretensions to military finesse or discipline, and what little ammunition they had was supplemented with pitchforks and other home-made weapons. But they had the advantage of the ground, Claverhouse having to station his troops in a morass, and they had boundless confidence in the justice of their cause. Advancing down the hillside they engaged the enemy with a vigour and energy which soon overwhelmed the disciplined ranks of Claverhouse's force. Some thirty soldiers were killed; the rest fled the field, Claverhouse narrowly escaping with his life, and the pursuit was kept up for several miles.[3]

The skirmish of Drumclog, as it came to be known, was a humiliation which Claverhouse never forgot: and many of his deeds of oppression in later years, it is said, may be traced to the desire to avenge this early defeat. For the moment, how-ever, Hamilton and his friends were triumphant. They sensibly decided that, since the government would be sure to react vigorously, their safety consisted in numbers. They resolved to keep together, to press home the advantage they had gained and to advance on the enemy's stronghold in Glasgow. But although their strength had now greatly increased, this proved to be too ambitious a target. The soldiers had had time to organize their defences and had no intention of meeting their victorious adversaries in the open country. After some futile attempts to break down the defences, Hamilton's men were forced to retire. It was, however, a merely temporary setback, because the news of their victory had now spread far and wide and was daily bringing in more adherents to their cause. Many of the new arrivals were quite unaware of the original causes of the rising, the deeply held principles which had motivated the public testimony at Rutherglen; they saw Hamilton and his followers simply as champions of the Presbyterian cause against tyranny and oppression, and they did not wish to see them left to the vengeance of the government. Throughout the following week large numbers from all parts of the west and south-west flocked to the standard. Among these were John Welsh and several of his fellow-ministers and supporters from Galloway. By the end of the week they had been joined by still others, including Donald Cargill.

For Cargill, the two weeks which followed were to prove a most unhappy experience. No sooner had he joined Hamilton's army than serious differences of opinion began to break out in its ranks. The immediate cause of the dissension was the drawing up of a declaration of policy, and the main ground of dispute was the Indulgence. Those who had made the public demonstration at Rutherglen were of one mind on the matter, but their new adherents viewed it differently. The Indulgence, they pointed out, had not been condemned by any church court; it had not been declared to be wrong by the church at large; and to denounce it publicly would merely alienate a large section of the people and diminish support for the army. Hamilton's party were at first able to resist the pressure, and on 6 June they published a short declaration testifying against 'popery, prelacy, Erastianism, and all things depending thereupon', the last phrase being intended as a

pointed reference to the Indulgence. But as the new adherents grew stronger and began to outnumber the other
party, dissatisfaction with this declaration increased and the
pressure for a more acceptable statement of policy grew
stronger.

Welsh's party, which included the majority of the ministers, produced a draft document in which they recounted at
length the miseries and distressed condition of the church and
people, asserted that they were now assembled in 'lawful and
innocent self-defence', and went on to give their aims as
'First, the defending and securing of the true Protestant religion and Presbyterian government founded upon the Word of
God; second, the preserving and defending the king's
Majesty's person and authority in the preservation and
defence of the true religion and liberties of the kingdom, that
the world may bear witness, with our consciences, of our loyalty, and that we have no thoughts nor intentions to diminish
his just power and greatness; and third, the obtaining of a free
and unlimited Parliament, and of a free General Assembly, in
order to the redressing of our foresaid grievances, for preventing the danger of popery, and extirpation of prelacy.'

The second of these reasons, acknowledging the king's
authority, was strenuously opposed by Hamilton and his
party, who contended that the king, by overturning the work
of reformation, disowning the Covenants, and persecuting
the church, did not deserve to be acknowledged publicly in
the manner proposed. It was not, they stressed, that they
wished positively to disown his authority, though some of
them were clearly ready to go that far, but merely to omit all
reference to him from the declaration. This, however, would
not satisfy Welsh's party, who maintained that to fail to
acknowledge the king would remove all hope of redressing
the grievances complained of, as well as alienating many who
would otherwise attach themselves to the cause. The draft
declaration was finally approved, amid some general confusion, and was published at the Cross of Hamilton on 13 June.
Hamilton and his supporters continued to oppose it after its
publication, and while not disowning it directly, maintained
that it had not been agreed in proper order and that its publication was in breach of an agreement that certain adjustments

would first be made to meet their objections. The publication of the declaration did much to exacerbate feeling between the two sides and it damaged still further the prospects of unity in the common cause.

In the meantime the Privy Council had been stirred to vigorous action. A series of proclamations had called the country to arms, and preparations to meet the challenge of the rising were well afoot. The charge of the army was committed to the Duke of Monmouth, a natural son of the king, who left London for Scotland on 15 June. By this time it had become obvious to all parties at Hamilton that a confrontation could not long be delayed. In preparation for this Hamilton and his party proposed a day of fasting, humiliation and prayer, an essential part of which would be a confession of the public sins which had provoked God's displeasure on the church and country. To this end they produced a short 'enumeration of public defections', including among other things 'ministers appearing at the court of usurping rulers and their accepting from them warrants and instructions (founded upon that sacrilegious supremacy) to admit them to and regulate them in the exercise of their ministry; their leading blindfold along with them many of the godly in that abjured course; their Indulgence becoming a public sin and snare, both to themselves and many others'. This uncompromising testimony was hardly calculated to gain the support of Welsh and his party, who opposed it vehemently. How would those proposing it, Welsh asked, react if he were to propose a fast because some ministers were dividing the church and preaching against the Indulgence when it had not been condemned by any church court? And so the disagreements intensified and the bitterness between the two parties continued to grow.

To no one did these divisions cause more distress than to Donald Cargill. He was himself a strong opponent of the Indulgence, he had preached against it publicly, and his sympathies naturally inclined to the side of Hamilton and his party. Indeed, he had personally taken part in drawing up the list of 'public defections' in which the Indulgence had been so strongly condemned. But he also had strong links with the other party: he had preached publicly with John Welsh and some of the others with whom he now found himself in such deep disagreement. It was a time of severe trial. At the risk of compromising his own position, Cargill did his utmost to reconcile the two sides. He talked privately with Welsh and his party, striving to convince them of the necessity of observing the public fast and pointing out the consequences which he was convinced would ensue from a failure to confess publicly the sins of church and state. At last, when all else failed, he stood up in the presence of the assembled ministers and army leaders and said, 'Gentlemen, it seems now that we must part, and I take you all to witness that the cause of our parting is that the rest of the ministers will not consent to a day of humiliation and fasting for the land's public sins. And let this be recorded for our vindication to posterity, that it may be a witness before the Lord for us, to after generations, and against them: that thereby any may see where this sin lies of forbearing so great and so necessary a duty.'

This move gave pause to Welsh and his party; they yielded so far as to ask for time to consult with friends who were shortly expected to join them and to seek God's guidance in prayer. There matters were left for the time; the final breach was averted and the appearance of unity preserved, but the divisions continued to run deep.

By this time Monmouth had arrived in Edinburgh and assumed his commission and was marching westwards with his army. The need to organize the forces against him was urgent. Hitherto there had been little semblance of order in the ranks. Hamilton and the other leaders had little military experience, and the lack of discipline was such that men came and went as they pleased. In the prospect of an imminent engagement, this state of affairs could clearly not be allowed to continue. On Saturday, 21 June the leaders convened to decide a plan of action and to appoint officers to command the troops. But once again the fatal divisions came to the fore. How could they, Hamilton and his party argued, expect the blessing of God on their cause if they did not appoint officers of right principle, whose honesty was known and attested? By this he was taken to mean those who, like himself, had declared themselves against the Indulgence, and so all the bitter disputes on that subject broke out afresh. The other party, who had now gained substantially in numbers, urged that in the present situation it was essential to appoint men of the best military ability, irrespective of their views on these controverted matters. An impasse was reached, and Hamilton, after solemnly protesting against the proceedings, withdrew from the meeting, followed by several others who had sided with him. Those who remained had little heart for the task, and no decisions on the appointment of officers were taken, but agreement was reached on another course which seemed to offer some hope of relief in their present desperate condition.

Monmouth, whose army was now only a few miles away, enjoyed something of a reputation for clemency, and on his arrival in Scotland he had declared his willingness to hear grievances. It was resolved to draw up a supplication to him, craving an audience, and an opportunity to lay before him the distressed condition of the church. An invitation was sent to Hamilton, and to the others who had withdrawn from the meeting, to associate themselves with the supplication and to send a representative to help in preparing it. Hamilton's reaction was at first hostile, but Cargill, clearly judging that he was taking too rigid a line, pressed him to accept. Eventually Hamilton yielded, and Cargill, gratified at the prospect of united action at last, was deputed to a small committee charged with drawing up the supplication. Early the next day the document was ready and was brought to Hamilton for his signature as commander-in-chief of the army. Hamilton duly subscribed it, though he was later to protest that he had done so in the mistaken belief that it was Cargill's work, and that he had been the victim of a deception.[4]

Monmouth's army had now arrived at Bothwell, on the north side of the Clyde, and was forming up in battle order before the narrow bridge separating it from the Hamilton side. A small party of Welsh's supporters was given a safe conduct to cross the bridge and present the supplication to the duke. In very conciliatory terms, this document acknowledged the 'most favourable providence' of Monmouth's presence at such a time, 'of whose princely clemency, and natural goodness, and aversion of shedding of Christian blood, we have had so savoury a report', assuring him that in redressing the grievances of the church 'Your Grace shall do that which

Bothwell Bridge

is most acceptable to the Lord, commend yourself to the generality of the people as a reliever of the oppressed, and a seasonable preventor of all the miseries and ruins that threaten this poor land, yea, and we doubt not shall bring upon you the blessings of many thousands, men, women and children, though not with us, yet sincere lovers of us, and favourers of our righteous cause.' Despite Hamilton's protestations there is no reason to suppose that Cargill did not associate himself with the final form of the supplication, and there is some evidence to suggest that he expected Monmouth to respond favourably.[5]

But while the duke replied that 'he reckoned their desires reasonable and just' and that 'he was very confident that he would be able to procure from His Majesty satisfaction to them, and would use his interest to the utmost with His Majesty', he would consent to nothing until they had first laid down their arms. 'And hang next,' was Hamilton's rejoinder when the envoys brought back their message, and amid the general uncertainty his was the voice that prevailed. After waiting in vain for an answer Monmouth gave the order to advance. The bridge was defended with great gallantry for an hour by some 300 men, but when their ammunition ran short, instead of being relieved, they were ordered to retire to the main body of the army. Monmouth, seeing the opportunity, immediately advanced his troops across the bridge, at the same time firing his cannon on the inexperienced cavalry opposite him. In attempting to reach higher ground they tangled hopelessly with the foot soldiers in the rear, throwing them into disorder, and amid general confusion, with no one able to exercise effective command, the entire force broke and scattered. Monmouth's troops, at last seeing the opportunity for action, kept up the pursuit mercilessly. At least 200 men were shot down in the fields and some 1200 taken prisoner. The prisoners were later herded to Edinburgh, where after being kept in confinement for some months in the Greyfriars Churchyard in insufferable conditions, some 250 of them were put on board ship for the plantations. It was a destination they were never to reach, for the ship carrying them was wrecked in a storm on the Orkneys and many of the prisoners perished miserably. Of the army leaders most went into hiding or fled the country. Two of the ministers, John Kid and John King, former preaching companions of Cargill, were less fortunate: they were captured, tried for treason and executed.

So ended the tragedy of Bothwell, a battle lost before it was fought, an example of a cause destroyed by the divisions within itself. The essence of the tragedy was that the main figures in it were all men of the highest integrity, seeking the good of the cause as they saw it, all loyal to the principles of the Reformation and Presbyterian church government, all motivated by the same opposition to the tyranny which was oppressing the church. It was a bitter irony that their final overthrow was brought about not by the persecution which they had come together to resist, but by their own inability to agree on the means to resist it.[6]

For Donald Cargill the events of these two weeks had been a bitter and sobering experience. In trying to reconcile the two sides, he had been under suspicion by some of those to whom he was most deeply attached, while he was openly reviled by some on the other side.[7] His sensitive nature was deeply hurt by these aspersions, but so long as there was any hope he continued to do his utmost to work for unity, and there were few who emerged from the disaster with greater credit. In the battle itself he received a dangerous wound in the head and escaped death or capture in a remarkable way: one of the soldiers who had struck him down demanded his name, and on hearing it another asked if he was a minister. On being told that he was, they immediately let him go. It was a deliverance which led Cargill to hope that despite the darkness of the hour there still remained work for him to do, and he later told friends that when his wound was being attended to he could not bring himself to ask if it was mortal, so great was his desire to live and to continue the work to which God had called him.

For the moment, however, the picture was bleak: the work dearest to his heart was at a stand; many of his friends were dead or in captivity; the church which he loved was rent apart by internal divisions. So despondent did he become that he fell into doubts and questionings about his calling to the ministry. Seventeen years earlier a promising ministry in

Glasgow had been cut short and there had followed a long period of enforced silence; now, after some six or seven years of preaching in the fields, it seemed that this ministry too was to be denied him. It was a time of much heart-searching and also, no doubt, of earnest prayer. Had he been too confident in the 'arm of the flesh' without seeking sufficiently the divine aid? Had he allowed himself to be led away from the things of God, to think of the issues in human terms, rather than to see the battle as the Lord's?

Questions of this kind must have filled his mind — misgivings about his part in the enterprise that had ended so tragically, doubts and fears about the future course of his ministry. He was now a declared traitor to his country, in common with the other ministers who had been at Bothwell, and in constant hazard of his life; anyone concealing or harbouring him was liable to the severest penalties. He had also become increasingly isolated from his fellow ministers. The divisions of Bothwell were to prove hard to heal, and his close association with Hamilton and the party from Fife had alienated him still further from many of those who had been his friends.

It was at this juncture, perhaps uncertain which way to turn, and in need of a period of rest and reflection, that Cargill received an urgent invitation from M'Ward and Brown in Holland to go over to join them. To him, at this moment of uncertainty and doubt, this must have seemed a direct answer to prayer, and he determined at once to accept. Apparently, however, there were others included in the invitation and time was pressing, for on receiving the letter Cargill wrote at once to Robert Hamilton, who was now in hiding in Galloway, to come to Edinburgh in all haste to meet him.[8]

Hamilton duly arrived, heavily disguised for fear of capture, and Cargill put the proposition to him. Hamilton, who was in daily danger of his life so long as he remained in the country, readily assented; and some time in mid-August he and Cargill appear to have left for Holland together. It had apparently been arranged that others of their friends would follow later, and this was duly accomplished.

Shortly before their departure, and probably as a result of Monmouth's influence, the government granted an indemnity for those who had been at Bothwell, with a further, third, Indulgence for ministers on surety being given for their good behaviour.

Cargill referred to these events in a letter written to some friends on the eve of his departure, when he also expressed feelingly his sorrow at leaving his native country and his submission to the will of Providence: 'Dear friends, I cannot but be grieved to go from my native land, and especially from that part of it for whom and with whom I desired only to live; yet the dreadful apprehensions I have of what is coming upon this land may help to make me submissive to this providence the better. You will have snares for a little, then a deluge of judgements. I do not speak this to affright any, much less to rejoice over them, as if I were taken, and they left, or were studying by those thoughts to alleviate my own lot of banishment, though I am afraid that none shall bless themselves long upon the account that they are left behind, but my design is to have you making yourselves prepared for snares and judgements, that you may have both the greatest readiness and the greatest shelters, for both shall be in one. Clear accounts, and put off the old, for it is like that what is to come will be both sudden and surprising, that it will not give you time for this. Beware of taking on new debt. I am afraid that these things which many are looking on as favours are but come to bind men together in bundles for a fire. I am sure, if these things be observed, there shall not be given long time for using of them; and this last of their favours and snares is sent to men, to show that they are that which otherwise they will not confess themselves to be. Tell all, that the shelter and benefit of this shall neither be great nor long, but the snare of it shall be great and prejudicial. As for myself, I think for the present he is calling me to another land, but how long shall be my abode, or what employment he has for me there, I know not, for I cannot think he is taking me there to live and lurk only.'

Cargill's fears about the future pattern of events proved only too true: it was not long before Monmouth fell from favour with the government and the persecution was resumed once more in full rigour. The letter is otherwise interesting as showing that Cargill had now regained something of his old assurance of his calling. It has about it that note of authority in spiritual matters which is to be seen still more strikingly in his later letters, particularly those to his friends in prison, where he draws on his rich fund of experience to impart Christian comfort and joy in the face of suffering and impending death. Cargill's letters, like his sermons, are remarkable for their intensity of expression and economy of language; they require close concentration, but their spiritual richness amply repays the effort. 'Short, marrowy and sententious' is Patrick Walker's assessment of Cargill's sermons, speeches and letters, 'which', he says, 'I wish from my heart that all the Lord's people would narrowly and seriously peruse; they have been very useful and edifying to me and to many others.'[9]

9.
Exile and restoration

Cargill seems to have arrived in Holland just after the departure from that country of Richard Cameron, who had gone
there in the previous May and so had missed being present at
Bothwell. Cameron had apparently been prevailed upon,
earlier in the year, to give a promise to forbear, for a time, his
preaching against the Indulgence.[1] This was a promise which
he later deeply regretted, and it was after giving it, and feeling
the spiritual barrenness which had come upon him as a result,
that he had decided to go over to Holland. Like Cargill,
Cameron knew that in Holland he could expect fellowship
with ministers who shared his views, for he had already had
messages of support from the two exiles.

Cameron's expectations were not disappointed. M'Ward
and Brown received him warmly, expressed their admiration
of his principles, and decided to give him ordination. Up to
now, though licensed, he had preached as a probationer;
ordination would give him the token of authority he needed
from the church and its seal of approval on his ministry.
M'Ward told him, 'Richard, the public standard is now fallen
in Scotland, and, if I know anything of the mind of the Lord,
you are called to undergo your trials before us, to go home
and lift the fallen standard and display it publicly before the
world. But before you put your hand to it you shall go to as
many of the field-ministers as you can find and give them your
hearty invitation to go with you, and if they will not go, go
alone, and the Lord will go with you.' The necessary quorum
for the ordination was obtained by the addition of a Dutch
minister, Koelman, and Cameron was accordingly ordained

in due form by the 'laying on of hands' of the two Scottish exiles and their Dutch colleague.[2]

After Brown and Koelman had lifted their hands from Cameron's head, M'Ward kept his in place and, with the prophetic insight for which he was noted, called out: 'Behold, all ye beholders, here is the head of a faithful minister and servant of Jesus Christ, who shall lose the same for his Master's interest, and it shall be set up before sun and moon, in the view of the world.' It was a prophecy which was to be only too exactly fulfilled, and in what remained of his life Cameron appears to have been very conscious that his time was short and that what he had to do was to be done with all his might. He returned to Scotland in the late summer of 1679, apparently just after Cargill had left it, and immediately made contact with as many of the former field-preachers as he could find. But the damaging effects of Bothwell still lingered: most of the preachers who remained were opposed to Cameron's stand on the Indulgence, and some of them even tried to prejudice the people against him. The few whom Cameron found sympathetic were unwilling to resume preaching in the fields, maintaining that it was now too dangerous and that it would give the government occasion to intensify still further the persecution against all the non-complying Presbyterians.

Cameron's mood at this time is reflected in a letter he wrote to M'Ward on 30 October, after consulting the ministers: 'This is the greatest strait and sharpest trial I ever yet met with, for their arguments do not satisfy me, my conscience telling me that the opportunity of a testimony is not to be slighted, as also I find that by forbearing it some are stumbled, others hardened, many take occasion to say that all the ministers are going one gate. I intend tomorrow out to the country again to consult the people. What I may do I know not. Oh for wisdom . . .!'

Cargill meanwhile was with M'Ward in Rotterdam, where his arrival no doubt gave much pleasure to his old friend and colleague. M'Ward was by now a rather lonely figure. John Brown, who had taken part in Cameron's ordination, died in September, probably just after Cargill's arrival, and James Wallace, one of M'Ward's closest companions in exile and the commander of the force at Pentland, had died the previous year. Cargill had opportunity to preach on several occasions in the Scots Kirk in Rotterdam, whose congregation was augmented at this time by those who had come over with him after Bothwell. These included Robert Hamilton, who was to remain in Holland until after the Revolution of 1688,[3] David Hackston of Rathillet, Henry Hall of Haughhead and several others. An incident which took place at this time between Hamilton and Cargill provides another example of Cargill's spirit of Christian charity and his desire to avoid division. The Rotterdam Church, though generally favourable to the exiles, decided to debar Hackston from the communion, presumably because of his involvement in the death of the archbishop. Cargill was due to officiate at the communion service the following day, 22 October, and Hamilton, on hearing of the church's decision, immediately went to tell Cargill of it, apparently expecting that he would refuse to take part. 'But', says Hamilton, 'he, with other friends, though resolving to resent it, yet could not determine on such a sudden to withdraw from the church, this being the first step of their ever appearing against us.' The next day, Cargill gave the communion as planned.[4]

It is not clear how long Cargill originally intended to remain in Holland, though it would seem from the letter he wrote before his departure that he envisaged a fairly lengthy stay. As events turned out, however, he appears to have been there for not more than three months. The immediate cause of his return may well have been an unfortunate disagreement which broke out in the Rotterdam congregation and which split the loyalties of the exiles into two camps. The dispute centred around Robert Fleming, an old fellow-student of Cargill's at St Andrews, who was now minister of the Rotterdam Church. Fleming, previously minister of Cambuslang, had been deprived of his charge because of his refusal to conform to the new ecclesiastical order in Scotland, and he was settled in Rotterdam in December 1677. On revisiting Scotland in 1679 he was arrested and imprisoned in the Edinburgh Tolbooth. Some time after Bothwell, however, he was set at liberty and in October of the same year, shortly after the other exiles arrived, he returned to his charge in Holland. Fleming, a man of judgement and moderation, could not bring himself to condemn those ministers who complied with the Indulgence, though remaining firmly opposed to it himself, and he pleaded with his congregation that such ministers should not be debarred from fellowship. Several of the newly-arrived exiles, Robert Hamilton in particular, were highly critical of Fleming's attitude and refused to countenance his ministry. M'Ward, though equally resolute against Fleming's position, continued to hear him and, instead of condemning him outright, tried by friendly argument to persuade him to change his view. As a result, M'Ward too was ostracized by Hamilton and by some others who sided with him. The disagreement caused M'Ward much distress and may well have hastened his end.[5]

Cargill's position in the controversy is not known, though his close friendship with M'Ward and his known similarity of temperament suggest strongly that he was of the same mind as his old ministerial colleague.[6] At all events it seems reasonable to conclude that Cargill, who abhorred controversy of this kind, found it impossible to remain in the increasingly acrimonious atmosphere of the Rotterdam Church and decided to return once more to Scotland. At the same time there was clearly another compulsion that was driving him home: the needs of the persecuted church lay heavy on his heart and the news of the oppressions exacted on the prisoners taken at Bothwell must have stirred him to the depths. On 21 November M'Ward recorded in a letter to Richard Cameron, no doubt to the latter's deep satisfaction: 'Mr Cargill went hence today, pressed in spirit to go home to preach in the fields.' Cargill was returning to his native land, ready once again to take up the work to which he had given his life, regardless of the cost.

Cargill was followed, or possibly accompanied, on his return from Holland by some of the other exiles, including David Hackston and Henry Hall, both of whom appear to have returned to Scotland towards the end of 1679. None of them was to see the friendly shores of Holland again, and for Cargill and M'Ward the parting must have been particularly painful, knowing, as both of them certainly did, that they were seeing each other for the last time. None of the returning exiles, least of all Cargill, had any illusions about the hazards

which lay ahead. The dangers they had confronted earlier
were little in comparison with what now lay in store for them.
They were greatly reduced in number; many former friends
had deserted them or been forced into submission; others
were imprisoned or exiled. The field-meetings, once so
numerous, had all but ceased, and most of the leading field-
preachers had fallen silent or left the country. John Welsh, his
spirit broken by the divisions at Bothwell, had withdrawn to
self-imposed exile in England. John Dickson thought field-
preaching now too dangerous and had advised Cameron
against it. Semple and Arnot too were silent, or preached
only privately in houses. Blackader had been laid aside by illness and for a time had to forego all his preaching work. With
the eclipse of the leading field-preachers it is perhaps not surprising that some of the less prominent began to show a
measure of compliance. Several of them, in the previous
autumn, had made it their business to persuade the prisoners
in the Greyfriars Churchyard to accept the bond for the peace
and to offer no further resistance to the authorities. At a
meeting of nonconforming ministers in Edinburgh on 16 September there had been general agreement that the bond
offered with the Third Indulgence could be accepted without
compromise of principle, and several of the former field-
preachers later accepted licence to preach on the government's terms. Through time, the path of non-resistance came
to be regarded as the norm, the mark of charity and moderation, while continued resistance became identified with
intolerance and extremism. The bitterness engendered at
Bothwell certainly played its part in this process and helped to
foster misunderstanding and mistrust. Increasingly, those
who stood firm came to be regarded as a separate party,
intolerant and fanatical, intent on political agitation rather
than religious struggle. Certain events soon to unfold gave a
show of credence to this view and helped to maintain the
popular belief. It was a ready conclusion that all who
continued to resist were at one with the zealots who had killed
the archbishop, or who had burned the government's acts at
Rutherglen. Scant regard was paid to the fact that for some
the issues remained on the same high spiritual plane where
they had always been, and the public standard of the rights

and liberties of the church was left in the hands of an increasingly maligned few.[7]

With these few Cargill did not hesitate to identify himself. It has become a somewhat popular view that at this stage of his life Cargill was driven, against his better judgement, from a previously moderate position into the hands of the extremists. But to say this is to do him a basic injustice. Inevitably, by choosing to stand firm, Cargill found himself in closer association with some who, for one reason or another, came to notice for some act of public defiance against the authorities. This did not mean, however, that his methods of making a public testimony necessarily coincided with theirs; indeed there is clear enough evidence to suggest the contrary. To the end of his days, often at the risk of his own reputation, Cargill refused to assent or adhere to anything that did not satisfy his own conscience as being motivated for the sole aim of God's glory and in accordance with his revealed truth. The principles for which he continued to stand were those for which he had ever stood: the spiritual independence of the church and the supremacy of Christ's kingly government. For him the issues were essentially spiritual, and would always be so, whatever the misrepresentation and misunderstanding to which he would increasingly be subjected from now on.

For some time after his return Cargill deemed it prudent to remain in concealment; he did not wish to expose himself to unnecessary danger and he clearly felt that care and deliberation were called for. During this time he took the opportunity to write to some of his friends in Galloway, sending them messages of spiritual comfort and consolation. One of these, dated 22 February 1680, was addressed to Lady Earlston the younger, who was a sister of Robert Hamilton and the wife of Alexander Gordon of Earlston, whose father had been killed at Bothwell Bridge. The Gordons were firm supporters of the Presbyterian cause and they had suffered much hardship, including the forfeiture of their estates, for their continued loyalty to it. Lady Earlston had apparently asked Cargill his opinion of Cameron, who had visited Annandale and Nithsdale the previous autumn, following his return from Holland. Cargill's tribute is whole-hearted: 'As for Mr Richard Cameron, I never heard anything from him, in the

Lord's truth, but I am both ready and willing to confirm it.'
And he adds, in a characteristic vein of self-depreciation: 'But
woe is me, that I have not more worth and authority for that
cause.' Here Cargill was referring, not for the only time, to
the apparent paradox of the ministerial calling — the treasure
hidden in the earthen vessel. But the unworthiness of the
messenger was no disparagement of the message, and so he
goes on: 'But truth itself, if it be rightly pleaded, will have
authority upon consciences.' It was God's Word, not his own,
that the minister proclaimed and so, despite his own weakness, he could claim to speak as the messenger of God. It was
this alone that could give worth to his words and authority to
his preaching.

Another letter, written from Gilkerscleugh House near
Crawfordjohn, a noted refuge for the persecuted, on 14 April
1680, was addressed to Alexander Gordon himself and
several of his friends. In it, Cargill tells them: 'Let all things be
little to you in respect of this, to have the land brought about
to be the Lord's and to have the Lord reigning in it . . . Seek
to be united to God, and to one another in truth and love: and
this cannot be without the pouring out of the Spirit, which
must be obtained by prayer. . . Fear not, for though fewer we
shall not be the less strong; and forget not to shut yourselves
up in a covenant with him, that if we must die in the common
lot, we may die with repentance and such purposes in our
heart, and leave a model to them that come after of the tem-
ple we minded to build to him, that those may go on according
to that pattern, and do well.'

For Richard Cameron, Cargill's return to Scotland meant
that he was no longer alone in his desire to resume preaching
in the fields and to make a public testimony against the sins of
the land and church. Cameron had met with no success
among any of the ministers whom he had approached and
Cargill's presence obviously brought him much support and
encouragement. It seems fairly clear that the two made contact very soon after Cargill's return and that plans were carefully laid for resumption of the work that had been at a stand
since Bothwell.

For his part Cameron kept ever before him the charge he
had been given by M'Ward, to 'lift the fallen standard and dis-

play it publicly before the world'. M'Ward, indeed, did not allow him to forget it, and he wrote several times encouraging Cameron to the work. Not unnaturally, M'Ward seems to have regarded himself as having a special responsibility for Cameron's ministry and he did not hesitate to exhort him to his duty in firm and almost peremptory terms. A letter which he wrote at the end of 1679 or the beginning of 1680 gives a typical example of his forthrightness of manner. It expresses his abhorrence at the reception given in Scotland in the previous November to the Duke of York, the king's brother, who was a professed Roman Catholic, and urges Cameron to the duty of calling a day of public humiliation and fasting for the deed. 'I would have you forthwith', M'Ward writes, 'without any further demur, procrastination or delay, speak to some of your more zealous and serious brethren, and awaken them unto the due and deep consideration of these things: that they and you may excite and stir up the people to give such a present signification of their hatred at and their abhorrence of this deed, as (1) you are to lay out yourselves by all means in informing the people of the guilt of this practice; (2) I would have you call all the godly in all the several corners of the nation to keep a day of solemn public humiliation. Up and be doing: go forward, as not fearing what flesh can do unto you.'

With the strength of M'Ward's exhortations behind him Cameron pressed forward with his plans, and he found in Cargill a willing and enthusiastic colleague. He was also encouraged by the return from Holland of Thomas Douglas, a field-preacher who had been active at Bothwell and before, and who now made common cause for a time with Cameron and Cargill.[8]

It was now no longer possible to hold meetings near the larger centres of population, and plans had to be made to meet in isolated and remote places where the danger of discovery was less likely. On a day in late April 1680 Cameron, Cargill and Douglas convened the first of the public fasts at Darmead, a lonely and desolate spot in the parish of Cambusnethan, some five miles to the south of the village of Shotts. For the first time since Bothwell the voices of the field-preachers rang out again, and for many who were present the occasion must have brought back poignant memories of past days. A comparison with those times, when upwards of forty ministers were actively preaching in the fields, would have emphasized the low condition to which the persecuted church was now reduced. As events were soon to prove, however, the work which was being resumed in such apparent weakness was destined to reach a height and achieve a fame surpassing all that had gone before.

10.
Queensferry and Ayrsmoss

The first public fast had laid the foundation of the work to which Cameron and Cargill now dedicated themselves. This was followed a month later, on 28 May, by another, larger meeting for the same purpose, this time at Auchengilloch, a particularly remote spot on the borders of Lanarkshire and Ayrshire. This was to prove a memorable occasion in the experience of many present, and for Cameron and Cargill it marked the start of a period of intense preaching activity. Cameron's text that day was Hosea 13:9-10: 'O Israel, thou hast destroyed thyself; but in me is thine help. I will be thy king: where is any other that may save thee in all thy cities? And thy judges of whom thou saidst, Give me a king and princes?' On this occasion Cameron declared himself openly for disowning the king, and appeared at times to be urging his hearers to something further still. Calling the king an 'enemy of God' and a 'vile adulterer', he went on: 'We must cry we will have no other king but Christ. If you would have him be for you, you must cut off this king and these princes and make able men be your rulers, endued with suitable qualifications both of body and mind, that may employ their power for the cause and interest of God. If we had the zeal of God within us we would not call him our king, and even with regard to the nobles and magistrates of this land we would not acknowledge them to be magistrates. I will tell you, sirs, if ever you see good days in Scotland without disowning the present magistrates then believe me no more. I know not if this generation will be honoured to cast off these rulers, but those that the Lord makes instruments to bring back Christ and to recover our liberties civil and ecclesiastical shall be such as disown this king and these inferiors under him. Are there none to execute justice and judgement upon these wicked men who are both treacherous and tyrannical? The Lord is calling men of all ranks and stations to execute judgement upon them. And if it be done we cannot but justify the deed, and such are to be commended for it, as Jael was.'

This was further than Cargill was ever to go, and the responsibility for it was Cameron's alone. His single-minded zeal sent his words speeding like arrows to their target, and his ardent spirit was untrammelled by the questionings which troubled the mind of his more mature colleague. Cargill well knew the misrepresentations which a public disowning of the king would cause and he fully recognized the difficulty of defending such a step. Above all, he feared the danger that the great issues for which he and the church were contending should degenerate into a civil and political quarrel, losing the spiritual and religious significance which formed their true background. For him the issues were not so sharply defined as they were for Cameron. The question of allegiance to the king had to be carefully weighed and balanced in the light of Scripture teaching, and only when he was fully satisfied that he was acting on this infallible rule would he dare to commit himself. To disown a sovereign was a serious, irrevocable step, and one not to be taken lightly; those who took it upon themselves to do so must be prepared to justify their action convincingly from Scripture and to show that they were not motivated by private resentment. It is not too much to say that Cargill was becoming increasingly unhappy at the way that some of his friends were approaching this solemn issue, and his misgivings were soon to be amply justified.

When his own turn came to preach, Cargill took a much more restrained line, dwelling mainly on the duty of the people of God in their present distress and warning of still greater hardships ahead. 'Sirs, sirs,' he exclaimed at the start of his sermon, striking his hand three times on his Bible, 'make good use of this; for the day is coming when you will be glad to get it at the back of a dyke.' He went on to speak of the need of steadfastness in face of the calamities that had come upon the church and he sounded a warning to his hearers of the dangers of complacency and compromise: 'Think you of possessing your enjoyments? It is a wonder, all things considered, how you can think of enjoying worldly things when not only Jacob, but the ark and people of God are now in the open fields . . . Many a man and woman I am afraid has looked a thousand times to their possessions since they looked once to their conscience. But maybe you will say, "Can we not get both our houses and our consciences kept?" But that you will not get done. Let enjoyments be as no enjoyments; let them be no snare; say to him, "Lord, I am as free to follow thee as the day when I had neither wife, children, house nor inheritance."'

But it might be asked, what was the point of making such sacrifices? Were the principles at stake worth all this effort of self-denial? Cargill's answer was definite: 'They will tell us that such and such is a little thing. But I say there is much in it: Christ and all the concerns of his church and the banishing him and his interest out of the land — no less is in it.'

But again, was not this a matter of the public testimony, of less direct concern, perhaps, to the individual Christian? Cargill had his answer ready: 'We never saw a minister prove effectual, without remembering the public case of the church, if it was in distress and stood in need of relief; and we find often, those who have most of the public concern have most of the private also. Put these two together, public zeal and tenderness of life and conversation: it is no zeal that has no tenderness, and it is no tenderness that has no zeal.'

What then was to be done? Cargill advised three things: sanctification, separation and renewal of Covenant engagements. The principle of separation from the ministers who had accepted the Indulgence was a particularly controversial point, and one for which Cargill had been severely criticized when he first dared to proclaim it, but he was clear that the time called for no less a testimony. There could be no fellowship with those who countenanced the denial of the interest of Christ. 'So, I say, separate fully: let not one hoof be left behind you. You think it is your duty to be charitable to them. We will not say but it is, but let it not appear to them in such a time as this. Keep your charity in your hearts. Open rebuke is better than secret love.' And in a final word of exhortation:

'You are now weaker than you were. Then strengthen yourselves with a new allegiance to Christ, and enter into covenant
with God; and enter more by faith than what you have before
done.' As he spoke Cargill seems to have had an increasing
presentiment of the terrible times that were to overtake the
church before the day of deliverance came — of the 'killing
time' of the mid-eighties when many were to suffer and die at
the hands of the common soldiers, summarily and without
trial, and when even to be seen in the fields on suspicion of
attending preaching could mean instant death.

Even now the forces of authority were bestirring themselves. Reports of the resurgence of the field-meetings had
reached the ears of the Council, and the agents of repression
were already active. Cameron and Cargill, considering their
own situation and the interests of the people, decided to separate, so that if one of them were captured the remnant would
not be left without a witness. Accordingly, after the meeting
at Auchengilloch, Cargill set out eastwards and made for the
vicinity of Bo'ness on the south side of the Forth. He was
accompanied, or was joined shortly after his arrival, by Henry
Hall of Haughhead, a Border landowner who had been prominent on Hamilton's side at Bothwell. Bo'ness was a noted
centre of support for the persecuted, and here it seems Cargill
had resorted on several occasions previously. On this occasion, however, it was a move that almost cost him his life.

Soon after reaching Bo'ness he was recognized by the
curates of Bo'ness and Carriden, who reported his presence
to Governor Middleton of Blackness Castle. The governor,
deciding that strategy was called for in dealing with so elusive
a rebel, arranged for a watch to be kept by his soldiers, and on
3 June he was informed that Cargill and Hall were riding on
the road between Bo'ness and Queensferry. Ordering his
soldiers to keep at a discreet distance, the governor followed
his prey into Queensferry, where they were seen to dismount
and enter an inn. The governor immediately sent back his servant to call up the soldiers and in the meantime presented
himself at the house where Cargill and Hall had entered,
making himself out to be a stranger and presenting his
respects to the two travellers. But the carefully laid plan mis-
fired. For some reason the soldiers did not appear, perhaps

through a misdirection by the servant, and eventually the governor, fearing that the golden opportunity was slipping through his hands, revealed himself in his true colours. Calling for help from the others present, in the name of the king, he drew his sword, and told Cargill and Hall to regard themselves as his prisoners. Only one man came to his aid — Thomas George, an excise officer, probably stationed at Queensferry to intercept contraband cargo from Holland. Hall, a man of strong physique and courage, grappled with the governor and allowed Cargill to make good his escape, and was about to escape himself when George struck him down from behind with a savage blow from a carabine. The uproar had by this time attracted the notice of the local people, and several of the women helped Hall, who was badly wounded, to escape to the house of a sympathizer about half a mile away. But word had also reached the ears of Thomas Dalyell, the redoubtable general of the king's forces in Scotland, at his nearby home at the Binns, and Hall was soon tracked down and arrested. He was immediately put under escort for Edinburgh to be brought before the Council, but the wound he had received proved fatal and he died on the way. In their frustration at Cargill's escape the Council left Hall's body for three days without burial, and eventually his friends were forced to bury it secretly by night.

In the struggle and confusion Cargill too had been wounded, though not seriously, and he was found in this condition by a local woman who tended his wounds and brought him to a nearby house, where he was given shelter in a barn for the night. The next day friends took care of him and arranged for his wounds to be tended by a physician. For this service one of them, William Punton of Carlowrie, was imprisoned in Edinburgh and heavily fined, and some of the women who had given assistance to Hall were similarly punished. A strict search was made for any who had been accessory to Cargill's escape and Dalyell was given instructions to bring any further suspects before the Council. John Park, curate of Carriden, who had been the main informer, found that his action had brought him into such odium with his parishioners that his life was threatened. He accordingly petitioned the Council, who recommended to the Bishop of

Edinburgh that he be transferred elsewhere for his own safety
and that at the same time he be given a reward for his good
service. Thomas George put in a similar petition for similar
reasons. Whether either of them was rewarded is not known.
What does remain on record is that Park was deposed from
the ministry some years later for gross misdemeanour.

But the incident at Queensferry was notable not so much
for the action itself as for the fact that there was discovered
among Cargill's or Hall's effects a paper or manifesto, drawn
up in the form of a covenant, and bearing on the most important of the controverted matters in church and state.[1] The
paper was unsigned and was obviously a draft. It was somewhat rough and unfinished in style and was clearly not
intended for publication in the form in which it was found.
But for the government it was a valuable prize, for now they
could let their loyal subjects see for themselves the true aims
of the 'fanatics' who were stirring up sedition among the
people and subverting their allegiance to the king. The paper
was speedily printed by order of the Council, and no effort
was spared to give it the widest publicity in order to bring the
greatest possible discredit upon its authors and the cause
which they represented. Who those authors were was never
revealed and will probably never be known for certain, for
though the paper was dubbed by the government 'Cargill's
Covenant' it would be wrong to regard it as being properly his
work. That he had a major hand in it cannot reasonably be
doubted; several passages are strongly reminiscent of his style
and there is a quotation from Calvin, his favourite author.
None of his contemporaries, even those who held him in the
highest regard, sought to deny his involvement in it, though
its principles were never accepted by the 'remnant' as a
whole. What is much less clear is how far these principles represented his own personal views, for several of them are contradicted by his preaching and practice. The contradiction can
only be resolved by the assumption that Cargill drafted the
paper, or assisted in drafting it, not on his own initiative but
at the behest of others whom he respected, but whose views
on certain controverted issues he did not fully share. If this is
so, his action should probably be attributed to a desire to

avoid factious controversy (of which he had already given ample evidence at Bothwell) rather than to any dilution of his own principles.

The paper evidently had its origin in Holland the previous year, when Cargill had been in the company of Robert Hamilton and the other fugitives after Bothwell. It was Hamilton and his friends Hackston and Balfour, who were also in Holland at that time, who had been mainly responsible for the Rutherglen Declaration in May 1679, following consultation with Cargill, and it is not at all unlikely that, knowing his skill at composition and his experience in legal styles, they had prevailed upon him to help in drawing up a paper which would express their principles in a more formal way. From a reference in Cameron's letter to M'Ward the previous October it appears that he too was eager to see such a statement prepared. Hackston had returned to Scotland towards the end of 1679, and it is likely that the paper owed its form largely to his influence and possibly also to that of Cameron. The intention appears to have been to send the draft over to Hamilton and the other exiles still in Holland for their advice on whether it should be used as a basis for a public declaration. Hall, who had himself not long returned from Holland, had apparently been chosen as a messenger for this purpose and was doubtless awaiting an opportunity to embark at Queensferry. Whatever the exact circumstances may have been, it is plain beyond doubt that Cargill, who never acknowledged responsibility for the paper, did not intend that it should see the light of day in the form in which it was drafted, and he no doubt hoped that through the influence of M'Ward and others in Holland some of its more contentious passages would be modified or omitted. However, before Hall could fulfil his mission disaster had struck and the paper in its unfinished state was in the hands of the enemy.[2]

The paper itself contained seven articles, or statements of policy, each linked to a separate declaration of intent. The first three articles dealt generally with the state of the church, affirming the loyalty of the authors to the Scriptures, the principles of the Reformation, Presbyterian church government and the Covenants, and pledging themselves to the overthrow of prelacy and Erastianism. The remaining four articles, particularly the fourth, fifth and sixth, were much more radical and intransigent in tone.

The fourth article took as its premise 'That the hand of our kings has been against the throne of the Lord, and that now for a long time, the succession of our kings, and the most part of our rulers with them, has been against the purity and power of religion and godliness, and freedom of the church of God'. It went on to rehearse the tyrannical acts of the government, their oppressions, persecutions and injustice, 'so that it can no more be called a government, but a lustful rage, exercised with as little right reason, and with more cruelty than in beasts, and they themselves can be no more called governors, but public grassators, [terrorists] and public judgements, which all men ought as earnestly to labour to be free of, as of sword, famine or pestilence raging amongst us'.

Pausing for a moment, the paper considered whether there was any hope of reclaiming the rulers to better ways. Its conclusion was in the negative: 'Neither can it be thought that there is hope of their returning from these courses, having so often showed their natures and enmities against God and all righteousness, and so often declared and renewed their purposes and promises of persevering in these courses.' The paper then went on to its climax. 'We then, seeing the innumerable sins and snares that are in giving obedience to their acts . . . and siding with God (who we hope will accept and help us to a liberation from their tyranny) against his stated and declared enemies, do reject that king, and these associate with him, from being our rulers . . . and declare them henceforth to be no lawful rulers, as they have declared us to be no lawful subjects . . . and that after this we neither owe, nor shall yield, any willing obedience to them . . . so that none can say that we are now bound in allegiance unto them, unless they will say we are bound in allegiance to devils, whose vice-regents they are.'

The fifth article went on to propound a more radical idea still: 'Being now loosed from all obligations both divine and civil to them, we do declare that we shall set up over ourselves and over what God shall give us power of, government and governors according to the Word of God, that we shall no more commit the government of ourselves, and the making of laws for us, to any one single person, or lineal successor, we not being by God, as the Jews were, bound to one single family; and this kind of government by a single person being most liable to inconveniences and aptest to degenerate into tyranny, as sad and long experience has taught us.' Here not only the king, but the whole concept of hereditary monarchy was being rejected. What was being propounded was a republican form of government, subject indeed to the laws of God, but assuming to itself the civil magistracy which had hitherto resided only in the king. This was the stuff of revolution, and it is hardly surprising that it was treated as such by the government. It was also plainly contrary to Presbyterian principles and was disowned even by some who later suffered for their faith. If it achieved nothing else, it showed the danger — of which Cargill, for one, was always deeply conscious — of fighting the spiritual warfare with carnal weapons, of giving the enemy an advantage by fighting on his terms and speaking in his language. In a public comment later on this passage, Cargill was careful to limit his interpretation of it to the necessity for kings to rule according to the law of God, and he had nothing at all to say of the assumption of magistracy which the paper had advocated.

Having thus dealt with the civil power, the paper went on in its sixth article to deal at length with the condition of the church, and particularly with the evil of the Indulgence. It denounced vigorously those ministers who had accepted 'that liberty founded upon, and given by virtue of their blasphemous, arrogated and usurped power', and who had thereby 'changed their masters, and of the ministers of Christ are become the ministers of men and bound to answer to them as they will'. Since those ministers had thus ceased to be ministers of Christ, they were no longer to be countenanced; the scriptural injunction was 'If any brother walk disorderly, from such to withdraw.' But the paper proceeded to advocate much more than a mere withdrawal from these ministers themselves: it included in its denunciations 'any who have encouraged and strengthened their hands by hearing and pleading for them'; 'all those who have trafficked for a union with them'; 'all that do not faithfully testify against them'; and 'all who join not in public with their brethren, in testifying against them'. This was an exclusiveness of a kind never advocated by the general body of the Presbyterians. It was of a piece with the exclusive spirit which had caused M'Ward so much distress in Holland the previous year, and which Cargill himself did his best to discourage. Cargill certainly believed that by accepting the Indulgence these men had proved disloyal to their calling as ministers of Christ and that they were to be discountenanced until they repented of their sin, but he continued to have fellowship with those who remained faithful, including Alexander Peden and others, however much they might differ from him in matters of conscience and individual judgement.[3]

The capture and publication by the government of this draft was undoubtedly an embarrassment to those who had hoped to use it as a basis for a public declaration, and they decided to publish without further delay a statement of policy on their own part. So it was that on 22 June, less than three weeks after the incident at Queensferry and on the anniversary of Bothwell, a party of horsemen, with Richard Cameron at their head, rode into the town of Sanquhar and, after the singing of a psalm, proclaimed and affixed to the market cross what was to become known as the Sanquhar Declaration.

This declaration was in some respects a condensed version of the Queensferry paper. It was much shorter and considerably more concise, and it left out many of the more contentious matters, particularly the disowning of hereditary monarchy and separation from the complying ministers. Indeed it did not mention the Indulgence, as such, at all; it dealt only very generally with the state of the church and its main orientation was towards matters of state. It was at one with the Queensferry paper in disowning the king — the first time this had been formally done — on the grounds of 'his perjury and breach of covenant with God and his church, and usurpation of his crown and royal prerogatives therein, and many other breaches in matters ecclesiastic, and by his tyranny and breach of the very *leges regnandi* in matters civil'. But the declaration went further than the Queensferry paper in the consequences of this action. 'As also', it went on, 'we being under the standard of Christ, Captain of salvation, declare war against such a tyrant and usurper, and all the men of his practices, as enemies to our Lord Jesus Christ, his cause and Covenants; and against all such as have strengthened him, sided with, or any wise acknowledged him, in his tyranny, civil or ecclesiastic — yea, against all such as shall strengthen, side with, or any wise acknowledge any other in the like usurpation and tyranny.' Here was a positive, militant resolution, a taking of the offensive against the enemy. The declaration went on to endorse the testimony of Rutherglen, to disclaim the Hamilton declaration for taking in the king's interest, to disown the reception of the Duke of York, the king's brother, and his succession to the crown, and to conclude by expressing the hope that 'After this none will blame us for, or offend at our rewarding those that are against us, as they have done to us, as the Lord gives opportunity.'

In these bold uncompromising sentences the declaration shows unmistakably the hand of Richard Cameron. It is virtually certain that Cameron drew it up himself, partly no doubt on the basis of the Queensferry paper, but mainly on his own initiative, and it bears the mark of his impassioned spirit. Cargill was apparently not consulted about the Sanquhar Declaration and he certainly never saw it before it was published. He never publicly expressed his opinion of it, but it is fairly clear that, however much he may have sympathized with its general intention, he did not fully endorse the manner of it. An indication of his sentiments can perhaps be gained by the answers given by Walter Smith, a young man who was much in Cargill's company in his later years, when asked about the declaration at his trial. Smith endorsed the principles of the declaration to the full, but did not accept that its authors were, as they claimed, 'the representatives of the true Presbyterian Church', nor that they were called, or were in a capacity, to declare war on the king. He felt that they had intended merely to justify lawful self-defence; otherwise, he thought, it might have been esteemed murder. Besides Smith's testimony there is evidence to show that others who were in close contact with Cargill at this time and afterwards entertained serious doubts about the grounds for disowning

the king which were expressed in the declaration, and it is difficult not to believe that these doubts were shared by Cargill
himself. [4]

The government's reaction to the Queensferry paper and
the Sanquhar Declaration was predictable. Not surprisingly,
the declaration was regarded as the 'more execrable' of the
two, since it dealt principally with the king and government,
was more uncompromising in its language and, unlike the
paper, had been formally published. On 30 June the Privy
Council issued a proclamation noting that Cameron and
Cargill, among others, had 'now at last shaken off all respect
to our laws, and their allegiance itself to us as their undoubted
sovereign', and had declared it to be 'not only lawful, but a
Christian duty upon all our subjects, to rise in arms against us,
and to murder such as are in any trust or employment under
us'. After expressing many similar protestations of horror,
the Council went on to declare both Cameron and Cargill
'open and notorious traitors and rebels', and 'for the better
encouragement of such as shall apprehend and bring in the
said traitors dead or alive', announced a reward of 5,000
merks for the capture of Cameron and one of 3,000 merks for
that of Cargill. The proclamation carried with it strict instructions to 'all our good subjects, as they will be answerable upon
their allegiance, to do their utmost diligence to discover the
said traitors, and to give timeous intimation with all possible
speed to the nearest officer of our standing forces'. In a large
area of the west and Galloway, covering seventeen parishes,
all the inhabitants over sixteen years of age were to be called
together on two days in July and August and required to state
on oath 'whether any of these traitors foresaid were in that
parish, and where and when'. Similar measures were to be
taken in other parts of the country where the 'said traitors'
might have fled, with heavy penalties for disobedience. Any
who did not appear to testify were to be 'holden and repute as
connivers at, and concealers of the said traitors'. To reinforce
these measures, troops were sent to the south and west to
hunt out any who did not appear at the courts and any others
who were suspected of disloyalty. The people in those parts,
who had already suffered much at the hands of the soldiers,
were now put to even greater hardships: their possessions

were seized, their houses and lands occupied, and some areas of the country were virtually desolated.

While the wrath of the government was directed mainly against Cameron, who was known to be the author of the Sanquhar Declaration, Cargill's life too was now in the utmost peril. For the first time he had been singled out for public denunciation as an 'open and notorious traitor and rebel', and the price of 3,000 merks now placed on his head meant that he had to move with the greatest caution. But whatever the danger, he was not deterred from the work which lay closest to his heart. On 6 June, only three days after his narrow escape at Queensferry, he was at Cairnhill in the south of Lanarkshire, where he preached from Hebrews 11:32: 'And what shall I more say? For the time would fail me to tell of Gideon . . . and of Jephthah.' It was a sermon for the times, dwelling much on the faith of which Hebrews 11 speaks, and stressing the need for such faith in face of the time of trial which he saw coming upon the church. 'The reason why we have chosen this scripture', he said at the outset, 'is to show what great things faith enables a man to do. The church of God has great things to do at this time, in order to her deliverance and raising up; our dangers are so great, our enemies so numerous, our friends so uncertain. We are now brought very low. But I will tell you, if ever the church be raised up, not only must it be by faith, but it must be by great faith.'

The earnestness with which Cargill spoke, and the marks he bore of his own recent escape from danger, prompted some of his hearers to remark to him, after his day's preaching was over, 'Sir, we think praying and preaching go best with you when your danger and distress is greatest.' It had been so, he agreed, and he hoped that it would continue to be so; indeed, he said, the more that ministers and all others had thrust at him that he might fall, the more discernibly the Lord had helped him. And he quoted to himself some words from the psalm that, like Martin Luther, he had made his very own, the 118th: 'The Lord is my strength and song, and is become my salvation.' The words of this psalm were to be on his lips to the very last.

Whatever his misgivings may have been over Cameron's

methods of making a public testimony, Cargill was at one with
Cameron in the main business to which they had set their
hand. The two days of public fasting held at the outset of their
ministry had set the course of their future work, and they now
dedicated themselves to full-time preaching. It was a work
attended from the start with remarkable and spectacular success. The impassioned fervour of Cameron, his powerful
challenges to the consciences of his hearers, and the earnest
and tender concern of Cargill, so different in style and yet so
similar in appeal, combined to make a deep and lasting impression. Even 200 years later, it is said, the memory of these
sermons had not completely died away in the places where
they were preached, and to some of those who heard them
they were as very heaven upon earth. 'I can say,' said John
Malcolm, one of those who was later to suffer for his faith,
'there have been as great days of the gospel in the west of
Scotland in the fields as were in Scotland, since it was Scotland. As much of Christ and heaven were found as finite
creatures on earth were able to hold, yea and more than they
could hold . . . The fathers will be telling the children of it,
when they are old men, that in the year 1680 there were great
days . . . it was then that I got the real impression of God on
my soul.'
    Another of those who were to suffer, John Potter, bore a
similar testimony: 'And now, when I am stepping out of time
into eternity, I declare that I adhere to all the doctrines that
ever I heard Mr Richard Cameron or Mr Donald Cargill
preach; and my soul blesses God that ever I heard either of
them, for my soul has been refreshed to hear the voice and
shouting of a king among these field-meetings, wherein the
fountain of living waters has been made to run down among
the people of God, in such a manner that armies could not
have terrified us.' If anything was to have set the seal of divine
approval on Cameron's and Cargill's mission it was surely
this. One of Cameron's sermons, on John 5:40, 'And ye will
not come to me, that ye might have life', was said to have been
blessed with more remarkable success than any sermon
preached in Scotland, with possibly one exception, since the
primitive times.[5] These were days which enriched the
memory of all who experienced them and who lived to pass on

the story, some of them, like Malcolm and Potter, when they were lying under sentence of death.

Cameron and Cargill had agreed at an early stage that they would normally remain apart for their own safety, but they arranged to come together on certain occasions, usually on alternate Sabbaths, when they shared the preaching between them. These became particularly memorable occasions. On one such day, 18 July, the meeting place was Kype Water in Avondale, where Cameron preached from Psalm 46:10: 'Be still, and know that I am God.' When the day's preaching was over, they agreed to meet as usual in two weeks' time at Craigmad, in the parish of Muiravonside in Stirlingshire. In the meantime they separated, Cargill going north towards Clydesdale and Cameron south towards the Water of Ayr. Conscious of the danger he was now in, Cameron had gathered around him a band of some sixty armed men, several of whom had subscribed with himself a 'bond of mutual defence' similar in terms to the Sanquhar Declaration.[6] This was a move dictated by the peril of the times; bands of soldiers were everywhere roaming the countryside, informers were active and Cameron and his men had to move with extreme caution.[7]

On the afternoon of Thursday, 22 July, after some days of constant travel, Cameron and his companions stopped for rest and refreshment at a desolate spot known as Ayrsmoss. But their movements had been betrayed, and scarcely had they lain down when they were suddenly surprised by a party of soldiers almost twice their number. There was no chance to prepare a proper defence. Cameron, determined to fight it out to the last, had time only to offer the hurried prayer, 'Lord, spare the green and take the ripe,' and immediately the soldiers were upon them. The fight was sharp and bloody. Cameron's men fought with an almost superhuman courage, but the superior numbers against them left the issue in no doubt. When all was over, nine of Cameron's party lay on the field, including Richard Cameron himself.

11.
Torwood

Cameron's death was a grievous blow to Donald Cargill. The fervour and zeal of his young friend and his natural buoyancy of spirit had strengthened and encouraged him in many a moment of despondency, and now that he was gone Cargill felt desolate.

On the following Sabbath at Shotts Cargill preached Cameron's funeral sermon from the words in 2 Samuel 3:38: 'Know ye not that there is a prince and a great man fallen this day in Israel?' They were words which expressed his deep and abiding regard for the young man whose career had been as bright and blazing as a meteor, and as quickly extinguished. His sense of sorrow was embittered some days later by the news of the cruel treatment meted out to those of Cameron's men who had been captured, and in particular by the fate of David Hackston, the leader of the party at Ayrsmoss, who was executed on 30 July in the most savage and inhuman manner which the ingenuity of the Privy Council could devise.[1]

Two days later, on 1 August, the day that he and Cameron had arranged to meet together to preach, Cargill kept the rendezvous alone and, taking as his text the doom pronounced on Jeconiah, King of Judah, by the prophet Jeremiah, ventured to make some predictions about the miserable end awaiting the king if he persisted in his present course. It is probable that he had by this time heard the news of Hackston's death and that he used it to add force and point to his sermon. This news also confirmed him in the belief that the conduct of the king and rulers had reached such a pitch of wickedness as to render them unreclaimable, a view that had been expressed in the Queensferry paper but which he himself had not previously asserted.[2]

About the same time Cargill sent an affectionate letter to John Malcolm and Archibald Alison, two of Cameron's followers who had been captured at Ayrsmoss and who were now under sentence of death in Edinburgh. It is typical of his letters, mingling comfort with exhortation, encouragement with a note of caution. 'Dear friends', he says, 'death in Christ, and for Christ, is never much to be bemoaned, and less at this time than any other, when these that survive have nothing to live among but miseries, persecutions, snares, sorrows and sinning, and where the only desirable sight, Christ reigning in a free and flourishing church, is wanting, and the greatly grieving and offensive object to devout souls — devils and the worst of the wicked reigning and raging — is still before our eyes. And though we had greater things to leave and better times to live in, yet eternity does so far exceed and excel these things in their greatest perfection, that they who see and are sure (and we see indeed, being made sure) will never let a tear fall, or a sigh go, at the farewell.'

The men to whom he was writing had ventured their all for God's cause, but as a true gospel minister Cargill urges them not to look to anything in themselves as the ground for their hope: 'Neither let the goodness of the cause you suffer for found your confidence in God and your hope of well-being; for were the action never so good, and performed without the least failing, it could never be a cause of obtaining mercy, nor yet commend us to that grace from which we are to obtain it. There is nothing now which is yours, when you are pleading and petitioning for mercy, that must be remembered, but your sins, for in effect there is nothing else ours. Let your sins then be on your hearts, as your sorrow, and let these mercies of God and merits of Christ be before your eyes as your hopes, and your winning to these as the only Rock upon which we can be saved. If there be anything seen or looked to in ourselves but sin, we cannot expect remission and salvation solely through free grace, in which expectation only it can be obtained. Look well then to your faith, that it be a faith growing out of regeneration and the new creature, and that it have

Christ for its righteousness, hope and rejoicing, and be sealed by the Spirit of God.'

He ends: 'Dear friends, your work is great, and your time short, but this is a comfort, the only comfort in your present condition, that you have a God infinite in mercy to deal with, who is ready at all times to forgive. Confess your failings to God, and look for his mercy through Jesus Christ, who has said, 'Whosoever loseth his life for my sake, shall keep it unto eternal life.' And let this not discourage you, that the work is great, and the time short; though this indeed should mind you of your sinful neglect, that you were not better provided for such a short and peremptory summons, which you should always have expected. Yet I say, let not this discourage you, for God can perfect great works in a short time; and one of the greatest things that befall men shall be effectuated in the twinkling of an eye. I assure you, he put the thief on the cross through all his desires: conviction, conversion, justification, sanctification, in a short time, and left him nothing to bemoan, but that there did not remain time enough to glorify him upon earth who had done all these things for him. Go on then, and be persuaded in this, that you have him as much and more hastening than yourselves; for you may know his motion by your own, they being both set forward by him. And, dear friends, be not terrified by the manner of your death, which to me seems to be the easiest of all, where you come to it without pain, and in perfect judgement, and go through so speedily; before the pain be felt, the glory is come. But pray for a greater measure of his presence, which can only make a pass through the hardest things cheerful and pleasant. I bid you farewell, expecting, though our parting be sad, our gathering shall be joyful again. Grace, mercy and peace be with you.' This was a letter which showed Cargill's pastoral care at its most tender, and to his two friends, now languishing in prison, it was calculated to bring much peace and comfort. Both of them, in their dying testimonies, gave ample proof of the faith and assurance of which he had spoken. They were executed together on 13 August.[3]

The calamity of Ayrsmoss and its consequences continued to oppress Cargill's spirit, and he felt it necessary for a time to give over his preaching work and to devote himself to prayer and meditation. He kept very much to himself and even in company he spoke very little. It seems clear that his communion with God became especially close at this time, and that he became increasingly convinced, and before long utterly certain, that God had a very special work for him to do. What that work was he confided to none but his devoted friend Walter Smith, the brilliant young theology student who had recently joined him from Holland and who was to be his constant companion in his closing days. He threw out hints at times to those around him, saying that the Lord had put a trumpet into his hand that was going to sound in the ears of many, but beyond that he would say nothing. It was clear nevertheless that not only was he grieving over the distressed state of the church, now at a lower ebb than ever before; he was preparing for something totally foreign to his previous practice, for some kind of positive, public act. This was something new for Cargill, who was never given to public demonstration or display, and it therefore promised to be all the more impressive when it came.

After some time, Cargill put an end to the suspense by announcing his intention to preach at Torwood, between Larbert and Stirling, on 12 September. The news of the meeting spread far and wide. Rumours of the hints that he had given had been widely circulated and it was generally believed that something sensational was to happen. When the day arrived an immense crowd gathered, many of whom were armed. Without doubt, many came out of a sense of curiosity, and out of a desire to be present at what promised to be a memorable occasion. They were not to be disappointed.

Cargill gave out his text from Ezekiel 21:25: 'And thou, profane wicked prince of Israel, whose day is come, when iniquity shall have an end, thus saith the Lord God; Remove the diadem, and take off the crown: this shall not be the same: exalt him that is low, and abase him that is high. I will overturn, overturn, overturn it: and it shall be no more, until he come whose right it is, and I will give it him.' The very reading of the text caused a commotion among his hearers. Raising his voice to make himself heard, Cargill called out: 'Now do not take prejudice, I say, do not take prejudice at us before you hear us speak.' With some difficulty he obtained silence;

some of his friends feared an attack from hostile elements in the crowd, and the landlord with whom he had spent the night took fright and fled. However, Cargill was not deterred, and after some time he was allowed to continue in silence.

He started by giving a short lecture or exposition of his text: 'This word', he proclaimed, 'gives assurance to all men that God is judge of all. He will judge oppression. If he will not relieve the oppressed, I doubt not that he will reward oppressors. God is a righteous judge. He will not suffer the wicked to pass away unpunished.' He went on, 'The words imply that the Lord is about to make a great change. And where he makes a great change, he will take away kings, he will take away nobles, he will take away princes, and he will lay waste many fair buildings. You may say, "Why will he make this great change?" If it were no more but because men have taken away his authority he will do it. Now he is saying to Britain, "Who rules here?" Ere it be long he will make them know who rules in Britain.'

He went on to deal in detail with his text: 'Now there is a great one fallen. It must not be an ordinary death, or ordinary fall: it would be too small a token of God's displeasure. He must stigmatize with more than ordinary brands. . . Oh, blessed shall we count that day, when sin and iniquity shall have an end and fall. We are persuaded that this joy is allowed devout souls. When the sinful lawgiver shall fall, and God shall arise, iniquity shall fall. Let them fall, be they who they will — be they father, mother, brother or be they what they will, if God arise, let them fall.'

He continued: 'The Lord stands by and gives orders to disrobe the profane wicked prince, to remove the diadem and take away the crown from him. There may indeed be much blood shed in keeping it on, and they may keep it for a while; but it shall fall and they shall never recover it again. The worst change in all the earth is not like this change of a wicked magistrate, for theirs is from the throne: they shall fall from the throne to eternal fire, from the crown to eternal fire. What regards the Lord a magistrate, when an enemy to him? "Thou profane wicked prince . . ." Here is a fell style given to a king, but sure I am of this, it does not belong to a faithful minister to give any king that is an enemy to God any other name. What means he by profane? It is either when a man neglects the worship of God altogether, or when he defiles all that he handles thereof. And what is called wickedness? Wicked men working enmity in their heart against God, against his way and against his people — that is wickedness: it is a stiff kind of sinning, they are never broken in their wills; they will not bow to God at all. Now see whether they be such or not who are called our rulers. Let every soul apply it without prejudice. Is not this the style that should be given them? But whatever be his confidence, his day is come, he shall be broken. It says this, his day is coming. There has been great lamentation for the death of kings, but he has been so great a burden to the people that there shall be as great singing and rejoicing. Lord, save us that we hear not that, that we be desired to die! Their death shall be desired, and when they are dead it shall be like the sea that has been long in a storm. In a word, now he will do to some as if a king took in a beggar from the dunghill and set him on high and put on his robes on him and caused him have an attendance and feasting, and after that he takes him out and disrobes him the next day and puts him where he was. When the greatest and highest fall, they become the greatest contempt; the more high they be, they shall be the more contemptible.' He concluded, 'They are sitting low indeed, whom he will set up, and pray that the Lord would seek them out, and that the Lord would make a way for them, and that the Lord would give success in mercy, as there has been success in judgement.'

His exposition over, Cargill went on to give a short 'discourse' in which he linked the words of his text with those of Paul in 1 Corinthians 5:13: 'Therefore put away from among yourselves that wicked person.' His theme was the ultimate sanction wielded by the church — that of excommunication. 'This', he said, 'being the highest censure of the church, and the sword of the Lord, to revenge all disobedience to God, must not be drawn out at all times, or against all sins, though we do acknowledge that it is the present generation's sin that it has been so long drawing out. Yet it shall have this advantage, that the longer it has been in doing, being deserved, it must be acknowledged to be the more just when done, and ought to have the greater weight. Nor yet must this sentence be drawn out by a private spirit or passion to revenge private injuries, but by the spirit of God, and out of zeal to God's glory. Who lives in him ought not to see his dishonour; that so we may stigmatize with this brand, and wound with this sword of the Lord, these enemies that have so apostatized, rebelled, mocked, despised and defied this our Lord and to declare them, as they are none of his, to be none of ours.'

The nature of excommunication he defined as 'a declaring that a man, by his sinning, though he still abide under the covert of the name of a Christian, and fear of God, belongs to the other body or corporation, whereof Satan is head, and not to that body whereof Christ is Head'. It was a 'taking away, a rending off of the insignia of Christianity; a ministerial punishment; a ministerial declaring of the mind of the Lord, that he quits formally these wicked persons, and divests them of that church and domestic relation of children they profess to have with him, and that he quits and gives them up to Satan as his own, to be tempted, tortured and punished by him at God's will'. 'And,' Cargill noted, 'it is very remarkable that where this sentence is just, that it passes the power of devils to make them such a life as they had before; for after that, they are still languishing, vexed and anxious in heart, as persons fallen from the highest and best condition, who are fallen under the worst of heads, and to the dreadfullest conditions and companies.'

The subjects of excommunication were 'those who either were or are the members of the true church, who were entered by baptism, and have fallen away by impieties, and not those who are without; all Christians, we mean one as well as another, the great as well as the mean, ministers as well as people; all people, priests, princes and kings are the subjects of excommunication. For excommunication, as it has causes, so it ought to follow upon the disobedience of the subjects to God, and that indifferently upon all, without respect of persons, as God, who is the Commander of this judgement will proceed himself in judgement, without respect of persons.'

The causes of this ultimate sanction were 'sins great and uncontrovertible, such as blasphemy, paganism, atheism, murders, adulteries, incests, perjuries, wilful and open profanation of the Sabbath, or where there is added contumacy to these sins, and obstinacy in regard to repentance'.

Finally the ends of excommunication were 'zeal to God's glory, that will not suffer such to abide in his house; that wickedness, which is like a leaven, which leavens the whole lump, may be stopped from further infection, and that the putrified member which is ready to infect the rest may be cut off before its infection spreads further; and to be a warning to those who are thus guilty and cast out, those censures being the forerunners and prognostics of ejection and banishment from God and eternal happiness, and a sorting of them to their own party and fellowship that they shall be eternally with, if they repent not'.

Cargill's audience were now well prepared for what was to follow. After closing his discourse and calling his hearers to prayer, 'that we may the better proceed', he came directly to the climax of his day's work. 'We have spoken of excommunication', he said, 'of the causes, subjects and ends; we shall now proceed to the action, being constrained by the conscience of our duty, and zeal for God, to excommunicate some of those who have been the committers of so great crimes and authors of so great mischiefs of Britain and Ireland, but especially those of Scotland, and in doing of this we shall keep the names by which they are ordinarily called, that they may be the better known.'

Cargill then pronounced: 'I, being a minister of Jesus Christ, and having authority and power from him, do in his name, and by his Spirit, excommunicate, cast out of the true church and deliver up to Satan, Charles II, king, and that upon the account of these wickednesses:

'1. For his high contempt of God, after he had acknowledged his own sins, his father's sins, his mother's idolatry, and had solemnly engaged against them in a declaration at Dunfermline, the 16th day of August 1650, he has notwithstanding of all this gone on more avowedly in these sins than all that were before him.

'2. For his great perjury, after he had twice at least solemnly subscribed that Covenant, he did so presumptuously renounce, disown and command it to be burnt by the hand of the hangman.[4]

'3. Because he has rescinded all laws for establishing of that religion and reformation engaged to in that Covenant, and enacted laws for establishing its contrary, and is still working for the introducing of popery in these lands.

'4. For commanding of armies to destroy the Lord's people who are standing in their own just defence and for their privileges and rights against tyrannies, oppressions and injuries of men; and for the blood he has shed on fields and scaffolds and in seas of the people of God, upon account of religion and righteousness (they being most willing in all other things to render their obedience, if he had reigned and ruled them according to his covenant and oath) more than all the kings that have been before him in Scotland.

'5. That he has still been an enemy to, and a persecutor of the true Protestants, a favourer and helper of the papists, both at home and abroad, and has hindered, to the utmost of his power, the due execution of just laws against them.

'6. For his relaxing of the kingdom by his frequent grant of remissions and pardons for murderers (which is in the power of no king to do, being expressly contrary to the law of God) which was the ready way to embolden men to commit murders, to the defiling of the land with blood.

'7. To pass by all other things, his great and dreadful uncleanness of adultery and incest, his drunkenness, his dissembling with God and man and performing his promises where his engagements were sinful.'

Cargill then went on to pronounce sentence 'by the same authority, and in the same name' on six of the king's leading officers of state: the Duke of York, brother of the king, 'for his idolatry'; the Duke of Monmouth, 'for leading armies against the Lord's people, and for refusing, that morning at Bothwell Bridge, a cessation of arms, for hearing and redressing their injuries, wrongs and oppressions'; the Duke of Lauderdale, the king's former commissioner in Scotland, 'for his dreadful blasphemy, his scoffing at religion, his perjury, his adulteries and uncleanness, his gaming on the Lord's Day, and his usual and ordinary cursing'; the Duke of Rothes, Chancellor of Scotland and President of the Privy Council, 'for his perjury, his adulteries and uncleanness; his allotting the Lord's Day for his drunkenness; for the heathenish, bar-

barous and unheard-of cruelty, whereof he was the chief
author, contriver and commander, to that worthy gentleman
David Hackston of Rathillet, and for his ordinary cursing,
swearing and drunkenness'; Sir George Mackenzie, the
king's Advocate, 'for his apostasy, his constant pleading
against and persecuting to death the people of God, his pleading for sorcerers, murderers and other criminals, and his
ungodly, erroneous, fantastic and blasphemous tenets'; and
Thomas Dalyell of Binns, general of the king's forces, 'for his
leading armies and commanding the killing, robbing, pillag-
ing and oppressing of the Lord's people; for his lewd and
impious life led in adultery and uncleanness from his youth,
with a contempt of marriage, which is an ordinance of God;
and for his other injurious deeds, in the exercise of his power'.

Cargill had now come to the close of his momentous work.
'I think', he said as he concluded, 'none that acknowledge the
Word of God can judge these sentences to be unjust. And as
the causes are just, so being done by a minister of the gospel,
and in such a way as the present persecution would permit,
the sentence is just; and there are no kings or ministers on
earth, without repentance of the persons, can reverse these
sentences upon any such account. God, who is the author of
that ordinance, is the more engaged to the ratifying of them,
and all that acknowledge the Scriptures of truth ought to
acknowledge them.' And he ended by applying to the case the
following words of Scripture: 'Should he deal with our sister
as with an harlot? Should they deal with our God as with an
idol? Should they deal with his people as murderers and
malefactors, and we not draw out his sword against them?'

For Cargill the consequences of the Torwood excommunication were incalculable. The news of it spread like wildfire
throughout the country; copies were posted up in prominent
places in Edinburgh and other principal towns, and the subjects of the sentence soon came to know of it. In a day when
ecclesiastical censures meant more than they do now, the significance of the excommunication was not lost upon the
authorities, for they recognized that those people who
believed that Cargill had divine authority for his action would
now regard themselves as loosed from their allegiance. Cargill well knew the dangers to which he had exposed himself

and the outburst of fury to which he would be subjected. He had entered on the work in the certain assurance that he was obeying God's command, and his utterance was characterized at every step by assertions of the divine authority. But there is evidence too that he was under intense mental strain: he forgot at first to include the Duke of Lauderdale in the sentence and was obliged to mention him separately in the afternoon, and also during his discourse he referred mistakenly to St Ambrose as Bishop of Lyons instead of Bishop of Milan. These were slips of which Bishop Paterson of Edinburgh took full advantage when writing later that week to Lauderdale expressing his horror at what Cargill had done.[5] But the fact that Cargill had taken this action was of itself of profound significance. For one thing it showed that it had been no empty gesture by a rash or impetuous spirit, for deliberation and forethought characterized all Cargill's public actions. Nor was he inclined by nature to the sensational or dramatic, or to any action which invited public attention. The mere fact that his work that day had been uncharacteristic and alien to his natural inclinations suggests strongly that he had been acting under a compulsion which overbore his own nature and which he clearly recognized as carrying divine authority.

Speaking some time later he said, 'I know I am and will be condemned by many for what I have done, but condemn me who will, I know I am approved of God, and am persuaded that what I have done on earth is ratified in heaven; for if ever I knew the mind of God, and was clear in my call to any piece of my generation-work, it was in that.'

Cargill did indeed come under heavy criticism, not only from declared enemies but from former friends. To many of those who had formerly sided with him he had now placed himself beyond the pale: 'Oh, whither shall our shame go, at such a height of folly are some men arrived!' exclaimed Robert Law, minister of New Kilpatrick, who had been ejected with Cargill in 1662 and had himself suffered for his nonconformity. Even otherwise friendly biographers have not hesitated to censure Cargill on this score.[6]

And yet, on any dispassionate analysis, Cargill's action can be seen as being fully in accord with the historic principles of Scottish Presbyterianism. As he had said, all baptized persons

— all members of the visible church, whatever their rank or
station — were subject to the discipline of the church and so
were potentially liable to her ultimate sanction. This had been
made abundantly clear in the Reformation standards of Knox
and his successors, which had stressed the essential unity and
catholicity of the visible church and her jurisdiction over all
within her pale, high or low, whatever their religious
allegiances or affinities might be.[7]

It was these standards, too, which had affirmed the divine
authority behind the office of the king or ruler, and his duty
to govern his people in righteousness.[8] Kings, to be sure, were
only human and subject to human frailty, and so, as Cargill
remarked on another occasion, 'There is nobody that rules,
but they are liable to failings in ruling; and therefore if all failings of rulers should be exactly looked to, there would be
none who would rule a day to an end, but we might find faults
in them, for which to depose them ere night.' But obstinate,
wanton disobedience was something quite different: 'It is one
thing to be failing in infirmity, and another thing to be in a
constant course of wickedness and enmity against God. The
first may be spared, but not the last.' To govern his people
according to God's law was an essential part of the king's
duty. 'We are sure,' said Cargill, 'we see this plain from the
Scripture, that this is the part of the office of a king, and he
that has no regard to this ought no more to be esteemed a
king, but a tyrant and enemy to God.'

In this there was no essential difference between Cargill's
position and that of the authors of the Sanquhar Declaration.
But at the same time there was a vital difference of emphasis.
For Cargill, the king's offence was not primarily against man
but against God. It was the sword of God, rather than the
sword of man, that had to be drawn out against him. Indeed,
in his reference in the excommunication to 'the sword of the
Lord' there may be a wistful reference to his own disillusion-
ment with those carnal weapons that had been drawn out, so
ineffectively, at Bothwell, or to the 'declaration of war' that
had been proclaimed at Sanquhar.

But who had the authority to draw out the 'sword of the
Lord' on his behalf against his enemies? Who other than
those having 'authority and power from him', those messen-

gers of his who were ordained to the ministerial office? Cargill, throughout his life, cherished the highest regard and respect for the office and work of the ministry. 'This is a great power indeed', he remarked on another occasion when speaking from Jeremiah 1:10, 'for a creature to have the power of heaven, power to plant, to pluck up and to destroy.' And so, as the offence had been against God, the sentence must be pronounced by one of God's servants at his Master's command. 'We shall only say this of it', said Cargill in his own defence, 'that ere all be done, great men shall know that there has been a prophet and a minister that has had the mind of the Lord in what he has done; and that as we have cursed or excommunicated, so the Lord has cursed or excommunicated.' What had been done by God's servant in his name on earth the Lord himself had ratified in heaven.

But was Cargill justified in acting without the concurrence of his fellow-ministers? Was he not arrogating to himself a function that properly belonged to the church as a whole and that was exercised only after the strictest investigation and enquiry? Cargill well knew that by the law of the Church of Scotland, going back as far as Knox's *Book of Common Order* in Geneva, excommunication was a corporate act of the church and not to be entered upon by any one person.[9] However, he had no hesitation in justifying himself on this score. He had sought the concurrence of other ministers, but could find none to side with him, and in these circumstances he considered it his duty to go on alone. He was well aware of the charges of arrogance which this would bring upon him. 'Pope-like', was how Robert Law described it. But he was prepared for this; he was utterly certain that he had been commanded by God to the work and, no matter what others might do, it was his duty to obey. 'And as to proof or probation of the offences, there needs none, their deeds being notorious and public, and the most of them such as they themselves do avow and boast of.' The conditions then, in these exceptional times, being fully met, the sword of the Lord was unsheathed and his enemies wounded with this 'more than ordinary brand'.

But it is possible to see in Cargill's action a deeper significance still. Ever since the Reformation, the Church of Scotland had had to contend in a particular way for the right of Christ to rule in his own house, for the church to have the oversight and jurisdiction of her own affairs independently of the state. This great principle, 'the most radiant pearl in the Church of Scotland's garland', as the *Cloud of Witnesses* calls it, had been a vital point of testimony in the post-Reformation church, and was of the very essence of Scottish Presbyterianism.[10] It was this principle the king had violated by taking away the liberties and rights of the church and arrogating to himself a supremacy which alone belonged to Christ. While Cargill's action had particular reference to the character of the king as a ruler and individual, it is quite legitimate to see in it a striking reaffirmation of the distinctive testimony of the church and a reassertion of her historic claim to spiritual independence.

The excommunication had been a stern work, and as soon as it was over Cargill returned to his more usual strain of preaching. That very afternoon he preached from Lamentations 3:31-32: 'For the Lord will not cast off for ever: but though he cause grief, yet will he have compassion according to the multitude of his mercies.' It was a sermon that had no application to the subjects of the excommunication, but was meant as a message of consolation and comfort for the suffering church and its persecuted members. Typical of Cargill's style are these extracts: 'We know not any Scripture that the Lord confirms oftener to us than this. Oh, it is a sweet word! But, alas, there are many sweet words that are hardly believed, because we are lying under much guilt. There is one thing sure, God will not cast off a remnant for ever. And if you be sure of this, that you once had him, we will make you sure of this likewise, that if you have had him, you shall yet have him. Has he ever been yours? If he has been within, I assure you he shall be within, he will return. Oh, the faithfulness of God! If he had dealt with us as we have dealt with him, what would have come of us? Oh, his faithfulness is strong! If his faithfulness had not been strong, we should have broken and run away from him and never returned to him again; we run from him, and he brings us back again. There is great love and affection in God towards his people. He will not only exercise his love upon himself and upon his own Son, but he will have a crea-

ture to exercise his love upon. Oh, that he should exercise his
love upon a creature! It is a wonder that we are not saying
every one to another, "I can never love but when I love him."
There is no creature that has an interest in him, but he has
reserved hope for them, that though there be an offcasting he
will return. I say there is none that have their foundation sure,
but he will return to them. Is your foundation sure? Have you
his tokens? Have you his earnest? Have you his seal? If you
have these, I assure you he will not cast you off for ever. But
you may say, "When will he return?" His returning will be
according to our diligence. If you can want [i.e., do without]
him, he will tarry the longer. When he is absent you never go
a right step till he comes again; you can do nothing without
him, but sin. Yet he will have compassion. He will have his
people up again, though he give them away for a while.
Though he cast down he will take them up again. Though he
cause grief he will not cast off for ever. There is nothing that
will make us sure of his return, but the compassion and mercy
of our God.'

Often, indeed, his preaching was of this kind, rich in
tenderness and consolation; at other times he would seek to
bring encouragement to his hearers from the very fact of the
sovereignty and authority of God, as in a sermon he preached
at Blackhill the Sabbath after Torwood on the words in Luke
18:7: 'And shall not God avenge his own elect'? His concern
on this occasion was to advise the persecuted members of the
church what to do in circumstances of sore trial, when
exposed to wrong and injustice: 'Oh, seek not avenging on
your own account, when you are wronged by others; for if you
do so, your avenging will be instead of God's avenging, and in
so doing you give your adversaries a great advantage. Give no
just cause of wronging you, but only righteousness; keep
down passion, keep down corruption, as much as in you lies.
Let the zeal of God be always uppermost in your soul.' And
the ground for this meekness of spirit lay in the identity of
Christ with his people: 'They are his in a very particular
manner, flesh of his flesh and blood of his blood, marked in
his image, and all that is done to them is taken as affronts
done to him. He is engaged on the account that they are his,
and that they are suffering on his account; for we are sure of

this, that we need not suffer this day as we do, were it not on his account. This cross would not be on us, were it not for Christ's sake.' And so, he counselled his hearers, in the confidence that they were suffering for God and his truths, the avenging of their wrongs could be left in God's hands. He would vindicate his honour; he would maintain his own cause.

12.
In the midst of dangers

Despite the increasing dangers now facing him, Cargill continued his labours undaunted. On 3 October he preached in
the fields at Craigmad, near Falkirk, from a text in Ezekiel
12:23: 'The days are at hand, and the effect of every vision.'
His message from this text was a sombre one, warning of the
judgements impending upon the land for its apostasy and
breach of Covenant. This was a theme which was to press
upon him increasingly from now on, and to which he gave frequent expression in his letters and sermons. Judgement he
saw as an inevitable retribution upon God's enemies, but at
the same time he was careful to remind his hearers that in
desiring to see God's truth vindicated upon persecutors they
must not be motivated by personal resentment: 'Oh that we
could when we pray for justice upon enemies, pray so that it
were not for our own private passion or wrath at them, or for
wrongs done to us, but only the love and zeal of God.' He
gave further emphatic affirmation to his action at Torwood:
'There are some that are condemning that just act of excommunication . . . what we have done, blame us as they will, but
though we be blamed by them yet with God we are sure that
we never shall be blamed, nor charged for what we have
done.' And, as if to seal his testimony to his momentous act,
he closed the meeting by asking his audience to sing part of
the 52nd Psalm, from the third verse to the end, words which
foretell the just doom of malicious persecutors.

The reality of the persecution was brought home to Cargill
in a particular way almost immediately afterwards. On his
way from the meeting — apparently making for Bo'ness,

where he often found sanctuary — he was waylaid by a troop
of soldiers at Linlithgow Bridge and very narrowly escaped
capture. His horse was shot under him and killed, and several
of his hearers who were with him were taken prisoner. It was
yet another of the providential escapes to which he had now
become almost accustomed, and it was to be by no means the
last. While this latest incident may have made him more circumspect in his movements, it certainly did not prevent him
from continuing to travel about to preach.

Three weeks later, on 24 October, he held a field-meeting
at Largo Law in Fife, attended by worshippers from as far
away as Glasgow and Edinburgh.[1] The strictness of the
searches for him had now forced him to travel only by night
and to remain in hiding during the hours of daylight. When his
day's preaching was over he retired to Kirkcaldy, staying privately with friends for the next two days and eventually
recrossing the Forth at Burntisland on the night of the following Tuesday. The next Sabbath, 31 October, found him again
preaching in the fields in the vicinity of Carnwath, near
Lanark.

Amid these varied hazards he found time on 8 October to
address two further letters to friends.[2] The recipients of these
letters are unknown, but it is probable that some of them were
in prison, for in one of the letters he remarks, 'Your condition
is sad and your danger is great, and you are destitute of mercy
and remembrancers.' In his other letter he reflects again on
the sad condition of the church — a theme never far from his
thoughts in these days — and on the prevailing neglect of the
things of God: 'Oh, let us never think that we have begun to do
anything aright till we have repented, not only of our abominations and evils, but that we have done so little for God and
have been so long in beginning to do! And let us therefore be
tender and zealous; keep these two, the one as a light to lead
us, and the other as a fire to warm us. Zeal without tenderness
is but like a flower broken off its own root and put in water; a
few hours will wither it. And tenderness without zeal is but a
fancy; for zeal is but an emanation of tenderness, and as it
were a speaking tenderness. And when we hear and see these
things, what tenderness can hold its peace more than the
earth can hold in its flowers and seeds at the approach of the

sun? There are such indignities done to God that could not
bring out zeal if tenderness were not within. For woe will be
to a man if he gets his own quiet and liberties and cares not
what little part God gets of the world. And blessed is that man
who if God get a large share cares not though he himself have
not a foot's breadth in it. All is now turned to a self zeal, a
man's zeal, a king's zeal. How great are the clamours that are
raised against some poor ones, as if they were the only
enemies to God and mankind for showing their dutiful zeal in
some holy things, as the only state confounders and state
disturbers; and a deep silence of the wrongs done to God.'
But black though the picture was, Cargill had a vision of a
future which would transcend the gloom, when the church
would be revived and shine forth more glorious than it had
ever been: 'He will suffer the church no more to hide in corners
and slavery, and his people to be at tyrants' courtesy for a
night's lodging and a peeping "on leave" profession; he will
exalt it above the tops of the mountains, and many people
shall flow to it. He will have it henceforth more large, more
pure, more glorious. The carnal ministers and professors
think these thoughts to be the height of fanaticism, and yet I
think it is now beginning to peep out and to come like the
morning . . . Providence will shortly speak and bring out the
wonderful contrivances which will at last, after it has made its
way through dreadful judgements, arrive at the purifying of
the Church of Scotland, a pattern for the world.'

With this vision to inspire him Cargill could look to the
future of the church with confidence. For the present, however, the harsh reality of the persecution continued. Since
Torwood his life had been in increasing peril; he had to look
to his own safety still more watchfully than before, and there
were few places where danger did not lurk. To no one would
his capture have given more satisfaction than to the governor
of Blackness Castle, from whose hands he had escaped so narrowly at Queensferry. The governor was not a man to give up
easily; ever since the Queensferry incident he had been plan-
ning ways of capturing the prey that had then eluded him, and
his resolution was strengthened by the publicity which had
followed Cargill's latest action.

At the beginning of November the governor decided on a

new strategy, even more devious than before. This time he used as his agent one James Henderson, a ferryman at Queensferry, whom he hired to search for Cargill and to present him with a forged letter, in the name of some of Cargill's friends in Fife, inviting him to come over to Fife to preach. Cargill had preached on the previous Sabbath, 7 November, in the moors above Falkirk, and the governor had apparently heard reports that he had afterwards moved with some friends into Edinburgh. After making some enquiries, Henderson duly tracked Cargill down there on 11 November to a house in the West Bow. Plausibly presenting the letter, though apparently without completely managing to conceal his insincerity, he offered to have a boat ready at the ferry the next day to take Cargill across to Fife. Though some of his friends were suspicious, Cargill accepted the offer, and on leaving the house Henderson immediately arranged for a party of the governor's soldiers to lie in wait about three miles out of the town. When the time came, Cargill took with him five friends — three men and two women. The women and two of the men went on ahead on foot, while Cargill himself and the third man, James Boig, followed some time later on horseback. The ambush was duly sprung, but one of the women escaped and managed to give the alarm to Cargill and Boig before they reached the spot. They immediately fled back to Edinburgh and safety. For the second time the governor's prey had eluded him, but Cargill's three friends were in the hands of the enemy and were shown no mercy. One of them, Archibald Stewart, who had been with Richard Cameron at Ayrsmoss, was cruelly tortured to extract information about Cargill's hiding-places. The other two, James Skene and Marion Harvie, were guilty of no crime other than hearing Cargill preach and of holding opinions about Bothwell and the killing of Sharp which the judges found treasonable. Stewart and Skene, with a third man, John Potter, were executed at the Cross of Edinburgh on 1 December. Marion Harvie, with another young woman, Isobel Alison, was executed in the Grassmarket on 26 January 1681.[3]

This incident and its consequences afflicted Cargill deeply. Skene, a young man of noble birth from Aberdeenshire, had come south only some six months before and Cargill had formed a high opinion of his worth. He wrote to him in prison, expressing his admiration for his uncompromising testimony before his judges and encouraging him in the hope of a future reward. Skene was a man of very strong principle and he had testified forcefully not only against the perjury and tyranny of the civil rulers but also against the compliance and unfaithfulness of ministers.[4] Cargill refers to both of these testimonies in his letter and expresses particular indignation at the harm done to the cause of Christ by the defections of its professed supporters. It is possible that he was particularly distressed by a report that one of his own former colleagues in Glasgow, John Carstairs, had strongly condemned Skene's principles before the Privy Council and had owned the king's authority and that of his courts.[5] This may go some way to explain the vigour of Cargill's language in his letter to Skene, which is uncharacteristically strong, and can only be put down to his deep indignation at the wrongs done to his friend by those who ought to have stood by him. He encourages Skene to stand firm: 'But go on, valiant champion: you die not as a fool, though the apostate, unfaithful and lukewarm ministers and professors of this generation think and say so . . . But neither regard their voices, nor fear, for God will neither seal to folly nor iniquity.'

He goes on to comfort and exhort his friend in the face of impending death: 'But forgive and forget all these private injuries, and labour to go to eternity and death with the heart destitute of private revenges, and filled with zeal to God's glory, and assign to him the quarrel against his enemies; and for yourself, whatever there has been either of sin or of duty, remember the one and forget the other, and betake yourself wholly to the mercy of God and the merit of Christ. You know in whom you have believed, and the acceptableness of your believing, and the more fully you henceforth believe, the greater shall be his glory, and the greater your peace and safety.' His closing words have in them a sublime beauty which has often been remarked upon: 'Farewell, dearest friend, never to see one another any more till at the right hand of Christ. Fear not, and the God of mercies grant a full gale and a fair entry into his kingdom, which may carry sweetly and swiftly over the bar, that you find not the rub of death. Grace, mercy and peace be with you.'

To Stewart and Potter he wrote in similar strain, dwelling again on the usurpation of Christ's rights and adding words of personal comfort and encouragement. He took the opportunity in this letter of vindicating once again his action at Torwood: 'If ever any excommunication is just, this is: and so far orderly as the times and state of affairs will permit, for the consent of the church cannot be expected in the perturbed state thereof, neither ought it to be waited for in a declined and corrupted state of the church.' His closing words to his two friends, soon to die, are in the same tender spirit as his farewell message to Skene: 'Dearest friends, go on then and secure other things, accordingly that as you have peace in your present quarrel because of your suffering, so men may have safety as to your future and eternal state. And blessed be God that I have somewhat wherewith to comfort you and to be comforted about you, besides the hope of a temporal life. And though he be able to give you the one as well as the other, yet let not the hope of this abate either the ardour in your preparation or the zeal in your testimony, and expect only his mercy in your duty. Go on then mourning for your sins, humbly creeping forward to the sceptre held forth, firmly believing in the sufficiency of a Saviour for the quenching of all challenges, and for the obtaining of a perfect righteousness, whereby you may stand unafraid before his tribunal.'[6]

While sending his friends these messages of comfort and reassurance, Cargill himself was in extreme danger. On 22 November, ostensibly as a result of information extracted from Skene, Stewart and Potter, the Privy Council issued a long proclamation in which the reward for his capture was increased from 3,000 to 5,000 merks. He and his friends were denounced as 'villainous and fanatical conspirators', and Cargill himself as 'one of their most seditious preachers'. It was by far the fiercest proclamation issued against him, and its tone gives some evidence of the indignation which his action at Torwood had caused. In the proclamation and in a covering letter to the king, the Council claimed with an exaggerated show of horror that Cargill had preached the lawfulness of killing the king and rulers, and that Skene and the others with him had met together in Edinburgh 'to consult with Mr Donald Cargill the best methods for putting the said abhorrent and hellish plot into execution'. The allegation that Cargill had preached the lawfulness of killing the king was, of course, entirely false, and the only evidence the Council could produce in support of it was a personal opinion expressed by Skene in his examination and a few statements extracted from Stewart under torture.[7] Nevertheless, these provided a sufficient excuse for the Council to vent their rage against Cargill on account of the excommunication, which they obviously resented bitterly. Gone for ever were the days when they had sought to conciliate him with the offer of an indulgence; he was now the declared enemy of the state, the most notorious rebel still at large, an open and declared traitor to His Majesty's person and government.

The shock of this latest incident, and the subsequent death of his friends, affected Cargill with the same grief of heart that he had experienced after Bothwell and Ayrsmoss. On this occasion, as then, he felt the need for a period of withdrawal from his preaching work and for meditation and reflection on his future course. This time he chose to retire into England, probably spending most of his time in Northumberland, where he seems to have stayed on at least one earlier occasion, and where he could apparently depend upon the loyalty of trusted friends. It is clear that during his time there his thoughts were much preoccupied with the condition of the church at home, and on at least two occasions this concern found expression in pastoral letters. The first of these, dated 16 March 1681, is the longest of his letters to survive and contains his views on many of the topical questions of the time. In many ways it is a written sermon, with numerous echoes of his preaching style. It seems to have been composed in some haste, as Cargill himself admits, and its literary quality falls somewhat short of the other productions of his pen. However, this is made good by the directness and naturalness of his approach as he counsels his friends on the personal and corporate duties of the day and encourages them with some characteristic devotional reflections. One of the most striking features of the letter is the facility with which Cargill was able

Covenanters Arrested

to quote and apply biblical texts to illustrate his theme, revealing how close and accurate was his knowledge of Scripture at every point.

Cargill begins by exhorting his friends to the cultivation of personal holiness: 'Loving friends, ponder that word in the 92nd Psalm, twelfth verse: "The righteous shall flourish like the palm tree, he shall grow like a cedar in Lebanon . . ." Oh, know ye the growth of the godly, sirs? Know ye what it is to grow up in all things into him which is the head, even Christ? (Ephesians 4:15). Know ye growth in grace and in the knowledge of our Lord and Saviour Jesus Christ? (2 Peter 3:18). This is the indiscernible growth of the cedars of Lebanon. O sirs, do not take your growth from men; remember that word in 1 Thessalonians 2:6: "Not of men sought we glory". Would you then know the end of the godly, when they are said to flourish? It is that they may be brought to the king in needlework, it is that they may be all glorious within (Psalm 45:13). O sirs, know ye the growth that is required of the king's daughter, and know ye the glory she shall have with her husband? I believe, sirs, there are a few of us that know it. It is this in a glimpse, eye hath not seen it, ear hath not heard it, neither hath it entered into the heart of man, to conceive the things laid up for the godly. Were you never brought to say with Peter in Matthew 17:4, "It is good for us to be here" when he had seen a glimpse of Christ's transfiguration? Were you never brought to it in your private retiring places, were you never brought to it in your family, were you never brought to it in your Christian fellowship, were you never brought to it in your meditation, were you never brought to it in villages walking alone, were you never brought to it in your singing, praying, reading the sweet Scriptures of Christ? If you have not been brought to say, "It is good for us to be here", you know not what it is to grow up like the tall cedars in Lebanon.'

Much of Cargill's letter is in this strain, rich in devotional exhortation and counsel. Later on he writes: 'Consider that word, "Come my people, enter into your chambers", and that other word, "Come my sister . . ."; well then, there are mansions prepared for the godly by sweet Christ Jesus. Oh, then run into him, and be hidden. Be up in the hill with him, even when you are here. Are none of your faces shining when you come down from him? Assuredly if you meet with him they will shine. Yes, they will shine in such a measure that others who are strangers shall know that you have been with Jesus of Nazareth. O sirs, know ye him who is altogether lovely, the chiefest among ten thousand? Can you not say, "This is my beloved"? O dear friends, be in heaven with him, for he is content to have you there.'

In exhortations like these, containing echoes of the sublime flights of devotion to be found in the letters of his old teacher, Rutherford, Cargill strove to bring the comforts of the Scriptures to his friends in their trial. He was also concerned, as he goes on to show, to remind them of the public duties of the time and to exhort them to continued public testimony. This would certainly be at the risk of suffering, and even death itself. But in the midst of this fiery trial there was the example of their Master: 'For a general comfort', Cargill advised, 'take that word in the fifteenth chapter of John, at the twentieth verse: "If they have persecuted me, they will also persecute you." You must not desire to be greater than your Lord, for if they called him Beelzebub, what will they not call you? I will say this, dear friends, that you have God's approbation.'

Cargill then goes on to deal at some length with the public affairs of the day, dwelling much on the apostasy of king and rulers, and with particular sadness on the defections of ministers. Understandably, the subject of the excommunication finds a place, though briefly: 'Purge yourselves of him called king, who is already cast out of the church, and purge yourselves of those that were delivered over to Satan with him, that they might learn not to blaspheme . . . Let divines, let professors say what they will, those are justly excluded, and much might be said here for the vindication of that act; but only take this one argument (for I may not stay here to multiply arguments), if there be not a mutual compact betwixt a king and people, as is between man and wife, master and servant, tutor and pupil? Then if the one violate it so that he opposes, kills, uses all kinds of malice against the other, may the other not lawfully defend himself and otherwise cast him off?' Cargill illustrates his argument — which again has strong echoes of Rutherford — by appealing to 2 Samuel 5:3 and 1

Chronicles 11:3, which record the league made between David and the elders of Israel before the Lord. He is careful to emphasize the words 'before the Lord' since they are central to his whole approach: 'Oh consider, sirs, that the compacts and covenants that were made with these persons in this land were made before the Lord and the host of heaven, sun moon and stars; yes, all these shall rise up in judgement and condemn this corrupt generation . . . Sirs, I desire to have charity, but I see that now it can hardly be given, when there is so much pleading for a wicked blood-shedding man; and I will say that one word, Luke 16:10: "He that is faithful in that which is least is faithful also in much, and he that is unjust in the least is unjust also in much."'

Cargill's concern extended not only to those in authority, but to all ranks of society in the Scotland of his day. The spiritual awakenings of the 1670s were fast becoming a memory, and it seemed that many of the people were relapsing into worldly unconcern and indifference. 'There are many', he observed, in a revealing comment on the popular interests of the day, 'that take greater delight in Bruce and Wallace, and ballads, than they do in the Word of God; they will spend days when they cannot get their labour gone about, and rise up early and sit up late, that they may discourse well in history. I do not disapprove of that, if it tend to the glory of God. But how few are there that have that end before them, especially some young folk, that know not what pains to be at, that they may acquire these ballads and romances. Oh, say some, we have the Bible on the Sabbath. Consider that word in Joshua 1:8: "This book of the law shall not depart out of thy mouth; thou shalt meditate therein day and night."'

The letter ends, as it began, with a series of devotional exhortations: 'Lastly, dear friends, look on this as a way to prevent God's wrath, and the peculiar duty of the day, and that is, Love God, and love one another. Oh will you take notice of that sweet word, Deuteronomy 7:7: "The Lord did not set his love upon you, nor choose you, because you were more in number than any people, for ye were the fewest of all people, but because the Lord loved you"? Oh, what will you do to the Lord for all his benefits? I will tell you: give him that love again which you have received from him. Psalm 31:23:

"Oh, love the Lord, all ye his saints." Oh, love him, love him, considering that it will be your exercise in heaven: love, praise, singing! Oh what sweet melody must it be . . .! Let the love of God be shed abroad in your hearts, according to that word in Romans 5:5: "Love one another." Dear friends, be united in the Lord. John 13:34: "Love one another; as I have loved you." Now, dear friends, farewell, and see that you have no companions to come in competition with sweet Lord Jesus. "Why should I be as one that turneth aside to the flocks of thy companions?" There are many that would be companions to our Lord and Master, but see that you neither follow them nor their flocks.'

There is nothing more typical of Cargill than the words with which he concludes his letter. 'Now, dear friends, remember that word, Luke 17:10: "So likewise ye, when ye shall have done all these things which are commanded you, say, We are unprofitable servants; we have done that which was our duty to do." I shall load you with no more. The Spirit and the Bride say Come. I rest, yours to command in the Lord.'

Cargill's second letter from England, dated eleven days later, on 27 March 1681, was addressed particularly to his old congregation in the Barony of Glasgow. It was now over eighteen years since he had been forced to leave his first and only pastoral charge. Yet there were some, and apparently not a few, who still cherished fond memories of these early years and who continued to keep in touch with him throughout all the testing times that followed. For those faithful members of his old congregation Cargill still was their minister, and for him the Barony was still his parish. It is not surprising therefore to find him, just before his return from England, writing at length to his old parishioners in terms of warm fellowship and affection. It is fairly clear from his letter that their friendship had not been limited to words only; it had found expression in many acts of kindness and generosity, for which he regarded himself as deeply in their debt.

But his main concern, as in all his letters, was to offer words of exhortation and advice, and to encourage his friends to stand fast in the faith. It was especially necessary that they should not be drawn aside by the example of those ministers who had accepted favours from the Council and had thereby done grievous harm to the cause of Christ. Cargill's horror of the Indulgence oppressed his mind as he wrote, but though he grieved over the defections it had caused he could still pity and pray for those ministers who had been ensnared and led aside. 'Some of them', he acknowledged, 'were in Christ before me' and he had some hope of their recovery. 'There being then a real difference we ought to acknowledge it in our compassion, tenderness and affection, and withal pray that they may be made to see what and whom they have relinquished. Oh that God would open men's eyes, that they may see how little good and how much evil it has wrought, how little it has done for the freedom and enlargement of the kingdom of Christ! They themselves, when come to themselves and sober, will see that it has not increased the treasure of God in themselves, because they stand in the way of gratifying a sinful power, of saving life on any terms, securing their quiet, and shunning the cross of Christ, who is calling all at this time to take it up.'

But Cargill knew too much of the human heart to leave matters there. Opposition to the Indulgence and the unfaithfulness of ministers was a commendable thing in itself, but it could quickly degenerate into a censorious formality if it was not accompanied with true heart religion. And so he goes on: 'Think not that rightness in these debated matters will do it, though I esteem much of that, and cannot but say that it looks like a spark of true grace; yet think it not sufficient without repentance. Let them see that you have as great a heart hatred of secret and private sins, as of public evils; by this you shall only be able to quit yourselves rightly, and let the world see that you are walking in all other things according to his commands, and that you are not making this a cloak for other sins, neither think that this discharges us of all or any one of the other duties of religion, but on the contrary that we are the more obliged to holiness in regard to the cause that we are to adorn.'

The times indeed were difficult and dangerous and called for faith and courage of no ordinary kind, but Cargill was not without hope that God would yet be gracious to his church, that he had not cast off for ever, but that he would yet return. 'For the present', he goes on, 'I have comfort in nothing, but that I think that I see his abode in the land, and it is a thing so wonderful, that I can hardly get it believed; yet, I say, I think I see his abode and glory beyond all these judgements. And oh that I knew how to warn, counsel, confirm and comfort you! Yet it is in his hand, who is infinitely more tender, and I leave it to him.' Cargill did not believe that either he or those to whom he wrote would live to see the time of the restoration of the church, but he was convinced that God was preparing for it. 'And, oh,' he exclaimed. 'how good it is to die having these desires, and to leave behind us the mould of such a fabric to our successors!' Here again was the note of self-denial to be seen in his earlier letters. To Cargill it did not matter if this glorious restoration did not take place in his time, since it would certainly take place in God's time; his duty meanwhile was to prepare the way for it by faithfulness to God's cause and perseverance in his service.

Cargill had not been in England long when the bloodhounds were once again on his track. On 22 January 1681 the king issued instructions to the Duke of Newcastle, as Lord Lieutenant of Northumberland, to search out and apprehend Cargill wherever he might be found and to deliver him up to the Scottish authorities.[8] Whatever action was taken to implement this proclamation was clearly ineffective, for Cargill continued in his refuge for another three months. It is unlikely that he remained silent throughout this period and he probably preached in houses as he had opportunity. But he never had the intention of making England his permanent home. Great as the dangers were, and they were greater now than ever before, his work lay in his native land. He could never bring himself to be absent from it for long. In April 1681 he returned to Scotland for the last time.

13.
The delusion of the Gibbites

On his return to Scotland Cargill suddenly found himself confronted with one of the greatest challenges of his life, not this time at the hands of enemies, but on the part of some who had been his friends. The leading figure in this was a certain John Gibb, a sailor from Bo'ness, who appears to have acted for some time as a courier between the church in Scotland and the exiles in Holland. He had come to the notice of the authorities for trying to bring in 'seditious books' and had got his employers into some trouble as a result. Gibb was not, however, a true adherent to the cause, as events were soon to show. It would be charitable to regard him as an extremist, or even a fanatic: he was merely a half-crazed megalomaniac, who did not scruple to distort the truths he professed in order to obtain for himself the position of influence which he sought.

Cargill's absence in England in the first few months of 1681 gave him the opportunity he wanted. It was easy for Gibb to proclaim, as he did with assiduity, that by withdrawing to England Cargill had deserted the cause and gone the way of all other ministers. Ministers could no longer be trusted. They had all proved false to their profession. It was now the duty of God's people to leave them, to have nothing to do with them or their works and to depend wholly upon God. Such was the doctrine Gibb proclaimed, and its plausibility, coupled with his own powerful personality, soon attracted a group of sympathizers. Among them were some, mainly women, who had formerly been among Cargill's most attentive hearers.

Calling themselves the 'Sweet Singers', Gibb and his followers moved around the country, singing mournful psalms over the state of the church's captivity, displaying napkins stained with the blood of Stewart and Potter and making a show of prayer and fasting for the sad defections of the times. Eventually, about the beginning of April, they took upon themselves to renounce worldly things altogether and settled in the Pentland hills to the south of Edinburgh, from where they expected to see the judgements of God poured out upon the wicked city. Some of the women carried their children with them, and to prevent their husbands from reclaiming them Gibb and one of his companions carried pistols at the ready.

This was the state of things which Cargill found when he returned from England about the middle of April. There were still a faithful few ready to welcome him, and they invited him to preach at Darmead the following Sabbath, probably 24 April. Gibb and his followers were known to be in the moors about a mile from the spot, and before he began the meeting Cargill sent two of his friends to invite them to meet him and discuss their differences. But Gibb was not to be moved. Cargill had left the land and deserted the testimony; they did not want him, or any other minister. Things had never been better with them than since they had parted from all the ministers.

Grieved as he must have been by this uncompromising reply, Cargill proceeded with the service. He opened it, appropriately, by singing the first verse of Psalm 37: 'For evildoers fret thou not', gave an exposition on 1 Kings 21:17-29, on King Ahab's outward humiliation before Elijah, and then preached from Amos 4:12: 'Prepare to meet thy God, O Israel.' His message from these texts was a sombre one, dwelling on the judgements he feared were coming on the land for its unfaithfulness.

When his day's preaching was over he made another attempt, this time with more success, to seek a reconciliation with Gibb and his followers. A meeting was agreed upon, and on the following day, in a barn on the hillside, Cargill listened patiently to Gibb's demands. Two things were required of him: that he would confess publicly his sin in leaving the country the previous winter and that he would agree to preach only to Gibb's followers and those who joined with them. Cargill refused to acknowledge it as a sin to have left Scotland when

he did, and in his circumstances; he had, he hoped, been useful to not a few during his stay in England. And as for setting
bounds on his preaching, it was not for them to do so. He had
a commission to preach the gospel to every creature and, he
asserted, if his trumpet would sound to the ends of the earth,
he would preach Christ to all. The debate was not resolved
that day, but Gibb invited him to stay on with them for the
night, and to this Cargill assented. No sooner had he lain
down, however, than he was seized with a presentiment of
danger. Rising up quickly he went out to the moor and stayed
there all night. It was bitterly cold. A chill mist shrouded the
mountains, and by morning he was wet and cold in body and
chilled and depressed in spirit. In that condition he was found
by his friends, who were eager to know how his conference
with Gibb had gone. 'My thoughts', he replied, 'are both bad
and sad. This man John Gibb is an incarnate devil. He might
have cut my throat this night, but I got warning of my danger.'
As for the others, one of them was 'a good scholar lost, and a
minister spoilt'; some would go 'to a greater length, but I
hope the Lord will reclaim some of them'. 'And now', he concluded, 'go all home, and pray that this snare may be broken,
for this is one of the most dreadful and dangerous snares that
has been in my time. But they run so fast, they will soon discover themselves.'

Events soon proved the truth of Cargill's prediction. At the
beginning of May Gibb and his followers were all seized by
the soldiers and carried to Edinburgh. The men were imprisoned in the Canongate Tolbooth; the women were consigned
to the 'correction house', the usual repository for the loose
and immoral of the city. After some weeks in prison Gibb
drew up a paper setting out his principles, which he presented
to the Council. It was a wild, unbalanced document, aptly
demonstrating the mind of its author and scarcely deserving
to be treated seriously. It denounced indiscriminately the use
of chapters and verses in Scripture, the metrical Psalms, the
translation of the Bible out of the original languages, the Confession of Faith and the Catechisms, the Covenants and the
Form of Church Government, the Queensferry paper, the
Sanquhar Declaration and even the names of months and
days of the week.[1]

This was not mere fanaticism: it was imbecility, but at least it helped to discredit Gibb in the eyes of many who had been deluded by his protestations of orthodoxy and his display of concern for the condition of the church. It was also of considerable help to Cargill in his self-imposed task of reclaiming his former friends, since he could now refute the delusions in Gibb's paper and expose its authors for what they were. Of Gibb himself and his three male companions he seems to have cherished little prospect of recovery. His conference with them had given him little to hope for in this respect. The women, however, he knew to have been imposed upon and led astray against their better judgement, and he now bent all his efforts to bringing them to a better mind. This he did by writing them a long and affectionate letter, in which he patiently pointed out the errors and fallacies of their ways.

Probably in no production of his pen does Cargill's Christian charity shine so brightly as in this letter; it is a model of self-restraint, of affectionate pleading and earnest concern. He does not denounce, but rather entreat; he does not dismiss contemptuously the opinions his friends had espoused, but deals with them considerately and carefully, refuting them with cogent logic backed by Scripture teaching. He is at pains to point out that he is not making this appeal to them in order to gain a following for himself. He would have written earlier, he tells them, and more fully, if he had not feared that they would harbour such suspicions of his motives. On the contrary, it is for the truth of God he is contending, and for that reason, and that reason alone, is he worthy of any credit. 'It has been my earnest and frequent prayer to God', he says, 'as he himself knows, to be led in all truth, and I judge in this I have been graciously answered; but I desire none, if they themselves judge it not to be truth, to adhere to anything that I have either preached, written or done.'

He assures them of his tender concern for their welfare, expressing his indignation at those who had led them astray: 'God having now shown you the ringleaders and authors of these opinions to be persons of such abominations, calls you not only to deny credit to them, but also to make a serious search of their tenets; which will, I know, by his grace bring you undoubtedly to see that these things are contrary both to

God's glory and truth, that they so much pretended to. And I cannot have great enough abhorrence of the persons, who knowing themselves to be of such abominations, did give out themselves to be of such familiarity to God, and of so clear illumination, as to make their delusions more passing with devout souls.'

He goes on to deal with some of the points in Gibb's paper by turn, pointing out the fallacy of each: 'You will join with none in public worship, but those who have infallible signs of regeneration. This seems fair, but it is both false and foul. False, because of its false foundation, that the certainty of our interest in Christ may be known by another, whereas the Scripture says: "That none knows it, but he that has it." Foul also, for this disdain has pride in it, and pride is always foul. You would have all to be prayed to eternal wrath, who have departed and made defection in this time; but this, I am sure, is not to give God his glory, but to take from him, and limit him in his freedom and choice in the greatness of his pardon. It is remarkable that the angels, in their glory to God, joined also with it good will to men. You have rejected the Psalms, with many other things; then you must reject all the other Scriptures, because the translation of them is man's work. You have not yet learned the original languages; you must betake yourselves altogether to the Spirit, and what a Spirit will that be, that is not to be tried by the Scriptures? As for the rest of your denying all your former covenants and declarations, this cannot be from God, they containing nothing but lawful and necessary duties. And your cutting off all that were not of your mind, and delivering them up to devils, was not justice and religion, it being done neither in judgement nor righteousness.'

But the point that grieved Cargill most was that Gibb had incited his followers to desert public preaching, which he goes on to call 'the great ordinance of God's glory and men's good'. It was not a liberty, but rather a temptation, that had led him to take such a step, 'especially to leave public ordinances at this time, when they are the only standards standing which show Satan's victory against Christ's kingdom in Scotland not to be complete'.

Much of Cargill's letter is taken up with words of exhor-

tation and caution. He graciously commends any good where
he can find it, but cautions against its misuse: 'I told you when
I met with you that there were some things you were owning
which were highly approved of God: such as an inward heart
love and zeal to God's glory, which I perceived to be in some
of you. I desire you then to retain your zeal; but see well to
this, that it be for his glory. Indeed, the more you are zealous,
and the further you go forward, so that the Word of God
direct your course, you are the more pleasing to God, and
shall be the dearer to us. And my soul wishes you well, though
it may be that I cannot here point nor lead you the way to well-
being; yet this I must say, that if I could lead you the way that
he has led me, I should let you see eternal life. Hold truth,
glorify God, be zealous to have him glorified; but think not to
desire the condemnation of any man, simply on that account
that they dare not come and continue where you are; or that
to put a bar by prayer between them and a return is a glorifying of God. We glorify him in this kind when, as he himself
desires, we acquiesce in his sentence when it is past, though
we wrestle against it before it be known to us. Dear friends,
let not the world have it to say that when you are become
right, you are become the less zealous; only take the right
object, and let your zeal grow. And think it not strange that
you have not such liberty in your return as you seemed to have
before; if you take the right way, and hold on, you shall find
it in his time greater and better and surer.'

Cargill well knew that by showing such a close concern
towards those who had been led astray by Gibb, he would be
in danger of being looked upon as one of themselves, and so
in a measure it proved. As his letter shows, Cargill utterly
repudiated Gibb and his views; but that fact did not prevent
him from being charged with the same delusions, and even to
this day his reputation has suffered as a result.[2] His compassion for Gibb's deluded followers, and his concern for
God's cause in the land, made him oblivious to these consequences, and there is evidence to show that his faithfulness
was in a measure rewarded. Many of the women were soon
afterwards set free, on surety being given for their good
behaviour, and the majority of them were successfully
reclaimed.

Gibb himself, on the other hand, fulfilled Cargill's predictions of him. After being liberated later in the year he and his remaining followers committed further extravagances, including publicly burning a copy of the English Bible. About three years later they were again arrested and put in prison, where Gibb's behaviour showed every evidence of mental derangement or, as some would have it, demonic possession. They were eventually banished to the American plantations where, says Patrick Walker, 'Gibb was much admired by the heathen for his familiar converse with the devil bodily, and offering sacrifices to him. He died there about the year 1720.'

Such was the end of the 'delusion of the Gibbites'. Though short-lived, it caused a great stir at the time, and its effects lingered on long after the movement itself had spent its force. From his recorded utterances about it, both in his letters and his public preaching, Cargill regarded the movement with great seriousness, and seems to have felt particularly keenly that it had been founded upon a distortion of those very truths — zeal for God's glory and separation from the evils of the times — which were most prominent in his own preaching. To Cargill, who always had a strong sense of the personal power of the devil, the episode was a direct challenge from the Evil One and an attempt to frustrate his work by stealth when he could not be diverted from it by persecution. His description of Gibb as a 'devil' was not therefore a mere piece of vituperation; he saw in Gibb's movement all the marks of demonic subtlety — the counterfeit orthodoxy, the pretended zeal, the plausible but spurious concern for God's cause. 'Satan transforming himself into an angel of light,' is how he describes it in his letter to the prisoners. Elsewhere in the same letter he remarks: 'The great sin, and pillar of Satan, that is in this snare, makes me tremble.' Although the enemy was successfully resisted and overcome, the snare exposed and the ensnared set free, the lessons of the episode were impressed upon Cargill's mind for ever afterwards, and it taught him the need for constant vigilance and unceasing and relentless exertion in God's service. Its immediate effect was to impel him to a period of vigorous and sustained activity, the momentum of which never slackened until his life's work was near its close.

14.
The lone standard-bearer

With the arrest and imprisonment of John Blackader in April 1681, Cargill had become the only active field-preacher now left. The news of his return and his resumption of preaching in the fields roused the government to fury, and their searches for him began to take on an appearance of desperation. No sooner was he reported to be in any place than parties of soldiers from miles around would descend upon it, scouring the countryside for any trace of him. He was obliged to seek refuge in woods, marshes and other secluded places, and only when the numbers of friends around him were sufficiently great to ensure safety did he venture into the open.

On 1 May, following his conference with John Gibb, he was in the Underbank Wood near Crossford, on the upper reaches of the Clyde, where he preached from Isaiah 62:6: ' I have set watchmen upon thy walls, O Jerusalem.' He dealt once more with the unfaithfulness of ministers, sorrowing over the sin of the church in ordaining to the ministry men who showed little evidence of spiritual life, and lamenting that so many had failed to stand firm in the time of trial. Intellectual prowess was no qualification in itself for the ministerial calling, and so he remarked, 'Oh the great and sinful rashness of taking young men from the schools to make them ministers, for no man naturally has the property of a good watchman till God give him it. There is much requisite in a good watchman: much concern, much tenderness, diligent labouring, much zeal for God, much acquaintance with God; and they will never be good watchmen if they be not in God's school. The work of a watchman is a work that will take up the greatest that ever was on earth, even one furnished with a full measure of the Spirit of God.'

Cargill stayed on in the wood for some days, in order to avoid the strict searches which were being made for him. There had been a prolonged spell of dry weather, which was to continue throughout the summer,[1] and he remarked one day to some friends on the parched appearance of the hillside opposite them, enquiring whether they saw any sign of rain. No, they replied, adding that if the Lord did not send it soon they feared for a scarcity of bread. 'I have been thinking upon that,' he told them, 'since I came into this wood; but if I be not under a delusion you need not fear that, so long as this persecution lasts; for the Lord has a greater respect to his own suffering people than to suffer such a rough wind to blow in the day of his east wind. For if that were so, the heavy end of the stroke would come upon his own people.' Again, the closeness of Cargill's communion with God had convinced him of this truth: God was bringing suffering and trial upon his church, not to crush or overwhelm, but to refine and purify. Despite the darkness of the hour Cargill still firmly believed in God's overruling providence: he would vindicate his own cause; he would glorify his name through his church.

On the following Thursday, 5 May, Cargill kept a public fast in the fields at Loudon Hill in Ayrshire, near the scene of the memorable triumph of Drumclog. News of the occasion had spread widely and a very large crowd gathered, some of them bringing young children for baptism. He spoke in the morning from Isaiah 9:16: 'The leaders of the people cause them to err,' once again dwelling on the theme of ministers' unfaithfulness. His lecture was not, however, merely an exercise in negative criticism, but was aimed rather at stressing the need for prayer that faithful guides might be given to the church. The unfaithfulness of some was no justification to cast off all, nor to forsake the ordinances of God. And so he went on: 'If you would be guided rightly, you must be seeking your leaders from the Lord by prayer and supplication, that he would give them as a mercy; for of necessity we cannot do without them. You should look on it as a mercy from the Lord to have true and faithful leaders agreeable to the Word of God contained in the Scriptures of truth, the Old and New

Testaments, Confession of Faith, Larger and Shorter Catechisms, Covenants and all our controverted Reformation. We must not cast off the ordinances of God. Leaders we must have, for it is not come to that yet, that we shall be able to lead and guide ourselves.' His recent encounter with Gibb and his followers was, of course, fresh in his mind as he spoke, but his words have been interpreted, and quite properly, as expressing his dislike of division or schism of any kind that would unreasonably disrupt the peace and well-being of the church.[2]

His exposition completed, he went on to preach from Matthew 19:28: 'Ye which have followed me, in the regeneration . . .' This was a message of encouragement for those whose faith had been sorely tried by bitter persecution. His counsel to them was to wait patiently for God, knowing that in his own time they would be fully vindicated: 'Now God be thanked, we know and are persuaded that his promise faileth never, and we shall have rest in him. He is a hiding-place and a covering from the heat, the shadow of a great rock in this weary land. He shall be a hiding-place to the faithful and their seed to many generations. Whatever they have forsaken for him, houses, lands, sister or brother, father or mother, they shall have a hundredfold, and in the world to come life everlasting. That is a reward that will fully pay you. Is it for God, and is it for the cause and interest of God and of Jesus Christ, that you are thus hunted and harried, spoiled and plundered? Is it so, that you forsake all in respect of him? Well then, you shall have much of God in this life, and eternal life as your reward, you that do not part with Christ and his glory. That is the thing that true sufferers must look to and have as the ground of their expectation, that wrongs will be thoroughly righted, and judged uprightly, in that day when our blessed King and Head shall be judging upon the throne of his glory.'

When he had finished his sermon and baptized the children, a privilege eagerly coveted for them by their parents, he was pressed to preach again in the afternoon. He had not intended to do so, but was eventually prevailed upon to give a short sermon. He took as his text Luke 23:28: 'Daughters of Jerusalem, weep not for me, but weep for yourselves, and for your children.' If Cargill was filled with a sense of foreboding

as he spoke, it was not without reason, for the news of the
meeting had meanwhile come to the ears of the forces in Glasgow and a large party of soldiers were hastening to the scene.
They had commandeered all the horses to be found in the city
and its neighbourhood, and in their frenzied dash through the
streets a young child had been run down and killed. Had Cargill's sermon been longer it is likely that the soldiers would
have arrived before he had finished; as it was, they came on
the scene just as he was offering the closing prayer and the
meeting was about to disperse. Even so, their arrival caused
great consternation. For some reason the meeting had been
undefended and the normal sentries were not on duty. Cargill
himself, in the confusion, found himself heading straight for
the enemy, but his friends quickly seized hold of him and hurried him to a place of safety. His congregation melted into the
moor, and although the soldiers fired after them none were
killed or captured. It was a remarkable deliverance to end a
remarkable day, the memory of which would remain in the
minds of his hearers for the rest of their lives.

In his afternoon sermon, for which he had been unprepared, Cargill had not spoken at any great length, and his
prayers too had been particularly concise. A few of his hearers, greatly prizing his ministry but disappointed at the brev-
ity of his preaching, felt impelled to remonstrate gently with
him on the subject. 'Oh, sir,' they pleaded, 'it is long between
meals, and we are in a starving condition. All is good, sweet
and wholesome which you deliver, but why do you straiten us
so much for shortness?' Cargill's reply was characteristic:
'Ever since I bowed a knee in good earnest to pray, I never
dared pray and preach with my gifts, and where my heart is
not affected, and comes not up with my mouth, I always
thought it time for me to quit it. What comes not from my
heart, I have little hope that it will go to the heart of others.'
And, as his way was, he repeated to himself the words of the
51st Psalm: 'Then will I teach transgressors thy ways; and
sinners shall be converted unto thee.' These were words
which illustrated perfectly the point he was trying to convey,
for they are immediately preceded by a prayer for self-
enlightenment: 'Create in me a clean heart, O God . . . cast
me not away from thy presence . . . restore unto me the joy of

thy salvation; and uphold me with thy free spirit.' Only through a personal experience of God's presence, Cargill was saying, could a minister hope to convey anything of God's truth to his hearers; whether few or many, his words must be impregnated with the Spirit of God before they could have any telling effect. They were words spoken from rich experience and they form a perfect apologia for Cargill's ministry.

It may have been about this time that a deprecating remark about Cargill's untiring efforts drew forth from him a memorable response. William Vilant, minister of Cambusnethan, who wrote a defence of the complying ministers, was present on one occasion when someone referred to Cargill's faithfulness and diligence. Vilant, who could hardly have found the conversation to his liking, remarked impatiently, 'What needs all this ado? We will get heaven, and they will get no more.' On learning of Vilant's comment, Cargill said, 'Yes, we will get more: we will get God glorified on earth, which is more than heaven.'[3]

Cargill's narrow escape at Loudon Hill in no way deterred him from continuing to preach in the fields. In the next few weeks he embarked on a round of activity as intense as any in the whole course of his ministry, going through Ayrshire and Carrick into Galloway, preaching and baptizing. Now that he was the only active field-preacher left he appears to have felt a responsibility to bring the Word to as wide an area as he could. Carrick and Galloway, where he had not been much accustomed to preach, had long enjoyed the ministry of men such as Welsh, Semple and Blackader, but their voices were now silent. As he left Galloway Cargill was filled with foreboding about its future spiritual condition: he foresaw a period of intense barrenness, which he feared would also affect other parts of the south and west. No detailed account survives of Cargill's visits to those parts, though he is said to have baptized twenty-two children in a barn at Meadowhead in Ayrshire, and a monument near the town of Maybole marks one of the places where he preached.

It was probably when nearing the end of this preaching tour that Cargill received word of the death of his old friend Robert M'Ward in Holland. M'Ward, who had been in failing health for some time, died on 26 May in Rotterdam, and was

buried in the land of his exile.[4] His death deprived the church
at home not only of an indefatigable correspondent ('this
poor scribbler' as he once described himself) but of an influential advocate for its cause in the land from which her
deliverance would one day come. An eloquent tribute to
M'Ward and his fellow-exile John Brown comes from the pen
of Patrick Walker: 'I have often thought through my life, that
it was a remarkably merciful dispensation (as the selling of
Joseph into Egypt) the banishing of these foresaid worthies
out of their native land. The enemies meant it for ill, but the
Lord turned it for good, considering how much of their time
they spent in praying for the Church of Scotland and her
sufferers, how useful they were with their pens, what influence they had upon all men who savoured of religion, and
built in Holland (as it were) a sanctuary for all sufferers who
fled there, being men of such piety and parts; whereby we
were more obliged to the prayers, and purses, of Holland
than all the world besides.' For Cargill, who had known
M'Ward since their student days at St Andrews, the loss must
have been particularly keen, depriving him not only of an old
ministerial colleague, but of a valued counsellor and friend
with whose views on the public issues of the time he was so
completely at one.

By the beginning of June Cargill was back in his favourite
Clydesdale, where he always confessed to finding the greatest
liberty in preaching. Scarcely pausing to rest after his journey
of the previous weeks, he announced his intention of preaching on a coming Sabbath, probably 12 June, at Tinto Hill near
Biggar. He stayed the previous night at a friend's house
nearby and in the morning went out to spend some time in
meditation alone. Unknown to him, however, the local landowner had changed the place of the meeting to another about
five miles distant, and he was obliged to make his own way
there on foot. The weather had now grown oppressively hot;
the way to the meeting-place lay uphill, and the heights were
steep. For a man now nearing his mid-fifties, prematurely
aged by wanderings and travel, the prospect was a daunting
one, but he saw the people flocking in crowds towards the
place and he did not hesitate. By the time he reached the spot
he was well-nigh exhausted, but not for a moment did he

allow his physical weariness to deter him from his spiritual duty. On his arrival he accepted a drink of water proffered to him in the bonnet of one of his hearers, and another between his sermons. He had tasted nothing before setting out in the morning and he was to taste nothing more that day. It was well won, he was wont to say, that was won off the flesh. In this department of life, as in every other, he had learned to make the earthly give way to the heavenly, the things of the body to the things of the spirit.

He went on to give an exposition and a sermon in the morning and then preached again in the afternoon. In his morning exposition he spoke on the words in Isaiah 6:8: 'Whom shall I send, and who will go for us?', the question addressed to the prophet when he was given his commission. Cargill was still oppressed by a sense of the spiritual deadness which he saw coming upon the church, and of which he had spoken during his visit to Galloway, and he gave further expression to his feelings when speaking from this passage. 'To speak with holy reverence, we see that the Trinity of heaven may be at a stand, where to get a fit messenger to carry the message. The prophet said, "Here am I, send me." But it is likely if he had known what he was to do, he would not have been so forward, for if an honest-hearted minister might refuse any errand that God sent him, it would be to denounce judgements upon a people, especially spiritual judgements. But the hand of God was here; and when he got his commission to preach to that people, and they grew more and more deaf and blind, he cried out, "How long?" And the answer was returned: "Until the city be without inhabitants, and the land utterly desolate."' Cargill looked at the hills, wild and desolate, all round him, and was filled with an infinite sadness. 'If I know anything of the mind of God,' he went on, 'this is the commission we are getting, and the commission that ministers will get, to preach the greater part of this generation more and more deaf and blind. And preach who will, and pray who will, this deafness and this blindness shall remain until many habitable places of Scotland be as waste and desolate as these mountains. But remember, I am setting no time to this: we know not what manner of spirits we are of; a thousand years appear in his sight as one day. But the longer it is delayed, the sorer it will

be when it comes.' It was spiritual desolation Cargill was
speaking of, a time of dearth and barrenness that was to
envelop the church before the bright vision of its future prosperity could be realized. But in even this dismal picture there
was one ray of hope: 'Yet in it', the prophet had said, 'shall be
a tenth.' And, said Cargill, as the Lord had preserved a
remnant through all the history of the church, so he would
preserve a remnant in Scotland that would ride out all these
winter storms.

Concluding his exposition, he went on immediately to give
the first of his two sermons. It was from Romans 11:20: 'Be
not highminded, but fear,' and was a characteristic study of
the Christian life, drawing richly on his own experience.
'Those who know themselves best', he declared, 'will fear
themselves most: and as it is hard to determine what length a
hypocrite may go in the profession of religion, so it is hard to
determine what length a child of God may go in defection,
having grace, but lacking its exercise. A Christian may go
through nineteen trials, and carry honestly through them, and
fall in the twentieth.' Cargill made it clear to his hearers that
he was speaking here of those who were true Christians, 'Not
of these wretched creatures, I mean John Gibb and his company. Woe to them, some of them are nothing but devils,
though many of them are misled. For the Lord's sake, look
not on them.' His conviction of the satanic power behind
Gibb's apostasy remained unshaken and led him to preach in
the afternoon from the words in Revelation 12:12: 'The devil
is come down unto you, having great wrath,' when he
expounded further on this theme.

With another full day's preaching behind him, Cargill
pressed on relentlessly, not sparing himself. It was as if in
these few weeks he had a presentiment that his time was
short, and that the work that remained to him to do was to be
done with all his might. The following Sabbath he was on the
eastern fringes of Clydesdale, where again he gave an
exposition and preached two sermons. His exposition was
based on Zechariah 2, on the high priest Joshua standing
before the angel of God. 'It was no created angel,' he began,
in characteristic strain, 'no, it was the Angel of the covenant,
it was the Mediator. Oh, blessed be he! Blessed be the

Messiah, for he has had mercy on us! Oh, if ever Christ be merciful to you, as it is sure he will be merciful to us, if we seek him for our Saviour, you will be made to say, "Blessed be he of the Lord for his mercy"! Oh how can we but love him, that stands so for man? We are sure we have great reason to love him that stands for us. The Mediator keeps by us; the devil would be in the Mediator's stead, but he stands against him. They are but poor sick sinful things with whom he takes part, that can do little for their own selves, yet he will help those that come to him.' He went on to speak of the influence of Satan in preventing men from coming to God. 'There is no man nor woman who rises and strives to be at God, but the devil stands to resist,' and yet of the imperative need for such action before help could come: 'We need not ever think that Christ will do anything to stir us or own us, if we sit still and never stir ourselves to labour to come back again. We will say that one word' — a very common expression of his when he wanted to say something with particular emphasis — 'the father met the prodigal, and welcomed him, but never before he began to come back.'[5]

For his morning sermon he took as his text the words in Psalm 45:3: 'Gird thy sword upon thy thigh, O most mighty,' words which speak of the power and authority of Christ. It was a memorable sermon, the first part of it cast in the richly devotional strain in which he excelled: 'The sooner Christ becomes sure to a soul, the next thing is to have him displayed to the view and uptaking of the whole world, for then they also would love him: for "Oh," says the soul that sees him, "woe is me that I must feed alone upon him, and not to have all the world to partake of this great feast of love that I have in the company of my Beloved!" You have found your Beloved; now have you any suit and desire to put up to him? And what is it? Is it not even this: "Gird thy sword on thy thigh, O thou most mighty"?' Love to Christ, Cargill was saying, could be the only true motivation of zeal for Christ's public glory, to see the Beloved One exercising the authority which was his due. And this, of course, was the motivation of Cargill's own resistance to the encroachments of the state, as it had been the motivation of the Reformers in whose steps he was treading; for the church in scriptural terms was the body

of Christ, and any injury done to the church was injury done
to Christ as its Head. Where the love of Christ was in the
heart, there could be neither indifference nor inactivity when
the interests of Christ were in danger, and his authority under
threat.

In the second part of his sermon Cargill went on to speak of
the security which Christ's authority brought to his people,
ending with some inspiring words of consolation and comfort:
'And finally, fear not to engage with Christ, and to take him
for better and worse. For he will defend you in all cases and
upon all hazards; for he carries the sword for that purpose, to
guard and defend his people from every hazard and danger
whatsoever, and to avenge himself upon all his enemies; and
the surest blow will unavoidably fall upon those that come
most near to hurt or annoy his people, and do them any harm.
We will say that one word, his sword is still drawn about his
church and people to keep them, lest anything should hurt
them, even as it was drawn out in the Garden of Eden to
guard and keep the tree of life.'

In the afternoon Cargill preached from Isaiah 10:3: 'And
what will ye do in the day of visitation, and in the desolation
which shall come from far?' This was a solemn sermon, speaking of judgement on rulers for their oppressions and God-dis-
honouring laws, and on subjects for giving obedience to them.
Now that the rulers had been cast off by God through the
excommunication, Cargill had no hesitation in urging his
hearers to the duty of disobeying them, if they were not themselves to come under God's displeasure. 'Let every man
look', he said, 'to what obedience he gives to powers, to
rulers, to tyrants, for they are no rulers but tyrants. It is true
they are powers, but not powers ordained of God, that are a
terror to evil works, and a praise to the good. Laws must be
stamped with justice and equity, and so have the authority of
heaven, as well as the authority of men; and if you obey them
without considering whether or not they have this mark, in
obeying them you disobey God.'

He went on to impress upon his audience the supreme need
for reconciliation with God, taking as an illustration a proce-
dure with which he was well familiar, the process for discharge of a debt: 'It is well if you can say these three: "I have

reckoned; I have judged myself; I have paid, not by myself, but by another; the Cautioner came in and paid for me, and God reckoned it up on my behalf. I have reckoned; I have paid; I am discharged." Oh, to have the seal of the living God to every discharge! There was wrestling before I got it, and I have laid it up, and kept it well, and when I take it out at the Great Day, he will acknowledge that it is his own hand.'

He ended his sermon with another vindication of Torwood, not without a tinge of irony: 'Oh, but it is wonderful to hear tell that ministers of the gospel should talk at such a rate! Where was ever such a thing as that heard? "What Scripture can you get," they say, "for excommunicating kings?"' He added his own answer: 'Are they not creatures and subjects to God? And are they not bound to be holy as well as the meanest? This word we shall say, unworthy are they, that ever they should be dressed with authority who do not follow God with it. Will not God judge kings? And should not ministers of the gospel excommunicate kings? The Scripture says, "Put away the wicked person from among you." And if a king be a wicked person, it says, "Put him away." For Cargill, then, the issue was simple and direct. The scriptural teaching on the matter was plain and the will of God was clear. He had never regretted the excommunication, and he never would regret it. His duty had been done.

Still keeping up his ceaseless activity, the following week he went over to Fife, where he preached on 26 June to a very large concourse of people at Dovan Common, a favourite preaching spot in the Lomond Hills. Again many children were brought to him for baptism.

He took as his text some of the last words of David, in 2 Samuel 23:5: 'He hath made with me an everlasting covenant, ordered in all things, and sure,' and went on to speak at some length of the covenant relationship between the Lord and his people. It was a theme dear to his heart, and he strove to bring home to his hearers the comfort of the assurance which it brought to himself. 'He hath made with me (Oh, the wonder, with me!) an everlasting covenant. And it is wonderful, first, because it makes poor man a party, and he may require of God. Oh, what an exaltation is this! And secondly, because it makes things sure to us, and not only sure, but immutable.

And third, as it is sure and immutable, we know what we may look for from God, and what we may require of God.

'"But," it may be thought, "how can a man covenant with God?" First, God himself has drawn up the covenant in the Scriptures: they contain the covenant, and they tell us, "This is the way, walk ye in it." Second, as he has drawn up the covenant, so he subscribes it, and so he has left room for you. Third, he has deposited his covenant in the hands of his ministers, and we are going about seeking your subscriptions to it. Now there are two or three things we must subscribe: first, to make God our God, to say, "I take him for my delight, the object of my worship, the object of my trust and faith." Second, we must take the righteousness of Christ for our righteousness, for God will have none to appear before him but by the righteousness of Christ. Third, we must take his law to be the rule of our actions; we must be ruled by the holy law of Christ. And further, we must subscribe his providence and pleasure, for the sum of the covenant is to please God and to labour to be pleased with God.

'Now the Holy Spirit shows us three or four qualities of this covenant. First, it is everlasting. We need say no more of this: if ever we be in covenant with God we can never fall out of it again, for this covenant will keep our souls here, and in heaven throughout eternity. Second, it is well ordered. It is well ordered because it has a sacrifice, for there could be no atonement for sin without a sacrifice: and it is a sacrifice the greatest and best. It is well ordered, too, because it has provided a surety. The first covenant had no surety, and so nothing came of it; now it will hold, for in whatever we come short the Surety will answer. And it is well ordered, again, because God undertakes it, not only for himself but for us: "I will put my law in their minds, and write it in their hearts." As he may require of us, so we may require of him. It is well ordered, then, in all: it has in it pardon of sin, heaven and happiness. And, lastly, it is sure. Sure indeed, for it is founded upon the oath of God and omnipotence. The sureness of the covenant depends only upon God."

Cargill did not stay in Fife long, but was soon back once more in Clydesdale, where he spent some days in the neighbourhood of Shotts. There two men from Galloway waited on him, and pressed him to go with them to Galloway to preach. But he had determined that his recent visit there should be his last, and so he declined the offer. He spoke much at this time of the troubles and afflictions he saw coming on the land, and more especially on the church, though he had a conviction that he himself would not live to see it. 'I do not know how the Lord's people will endure it,' he would say, 'who have to meet with it; but the foresight and forethought of it makes me tremble.' And he was heard to add, as if in the prospect of the fate he saw in store for himself: 'Short, but very sharp.' He was much in meditation in these days, spending little time in conversation or company; the prospect of the future filled him with anxiety and he was depressed as he saw the easy compliance of so many with the impositions of the government. To two young men who were with him at this time he spoke of great trials and hardships ahead, and for the Scottish nobility in particular he foresaw a time of sad decline because of the compliance of so many of them with the persecution of the church and their resistance to the cause and interest of Christ.

But he did not allow these gloomy forebodings to curb him in carrying out the duties of the ministry. So long as he was able, he was determined to press forward with his work to the end. On 3 July he went south to Auchengilloch, the scene of one of his public fasts with Richard Cameron, and preached again to a large multitude. He returned once more to his beloved Clydesdale, taking up his abode for some days in the Lee Wood, a little way downstream from Lanark. During his stay there he performed a marriage ceremony, though not without some misgivings: he had a presentiment that the partner the young man had chosen would lead him aside from his profession of the faith, and this was later sadly verified. The performing of marriage Cargill accepted as part of the ministerial office, and he never declined it when asked, but as he looked to the future he well knew that for the married, with their wives and families to consider, persecution would come with an added sharpness and sorrow and would bring its own particular temptations.

While he was resting in the wood Marion Weir, the wife of a friend in the neighbourhood, brought him some food and pressed him to eat. 'Let alone', he replied, 'I cannot be pressed; for I took not that meal of meat these thirty years, but that I could have taken as much when I rose as when I sat down.' Here again was the subjection of the flesh, the 'keeping under of the body,' as the apostle Paul describes it, which Cargill had made an inflexible rule of his daily living.

It was now high summer, and with the days at their longest Cargill's dangers had increased. The long hours of daylight, coupled with the continued fine weather, gave an important advantage to his pursuers, and he was increasingly forced to confine his movements to the short hours of darkness. There was, of course, the incentive of the 5,000 merks reward, which had been outstanding since the previous November, and while the great majority of the people — including many who never publicly sided with him — could never have brought themselves to betray him to the enemy, there were inevitably a few who longed for the opportunity. To none did the lure seem more attractive than to James Irvine of Bonshaw, who appears to have set his heart on capturing Cargill. Irvine, or Bonshaw as he was commonly called, had engaged in illegal horse-trading in the Border country and, apparently to save himself from the consequences of discovery, had offered to place his knowledge of the country at the disposal of the authorities. He had been given a commission, though he was not himself an officer, and had a party of dragoons placed under his charge. He had already been at great pains in his searches for Cargill, he had lost several horses and incurred considerable expense. So far his prey had eluded him, but he watched and waited for every opportunity.

Cargill, who seems increasingly to have had a presentiment of his end, was meanwhile preparing for yet another Sabbath's preaching. The place he chose was Dunsyre, outside Clydesdale proper and virtually in the shadow of the Pentlands. It was 10 July 1681. Another great congregation awaited him.

He began his day's preaching with an exposition of the first chapter of Jeremiah, in which he dealt with the duties of the ministerial office and the solemn responsibility of those whom God had called to his service. It was a deep, searching examination of a subject that was always close to his heart. In it, he spoke of the awesome responsibilities of those who had been called by God to preach his Word, of the sheer impossibility of doing it in their own strength and yet of the fulness and abundance of God's promise: 'Lo, I am with you alway, even unto the end of the world.'

He dwelt on the absolute necessity for the messengers to be assured of their own salvation before preaching to others: 'Till this be once sure, they are ever unable for the public work of the ministry, and this being once made sure, they are to lay it by till they go before the tribunal of God. There are many who come out at random to the ministry, but what comes of them? Some run one way and some another, and when brought into any eminent piece of service they soon turn aside. And what is the cause of it? Is it not because they were not sure themselves, and so could not deal with others, being unprepared for the work?'

Finally, he spoke of the power and authority of the ministers of the gospel, going on by a logical progression to apply this truth to a further, and final, vindication of his action at Torwood. In vindicating himself in this way Cargill was not displaying mere vainglory: he was asserting an absolute conviction that the mind of God had been declared, the judgement of heaven had been pronounced; he himself had merely been the instrument, the divinely appointed mouthpiece, by which the will of God had been made known. From that conviction he never was and never would be shaken.

It was now time for him to give his sermon. He gave out his text, Isaiah 26:20: "Come, my people, enter thou into thy chambers, and shut thy doors about thee: hide thyself as it were for a little moment, until the indignation be overpast.' Among the huge crowd there was an eager mood of anticipation. Some had travelled great distances to be present, even up to forty or fifty miles, and the younger among them would cherish the memory of this day for the rest of their lives. Among them was Patrick Walker, then a youth of fourteen or fifteen years of age, who many years later, as an old man, recorded his recollection of this supremely memorable occasion: 'I had the happiness to hear blest Mr Cargill preach his last public sermons (as I had several times before, for which while I live I desire to bless the Lord) in Dunsyre Common, betwixt Clydesdale and Lothian, where he lectured upon the first chapter of Jeremiah, and preached upon that soul-refreshing text, Isaiah 26, the two last verses: "Come my people, enter into your chambers." Wherein he was short, marrowy and sententious, as his ordinary was in all his public sermons and prayers, with the greatest evidences of concernedness, exceeding all that ever I heard open a mouth, or saw open a Bible to preach the gospel, with the greatest indignation at the unconcernedness of hearers. He preached from experience, and went to the experience of all that had any of the Lord's gracious dealings with their souls. It came from the heart, and went to the heart; as I have heard some of our common hearers say, that he spoke as never man spoke, for his words went through them. He insisted what kind of chambers these were of protection and safety, and exhorted us all earnestly to dwell in the clefts of the rock, to hide ourselves in the wounds of Christ, and to wrap ourselves in the believing application of the promises flowing therefrom; and to make our refuge under the shadow of his wings, until these sad calamities pass over, and the dove come back with the olive leaf in her mouth.' Patrick Walker's recollection is verified by the fragmentary record of that sermon which has survived from the notes of other hearers. In it, Cargill spoke of the justice and judgement of God, soon to be poured out for the wrongs done to him; but he also spoke words of rich comfort and peace to those who could claim God himself as their refuge.

The written record of this sermon hardly does justice to the memory of the occasion, but it is still possible from it to capture something of the solemnity of Cargill's final appeal as, with supreme simplicity, he brought his sermon to a close: 'Come, my people. Oh, but God is tender of his people's safety! But alas, there are few of them so tender of it themselves as to hear God speaking kindly to them, to make haste into their chambers. There are chambers for you; oh, then like doves fly in at your windows! We see some great work God has to do, and he would have his people providing for it. He commands you to lay by all other things, and to labour to get a place of refuge near God, for he has a great work to do, and he would have you providing against an approaching storm. Labour to get a secret hiding-place, a place of retirement from all dangers. Enter into your chambers, says he. There is a warning. What more? Shut thy doors about thee, make all fast. Make sure both before and behind thee, and leave no open doors, for justice will make a wonderfully narrow search, and will pry into the least cleft or recess, and therefore make sure. Hide thyself. It is good for us; it is our advantage to be there, until the wrath be over, until the indignation be overpast; and we are never to come out from thence. Oh, thrice happy they that shall never come out of these chambers! We are sure, we are persuaded, it shall ever be well with them, who are once entered into these chambers of safety.

'Now wherefore are they called chambers? They are called chambers upon these accounts, that they are chambers for presence and delight, and for strength, protection and defence. So that they are chambers of safety and pleasure too. In a word, they are God himself, who is all in all to the believer. We may say this of them, they are a place of defence from the wrath of God, for it never pursues a man within these chambers. They are places of delight, safety, security and strength.

'Now there are three things that the people of God must do if they would have his assistance in their duty; they must all supplicate him for help to do these things. First, there must be an entering in, that is, a committing ourselves to God, and a covenanting with him by faith. So you see faith must go before an actual covenanting with God. Then you must commit and resign yourselves over to him in time, that you shall no more go back to the entanglements of the world. But alas, there are few or none in the land who are afraid, either for the devil, or the severity of justice.

'Secondly, "Shut thy doors about thee." What is that? Why, it is to make all sure behind you. Wrath will pursue you, and if you be over-long fleeing into these chambers, wrath will overtake you. Many have but loose grips, and have not made all sure behind them, and the wrath of God will let them see that they have neither shut doors nor windows behind them; and where there has been nothing of this done there are open doors, and wrath will enter. But we are sure that the wrath of God will never come at any person who has once got into these chambers, and has got the doors shut behind him. Well then, shut the doors, and make all sure behind you by a covenant engagement; if you do not, a black and gloomy reckoning awaits you. For justice will try you strictly; if you leave but a window unshut, he will find you. Therefore make all sure in time.

'And lastly, "Hide thyself as it were for a little moment." Hide yourselves. Enter in. Hiding and entering in make all one thing. This makes all sure with God. Where will you hide yourselves? In him, for there is no other hiding place than in him. "A man shall be a hiding-place from the wind, and a covert from the tempest: as rivers of water in a dry place, and as a shadow of a great rock in a weary land." We shall add, they are chambers of defence, and well they are furnished. We would lay it at your door, that you would be serious for yourselves, and make all sure. Shut the doors behind you, and God will never bid you go out again. Rest you there till the dove come back to the ark with the olive leaf in her mouth.' They were the last words of his last sermon.[6]

As the congregation melted away, Cargill and a few friends remained. It was not safe to venture away until nightfall: the roads were closely watched, and to travel in the open during daylight would invite almost certain risk of discovery. Cargill and his two faithful friends, Walter Smith and James Boig, had spent the previous night at a friend's house some miles from the place and they decided to return there when darkness fell. They reached their objective in safety and found a safe lodging for the night. It seems that they stayed in this refuge for a further day and a night, until the following Tuesday, and perhaps they intended to continue longer. The rest would certainly have afforded Cargill an opportunity to refresh himself after his recent exertions and to recover something of his strength. On the Tuesday, however, an invitation reached them from the proprietress of the estate of St John's Kirk, in the vicinity of Tinto Hill, offering them the hospitality of her home for some days, perhaps with a view to having Cargill preach there on the following Sabbath. Cargill was not impressed with the spiritual qualities of his intended hostess, though she had frequently attended his preaching, and he was unenthusiastic about accepting her offer. Moreover, he had an increasing presentiment of danger, but at the request of his two friends, who interceded with him on her behalf, he finally agreed to go. The journey had, of course, again to be performed at night and probably involved about two hours' travel. As they proceeded, Cargill's misgivings increased, and when they reached Covington Mill, about three miles north of St John's Kirk, he would go no further. Covington was the home of Andrew Fisher and his wife, two loyal sympathizers, and there Cargill and his friends found shelter for what remained of the night. Whether they intended to stay longer is not clear; at all events it was a move that was destined to have fateful consequences.

15.
The final triumph

Cargill's suspicions were to prove only too true. Twenty miles away at Kilbride, Irvine of Bonshaw was stationed with a party of soldiers. His thoughts were not for the moment on Cargill. One of Bonshaw's men had recently been killed in an encounter with one of the country people, and he was determined to track down the fugitive and bring him to justice. Late on that same Tuesday, he decided to pursue his search in the area of Tinto Hill, to which Cargill and his friends were at that moment heading. If, as he suspected, the wanted man was being sheltered by one of the local sympathizers, it was important to gain the advantage of surprise, and so, gathering his men together, he decided to set off for the place overnight and to begin his search at daybreak. His first objective was St John's Kirk, whose owner's sympathies were apparently well enough known, and he and his troops duly arrived there at first light on the Wednesday morning. A thorough search of the house was made, but without success. Bonshaw, however, was not a man to give up easily: he well knew who the local sympathizers were, and he may have gained the feeling, in the course of his search, that an important prize was almost within his grasp. He led his men to the farm of Muirhouse, a mile to the north, and made another exhaustive search there. And then, as if guided by some fatal instinct, he led them the two miles further to Covington. In the house, Cargill and his friends had not long retired to rest; they had probably spent some time in conversation after their journey, and they still lay awake. The house was surrounded without a moment's warning, leaving no possibility of escape.

Bonshaw himself was foremost in the search, and he it was who made the momentous discovery.[1] His exultation and amazement knew no bounds: 'O blessed Bonshaw, and blessed day that ever I was born,' he exclaimed, 'that has found such a prize!' He could scarcely believe his good fortune; he must instantly ensure that the precious prize did not slip from his grasp. Not a moment must be lost, in case word of the capture would spread and an attempt be made at a rescue. With frantic haste he had his prisoners brought out and carried the six miles to Lanark, where he put them in the town jail while he and his troops got some much-needed refreshment. Horses were brought, and the prisoners set upon their bare backs. Not trusting the task to anyone else, Bonshaw tied Cargill's feet under the horse as hard as he could, without any regard for his comfort. Cargill looked down at him sadly. 'Why do you tie me so hard?' he asked. 'Your wickedness is great. You will not long escape the just judgement of God, and if I be not mistaken it will seize upon you in this place.' Once again, time was to prove Cargill a true prophet.

From Lanark, the sixteen miles to Glasgow were covered at high speed, in growing fear of a rescue attempt. Once in sight of the city, where he could get reinforcements for the final stage of the journey to Edinburgh, Bonshaw felt more secure. He turned his entry into something of a triumphal procession: he had Cargill placed backwards on the horse, and led into the city as a vanquished enemy. It was a sight which made many of his old parishioners weep bitterly. For some, however, it was a matter for merriment, and one of them, John Nisbet, the archbishop's factor, could not refrain from taunting Cargill openly. 'Mr Donald,' he called out to him three times as Cargill was led into the Tolbooth, 'in effect, will you not give us one word more?' He was alluding to the mannerism with which hearers of Cargill were well familiar, for the expressions 'I have one word more to say', or 'In effect we will say that one word,' were frequently on his lips. Nisbet's knowledge of this fact suggests that he himself may at one time have been a hearer of Cargill who had become an apostate, and Cargill may well have realized that only from such a source could come words of such cruel contempt. He looked at Nisbet for some time in silence, then said solemnly:

'Mock not, lest your bands be made strong. The day is coming when you shall not have a word to say, though you would.' A well-authenticated record confirms that Nisbet was seized some time afterwards with an illness which proved fatal and which left him speechless for the last few days of his life.

Cargill and his two friends were kept bound in the prison all night and were not even allowed to pray together. The next day, Thursday, 14 July, they were put under guard for Edinburgh. The journey passed uneventfully. By the time Linlithgow was reached, probably by late afternoon, Bonshaw felt sufficiently secure to give his prisoners a little liberty and they were allowed time for some prayer and conversation. From there, their journey was soon completed. Once in Edinburgh, Cargill was securely lodged in the Canongate Tolbooth under an armed guard. Bonshaw's task was now accomplished and Cargill was in the hands of the Privy Council. But Bonshaw was to find that his masters were not so keen to part with their money as they had been to offer it. By May of the following year he had still not received the reward and he petitioned the Council in an aggrieved tone, pointing out 'the great search, travel and expense,' which it had cost him to bring Cargill to justice. Two months later, when nothing had happened, he petitioned the Council again in stronger terms, mentioning 'his great pains and loss of horses,' and urging that the Council honour their promise, 'which', he pleaded, 'will not only encourage the petitioner but likewise others in the future to use all endeavours to apprehend rebels and traitors'. If Bonshaw got the reward, he did not live to enjoy it long: he was stabbed to death a year afterwards in a brawl with a fellow-soldier at Lanark, not far from the spot where he had bound Cargill to the horse and had heard from him the prophecy of his own doom.

The Privy Council was much occupied at this time with preparations for the new session of Parliament, which was to be opened on 28 July by the king's brother, the Duke of York, later to be James II and VII. The duke, who had been admitted a member of the Council some eighteen months earlier, was already in Edinburgh and was a regular attender at the Council. The Council's president, the Duke of Rothes, who was also Chancellor of Scotland, had been absent for some time because of illness and his place was being taken by Charles Maitland of Hatton, who held the office of Lord Treasurer Depute. Both York and Rothes were among those excommunicated by Cargill at Torwood; two others, Dalyell and Mackenzie, were also members of the Council. It was clear that from these four Cargill could expect no mercy. Rothes in particular had been incensed by Cargill's action and, though now seriously ill, he summoned the strength to confront Cargill when he was brought into Edinburgh. Maliciously he gloated over his fate, assuring him he could expect torture and a violent death. Cargill was not moved: 'My Lord Rothes,' he replied, noting his persecutor's sickly appearance, 'forbear to threaten me, for die what death I will, your eyes will not see it.' It was a remark which those who heard it had cause to recall vividly before very long.

The next day the Council, with Maitland presiding, were ready to question Cargill. They well knew what his principles were and what answers to expect, but now that they had him in their power they were eager to exploit the opportunity to the full and to enjoy their long-awaited triumph. Cargill, for his part, was determined to give them as little satisfaction as possible; he knew that it would be to no purpose to use reasoned argument in his defence and he contented himself with giving brief, almost perfunctory answers.

The account of his interrogation stands in the Council's records thus: 'Edinburgh, the 15th July 1681. In presence of His Royal Highness, His Majesty's High Commissioner and Lords of his Majesty's Privy Council, the examination of Mr Donald Cargill, prisoner. Mr Donald Cargill being examined and interrogate if he owns the king's authority and the king as his lawful prince, answers, as the magistrate's authority is now established by the Act of Parliament anent Supremacy and Explanatory Act, he denies the same. Being interrogate if he owns the king as his lawful prince, yes or no, refuses to give any other answer than as aforesaid. Being interrogate if he kept a conventicle at Torwood in October 1680,[2] confesses the same. Being interrogate if he excommunicated the king there, answers, that question being a question merely anent an ecclesiastical matter, declares that he cannot answer it before the Council, being a civil judicatory. Being pressed to give a direct answer, yes or no, he refuses to make any further answer. Being interrogate whether he saw any of those that killed the archbishop, or knew anything of the intention of doing it before it was done, declares he knew nothing of the intention before it was done, being then at Glasgow, and confesses he knew Balfour, Henderson and Russell, but thinks he did not see Balfour of Kinloch these two years, but did see the other two within these twelve months or thereby to the best of his knowledge. The copy of the sermon alleged preached by him at Torwood being produced, and he asked if that was the copy thereof, desires a time to consider thereof before answer. Being interrogate if he thinks the rising at Bothwell Bridge was a rebellion against the king and his authority, declares he owns defensive arms in case of necessity, and thinks those that rose at Bothwell Bridge were not rebels and that he thinks they were oppressed, and rose in their own defence. Being interrogate if he was with those who were in arms at Ayrsmoss, refuses to answer and desires it may be made out against him. Being interrogate if he was with those who were in arms at Bothwell Bridge, he makes the same answer. Being interrogate if he was at the emitting of the declaration at Sanquhar, denies he was. Being interrogate if he had any accession to the drawing up of that declaration, or penned the same, refuses to give answer thereupon. Being interrogate anent that paper called the Declaration at Sanquhar and if he owns the principles therein contained, refuses to make answer and desires time to consider thereof. That paper called the Fanatics' New Covenant, or Cargill's Covenant, being also read to him, and being interrogate if he owns the principles therein contained, makes answer as aforesaid. Being interrogate if at his preaching at Torwood his lecture was upon Ezekiel 21 vv. 25 to 27, confesses it was. Being interrogate where his text was to his sermon, declares he remembers not. Being interrogate if he thinks the killing of the Archbishop of St Andrews was a murder, declares he cannot give his sense thereof. Being interrogate whether he thinks the king by his falling from the Covenant has lost his civil right as king, he declares he thinks it a matter ecclesiastical and cannot answer, but that he is not obliged to obey the king's government as it is now established by the Act of

Supremacy. Being interrogate where he was the night before and after he was at Queensferry, declares he does not remember, but seeing it may concern others he thinks he is not obliged to answer. Being interrogate when he was in Fife, confesses he was there upon Sunday, was a twenty days or a month, and preached in Dovan Common in the fields. Being interrogate if any of the Hendersons, sons to Henderson, tenant in Kilbrachmont, was present at that meeting, confesses there was one John Henderson there but whose son he is he knows not; he thinks he was a man about thirty years.[3] Being interrogate when he was in Stirlingshire or Craigmad, declares he was not there these twelve months; denies he was in Angus these three or four years past.'[4]

On being given an opportunity to read over the account of his examination when it had been drawn up by the clerk, Cargill asked for a number of changes to be made. First, he amended his answer about the meeting at Torwood to say that 'he preached at the Torwood in the fields,' thus avoiding any implied acceptance of the pejorative word 'conventicle' used by his questioners. On the excommunication itself he added 'that he was content privately to give an account of all the excommunications that he ever made or pronounced'. On the Sanquhar Declaration he affirmed 'that he did not see it till after it was proclaimed' and that he was 'not unwilling, upon time given him, to declare his judgement thereupon'. Finally, feeling that his answer on the death of the archbishop was not sufficiently explicit, he declared 'that the Scripture says, the Lord giving a call to a private man to kill, he might do it lawfully, and instances the case of Phinehas and Jael'. After some other minor changes had been made, at his request, he signed the account of his examination as a true record.

Cargill's demurring to assent to the Sanquhar Declaration and Queensferry paper was without doubt the part of his answers which most surprised his questioners. He was, of course, commonly regarded as the author of the Queensferry paper, and so was expected to own its principles. Moreover, many of those whom the Council had recently questioned and who had owned acquaintance with him had given their unequivocal assent to both the paper and declaration. Not a few therefore concluded that Cargill was willing to com-

promise his principles in order to gain favour from his judges.[5]
This charge was, of course, completely false, since his denial
of the king's authority was in itself sufficient to condemn him.
Rather Cargill was acting under the dictates of both honesty
and charity: on the one hand he could not have given an
unqualified assent to the two papers, on which he had already
given some hints of his feelings, while on the other he was not
prepared to question publicly, as Smith was later to do, the
motives of their authors.

However, the contrast which he drew between the papers
and the excommunication was significant, and instructive: the
papers he was content to regard as civil matters, on which the
Council were at liberty to question him, and he to answer; the
excommunication was an ecclesiastical matter, an act
sanctioned by the authority of heaven, over which no civil
court could claim jurisdiction.

The Council, dissatisfied with his replies, decided to question him once more in the hope of getting more specific
answers. On Tuesday, 19 July, his second examination began.
It stands in the records as follows: 'Edinburgh, 19th July 1681.
In presence of His Royal Highness, His Majesty's High Commissioner and Lords of Privy Council, Mr Donald Cargill
being called and examined if he owned his sermon preached
at Torwood in which he excommunicated His Majesty and
His Royal Highness and others, and if he owns the excommunication of the king and doing of it under the name of
Charles Stuart and as a tyrant, answers, if there was an
excommunication he could not answer for it but before an
ecclesiastical court, it being an ecclesiastical act. Being asked
if in that excommunication he named His Majesty under the
name of Charles Stuart, and as a tyrant, abstract from the
excommunication, refuses to answer. Being interrogate if he
owns the principles expressed in the paper called "Cargill's
Covenant" and the words therein relating, declares he has not
yet had sufficient time to consider thereof, and cannot
answer. Being interrogate if he owns these principles mentioned in that paper called the Declaration at Sanquhar, and
if he saw it before it was published, to the first will not answer,
but declares he did not see that declaration before it was published. The Sixth Article of that paper called Cargill's Coven-

ant being read to him, he refuses to make answer. Being interrogate who was the author of that paper, and who wrote it,
refuses to answer.'

For the Council's purpose this examination was clearly no
more satisfactory than the earlier one, and they concluded
that no useful purpose would be served by questioning Cargill
further. As soon therefore as his second examination was
over, they instructed the king's advocate, Sir George Mackenzie, to pursue a criminal process against him before the
Lords of Justiciary. Similar instructions were issued in respect
of his two friends, Smith and Boig, and two others, William
Thomson, of Frosk in Stirlingshire, who had been captured
when returning from Cargill's field-meeting in Fife on 26
June, and William Cuthill, a sailor from Bo'ness, who had
also been a follower of Cargill's preaching. With the new Parliament due to open on 28 July, the Council were anxious to
lose no time, and indictments against all five were ordered to
be drawn up without delay. At the same time, notices were
sent to thirty-seven heads of households in Edinburgh and the
surrounding district to present themselves for jury service,
under the statutory penalty of 100 merks.

By Friday, 22 July, three days after the Council's instructions were issued, the indictment against Cargill, Smith and
Boig was ready. Mackenzie, founding the charges on their
confessions before the Council, adduced against Cargill his
denial of the king's authority, as expressed in his confession,
and also charged him with having been present at Bothwell
Bridge. To prove this latter charge he needed the help of
witnesses, and so summonses were served on three residents
of Hamilton to testify that Cargill had been seen in company
with the rebels there.

Not content with pressing the criminal charges, Mackenzie
also included in the indictment certain allegations of his own
against Cargill's character and conduct, calculated to do him
the most damage and evincing a spirit of spitefulness that was
obviously born of a deep-seated personal resentment. 'You
have', he charged, 'drunk in popish and jesuitical principles of
exauterating [i.e. dethroning] and killing of kings, and to
make them the better take up with your zealous and ignorant
disciples you did most treasonably excommunicate your

native sovereign and some of his officers, and you have by that contagion poisoned and infected many poor and ignorant people, and have given occasion to popish emissaries to co-operate with you in this despicable and antichristian work. You have brought your disciples to the scaffold owning these jesuitical and treasonable principles, whereby you are guilty of their blood. You have advanced that to which you pretended enmity, and have destroyed, as far as in you lay, that to which you pretended friendship. You have wrested and strained the gospel of peace, which teaches obedience to magistrates for conscience' sake, into rebellion and disobedience, to the great scandal and disadvantage of the Protestant reformed religion. You also teach your disciples to die for that which you shift and shrink to own.' This last accusation was, of course, a reference to Cargill's withholding of his assent to the Queensferry paper and Sanquhar Declaration in his answers before the Council.

The indictment duly prepared, that same day James Dunbar, herald pursuivant of Court, attended by William Trotter and Robert Dalzell, officers, proceeded to the Canongate Tolbooth, where Cargill and his friends were held, and there with sound of trumpet and all due ceremony summoned them to appear before the High Court on Tuesday, 26 July, to answer to the charges. As required by the law, copies of the indictment and the lists of witnesses' and jurors' names were served on them by the officers. When the trumpets had finished sounding, Cargill remarked to his friends: 'This is a weary sound, but the sound of the last trumpet will be a joyful sound to me, and all having on Christ's righteousness.'

He now had four days to prepare himself for the trial. In the meantime, rumours about his fate spread rapidly. Some spoke of cruel tortures being got ready, 'of a barrel with many spikes, and an iron chair to be heated red hot'. Cargill was unmoved by these tales, though he well knew the end that lay in store for him and he now awaited it with calm resignation. He was able to share the fellowship of his two friends, Smith and Boig, and it gave him particular satisfaction to find that Boig, who some months earlier had been estranged from himself and Smith, was now fully reconciled to both of them and expressed his sorrow for his fault.[6] He was also allowed visitors; one of them was his old friend James Wodrow, father of the historian, with whom he had occasionally preached in the fields. Wodrow had fallen silent while Cargill had soldiered on, but though he was out of sympathy with much of what Cargill had done, and particularly with the excommunication, he had continued to cherish the memory of these early days and he held a high regard for Cargill's character. Wodrow was anxious to know how his old friend was faring. Cargill reassured him: 'As to the main point, my interest in Christ and the pardon of my sins, I have no doubts there, neither have I been ever shaken since the Lord's condescension to me in my extremity about twenty-five years ago, which I communicated to you a little after; and no thanks to me, for the evidence was so clear that I could never since once doubt. But then as to many other things, I have sad fears and damps. I see a dark and heavy cloud coming on the Church of Scotland, and our trial is not yet at its height.' For the church, and for the church alone, Cargill grieved and trembled; his personal salvation, ever since that memorable morning in his youth, was something that he could 'lay aside as asssured', so that he could devote all his attention to his Master's public work.

Eventually, on Tuesday, 26 July, before five Lords of Justiciary, the trial duly began. Its proceedings were a formality, and its result a foregone conclusion. By remitting Cargill to the High Court, the Council had to all intents and purposes fixed his sentence: the court at this time was merely their instrument, and on at least one previous occasion — in the case of Hackston — they had actually passed the sentence themselves and then got the court to ratify it. But, as always, the proper forms had to be observed and the court convened with all due solemnity. The jury was empanelled, fifteen in all, most of them ordinary working men: Hugh Blair, vintner; John Calendar, smith; William Bruce, stabler; Robert Miln, mason; Alexander Isaac, plumber. Two of those summoned, Andrew Fowler, a vintner, and James Bain, a wright, failed to appear, and were fined the 100 merks penalty. The lengthy indictment against Cargill and his fellow-prisoners was read, and found relevant.[7] Mackenzie, leading the case for the Crown, adduced the record of Cargill's examinations before the Council and in particular his own denial of the king's authority. Cargill, on being given an opportunity to speak in his own defence, added a brief word of explanation of his denial, and the grounds on which it had been made. The Explanatory Act, he asserted, gave the king a right to the authority of Jesus Christ, and the supremacy so given him was against right. And as for Bothwell Bridge, those who had been in arms there were not rebels, but had been raised by oppression. There he stopped and declined to say more. He saw that his audience, both judges and spectators, were hostile to him and ready to catch and misconstrue his words, and he saw no purpose in asserting his principles, or attempting to defend himself, at any further length. And in this he was clearly right, for when Smith, succeeding him, ventured to denounce the tyranny of the king and government he was subjected to the general ridicule of the whole court. When Smith was speaking, Cargill placed his hand on his shoulder and urged him to desist; he was grieved that the great issues for which they had fought should be made a matter for mockery and he knew that in the face of judges such as these the best answer was silence.

It remained merely for Mackenzie to go through the formality of calling witnesses for the prosecution. Maitland, as acting president of the Council, testified that the account of Cargill's examination was a true record of his answers as he had given them to the Council. Hugh Stevenson, the Council clerk who had written the document, gave a similar testimony. Two witnesses were then called to support the charge that Cargill had been present at Bothwell. James Hamilton, a married man of forty-three, declared that he saw Cargill several times, with sword and pistols, riding with the rebels in Hamilton and Hamilton Moor on a grey horse between the fight at Drumclog and the battle at Bothwell, and that to the best of his knowledge Cargill had been at the Cross of Hamilton when the declaration there was proclaimed. Gavin Wood, a youth of twenty, told a similar story about the arms and the grey horse and added the information that about a week before the battle he had heard Cargill preach to the rebels in the park at Hamilton, with a sword about him. No further evidence was brought; a third witness, John Mark, failed to appear.

The jury were then asked to retire and consider their verdict. On the evidence before them there was no doubt what it would be. They did not deliberate long. The verdict was unanimous. William Dunbar, their foreman, announced it to the court: Cargill was guilty of being at the rebellion at Bothwell Bridge and of treasonably declining the king's authority. For such a crime there could be only one sentence.

The final moment had now come. In accordance with custom the duty of announcing the judgement was passed to the 'doomster' or 'dempster' of court, Andrew Cunningham, who in solemn tones read the words of the sentence: 'That the said Mr Donald Cargill be taken to the Mercat Cross of Edinburgh tomorrow, being the 27th inst., betwixt two and four o'clock in the afternoon, and there be hanged on a gibbet till he be dead, and thereafter his head to be severed from his body and affixed on the Netherbow; and his name, memory and honour to be extinct, and his arms to be riven forth and delete out of the books of arms; that his posterity never have place nor be able hereafter to brook or joyce any honours, offices or dignities within this realm in time coming, and to have forefaulted, omitted and tint all and sundry his lands, heritages, tenements, rents, offices, titles, dignities, tacks, steadings, rooms, provisions, goods and gear whatsoever pertaining to him, to our sovereign lord, to remain with His Highness in perpetuity: which is pronounced for doom.'

Similar sentences were passed on Smith, Boig and the two others. The sentences were then signed in due form by the five judges, Sir Richard Maitland, Lord Justice Clerk, Sir James Foulis, Sir David Balfour, Sir David Falconer and Sir Roger Hog. And so, the final formality over, Cargill and his friends were returned once more to prison.

There was now only one day left. But before it dawned another of Cargill's predictions had been fulfilled: Rothes died that night, attended on his deathbed by two Presbyterian ministers and expressing bitter remorse for the evils of his past life. To many it was a startling vindication not only of what Cargill had said to him the previous week but also of the

sentence pronounced upon him at Torwood, and the event
cast an even greater solemnity over the happenings of these
final days. According to one account, it even prompted some
members of the Council to make a last-minute attempt to save
Cargill's life by commuting his sentence to life imprisonment
on the Bass, but if any such attempt was made it proved
unsuccessful.[8]

Back in prison Cargill set about writing a last testimony,
vindicating his life and ministry and dealing at some length
with the great issues for which he had fought. That night,
before he had an opportunity to finish it, the paper was taken
from him by the keepers and pen and ink denied him. But
somehow, and at great personal risk, a friend contrived to
pass writing materials in to him on a string through his cell
window, and in the early hours of the morning, just as dawn
was breaking, he completed a second, shorter, testimony
which was successfully smuggled out of the prison. In some
ways the loss of the original testimony was a blessing in dis-
guise, for into this second document he compressed such a
wealth of 'admirable and very rare sentences' — the phrase is
Patrick Walker's — as make it one of the choicest pieces of
personal testimony ever penned. It is a triumphant sum-
mation of a life spent in close fellowship with God and complete submission to his will. The assurance of faith breathes in
every sentence, pointing forward to the everlasting joys of
heaven.

'This is the most joyful day,' he wrote, 'that ever I saw in my
pilgrimage on earth. My joy is now begun, which I see shall
never be interrupted. I see both my interest and his truth, and
the sureness of the one and the preciousness of the other. It is
near thirty years since he made it sure,[9] and since that time,
though there has fallen out much sin, yet I was never out of an
assurance of mine interest, nor long out of sight of his presence. He has dandled me, and kept me lively, and never left
me behind, though I was oft times turning back. Oh, he has
showed the wonderful preciousness of his grace, not only in
the first receiving thereof, but in renewed and multiplied pardons! I have been a man of great sins, but he has been a God
of great mercies, and now, through his mercies, I have a conscience as sound and quiet as if I had never sinned. It is long

since I could have ventured on eternity, through God's mercy and Christ's merits, but death remained somewhat terrible, and that now is taken away; and, however it be with me at the last, though I should be straitened by God or interrupted by men, yet all is sure, and shall be well. I have followed holiness, I have taught truth, and I have been most in the main things; not that I thought the things concerning our times little, but that I thought none could do anything to purpose in God's great and public matters, till they were right in their conditions.'

'Most in the main things' is a phrase which perfectly sums up Cargill's life, a life spent in devotion to God and service to his church, a life which ever kept at its centre the great theme of God's glory, and was never diverted from this supreme aim.

'My preaching has occasioned persecution', he went on, 'but the want of it I fear will occasion worse. However, I have preached the truths of God to others, as it is written, "I believed, and so I preached", and I have not an ill conscience in preaching truth, whatever has followed: and this day I am to seal with my blood all the truths that ever I preached; and what is controverted of that which I am professing shall ere long be manifested by God's judgement in the consciences of men. I had a sweet calmness of spirit and great submission as to my taking, the providence of God was so eminent in it; and I could not but think but that God judged it necessary for his glory to bring me to such an end, seeing he loosed me from such a work.'

He ended his written testimony with a specific declaration of the reasons for his suffering. In this, he was again at pains to show that his refusal of the king's authority was linked inextricably with the declaration in the 1669 Act that the king had supreme authority over the church as an inherent right of the Crown. Since the Crown was one and indivisible, there was no way in which the king's authority could be recognized in one sense and not in another: it was impossible for his authority to be admitted in civil matters and not in ecclesiastical. Denial of one was denial of the other and both were equally treasonable in the eyes of the law. For Cargill there was no evading this basic issue. The king or Christ — one or other it must be. There was no room for temporizing or manoeuvre.

And so he wrote, 'This is the magistracy that I have rejected, that was invested with Christ's power. And seeing this power, taken from Christ, which is his glory, made the essential of the Crown . . . there is no distinction we can make that can free the conscience of the acknowledger from being a partaker of this sacrilegious robbing of God; and it is but to cheat our consciences to acknowledge the civil power, for it is not civil power only that is made of the essence of his crown. And seeing they are so express, we ought to be plain; for otherwise it is to deny our testimony, and consent to his robbery.'

It was not then for a theoretical principle, or an abstruse point of doctrine, that Cargill had been brought to suffer: the living reality of Christ, to which his words bear such firm witness, was at all times the driving force. And the Christ he knew, the Christ preached by the Scottish Reformers, in whose tradition he stood, was complete in all his offices, as Prophet, Priest and King. This issue then was the mirror image of the other: to deny Christ's supremacy in one sphere was to deny it in all; to deny him as King was to deny him also as Priest and Prophet. Again the issue was plain and unmistakable, and again there was no room for doubt. On that note, perhaps cut short by pressure of circumstances, his written testimony ended.[10]

The summer day was lengthening into afternoon when Cargill was brought out to die. It had been a long way from the early days in Rattray, from the young ministry, bright with promise, in the Barony of Glasgow, through the years of confinement and then of untiring public testimony. He had many memories to treasure: the few memorable months with Richard Cameron in the summer of 1680, preaching to multitudes with evidence of remarkable blessing, the loving devotion of the old flock in Glasgow, the fellowship with faithful friends. And he had his sorrows too to remember: the deep personal grief of his wife's early death, the bitter public tragedy of Bothwell, the pernicious evil of Gibb. But all these were now behind him, and in this final, supreme, hour his mind was at peace. He was led through the immense crowd thronging the High Street to where the scaffold stood at the east end of the High Kirk. He turned to face the multitude. And then, taking his old weatherbeaten Bible,[11] the companion of all his

years of wandering, he turned to the 118th Psalm, that great
song of victory and triumph, and sang these words in the old
Scottish metrical version from the sixteenth verse to the end:

> The right hand of the mighty Lord
> exalted is on high;
> The right hand of the mighty Lord
> doth ever valiantly.
>
> I shall not die, but live, and shall
> the works of God discover.
> The Lord hath me chastised sore,
> but not to death giv'n over.
>
> O set ye open unto me
> the gates of righteousness;
> Then will I enter into them,
> and I the Lord will bless.
>
> This is the gate of God, by it
> the just shall enter in.
> Thee will I praise, for thou me heard'st
> and hast my safety been.
>
> That stone is made head corner-stone,
> which builders did despise:
> This is the doing of the Lord,
> and wondrous in our eyes.
>
> This is the day God made, in it
> we'll joy triumphantly.
> Save now, I pray thee, Lord: I pray
> send now prosperity.
>
> Blessed is he in God's great name
> that cometh us to save;
> We, from the house which to the Lord
> pertains, you blessed have.

> God is the Lord, who unto us
> hath made light to arise:
> Bind ye unto the altar's horns
> with cords the sacrifice.
>
> Thou art my God, I'll thee exalt;
> my God, I will thee praise.
> Give thanks to God, for he is good:
> his mercy lasts always.

As he finished singing he looked up smilingly at the multitudes thronging the windows of the houses opposite and in the street around him. He motioned for silence, for he had a few words to say, which he said, 'I shall direct to three sorts of folk, and shall endeavour to be brief'. His first words were to the persecutors of the work and people of God: 'Oh, beware for the Lord's sake, and refrain from such courses, as you would escape wrath eternally.' At this, which was taken to refer to the king and Council, the soldiers stationed round the scaffold were ordered to beat their drums to drown out the rest of his words. Cargill waited patiently until they had stopped, then remarked, 'Now you see we have not liberty to speak, or at least to speak what we would, but God knows our hearts.'

He went on to address a word to ministers, his last word on a subject that lay heavy on his heart: 'Oh you that are called ministers in the Church of Scotland, who are wearied in waiting upon the Lord, and are turned out of his way, and run into a course of gross defection and backsliding, truly, for my part, I tremble to think what will become of you; for either you shall be punished with sore affliction (I mean in your consciences, because of sin) or else you shall be tormented eternally without remedy, which shall be shortly, if mercy prevent it not; which I pray God may be the mercy of all those to whom he has thoughts of peace.'

His third word was to 'the poor remnant, who fear sinning more than suffering, and are begging for his returning into Scotland to wear his own crown and reign as King in Sion, in spite of all that will oppose him, whether devils or men. I say to you that are thus waiting, wait on, and you shall not be disappointed; for either your eyes shall see it, or else you shall die in the faith of it, that he shall return, and "if you suffer with him you shall also reign with him", which reign shall be glorious and eternal.'

His words of admonition done, he went on to vindicate his work of public testimony: 'I come now to tell you for what I am brought here to die, and to give you an account of my faith, which I shall do as in the sight of the living God before whom I am shortly to stand. First I declare I am a Christian, a Protestant, a Presbyterian in my judgement; and whatever has been said of me, I die testifying against popery, prelacy, Erastianism, and all manner of defection from the truth of God, and against all who make not the Scriptures, which are the Word of God, their rule, that so they may commend Christ and his way to strangers by a holy and gospel conversation. The cause for which I am sentenced to die here this day is my disowning of authority in the unlawful exercise thereof, when they, instead of acting for God, are fighting against him and encroaching upon his prerogatives, by that woeful supremacy which my soul abhors, and which I have testified against since I was apprehended, and now again I disown all supremacy over the consciences of men and liberties of Christ's church.'

At this, which was taken as another attack on the king, the drums were again beaten. Cargill remained silent for some time after they had ceased, then said, 'Of this subject I shall say no more. Only I think the Lord's quarrel against this land is because there has not been so much heart religion and soul exercise among ministers or professors, as there seemed to be when the land owned Christ and his truth. I wish there were more true conversions, and then there would not be so much backsliding, and, for fear of suffering, living at ease when there are so few to contend for Christ and his cause.'

He had now come to the closing part of his speech. He devoted it to a few stirring words of personal testimony: 'Now, for my own case: I bless the Lord that for all that has been said of me, my conscience does not condemn me. I do not say I am free of sin, but I am at peace with God through a slain Mediator, and I believe that there is no salvation but only in Christ. I bless the Lord, that these thirty years and

Covenanters on scaffold

more I have been at peace with God, and was never shaken loose of it; and now I am as sure of my interest in Christ, and peace with God, as all within this Bible and the Spirit of God can make me, and I am no more terrified at death, nor afraid of hell, because of sin, than if I had never had sin, for all my sins are freely pardoned and washen thoroughly away, through the precious blood and intercession of Jesus Christ. And I am fully persuaded that this is his way for which I suffer, and that he will return gloriously to Scotland, but it will be terrifying to many. Therefore I entreat you, be not discouraged at the way of Christ, and the cause for which I am to lay down my life, and step into eternity, where my soul shall be as full of him as it can desire to be. And now, this is the sweetest and most glorious day that ever my eyes did see. Now, I entreat you, study to know and believe the Scriptures, which are the truth of God; these have I preached, and do firmly believe them. Oh, prepare for judgements, for they shall be sore and sudden; enemies are now enraged against the way and people of God, but ere long they shall be enraged against one another, to their own confusion.'

He was allowed to continue no longer. The drums were beaten a third time, forcing him to stop, and he was led round to the side of the scaffold while one of the others, probably Walter Smith, took his place at the front. There he remained while Smith sang a psalm and spoke to the people. He was then led round each side of the scaffold in turn, alternately offering silent prayer and speaking a word to those around him as he had opportunity. The presentiment of coming judgement on the church continued to oppress him even now. 'I entreat you', he was heard to say, 'prepare for a stroke: for God will not sit with all the wrongs done to him, but will suddenly come and make inquisition for the blood that has been shed in Scotland.'

At last, when all was ready, he was ordered to climb the ladder. As he set his foot on it he remarked: 'The Lord knows, I go up this ladder with less fear and perturbation of mind than ever I entered the pulpit to preach.' It was a remark in which his entire character was epitomized: the reticence and reserve of the natural temperament, the sensitivity to the awesomeness of the ministerial calling and yet the unshake-

able assurance of faith in God. He mounted the ladder and
seated himself at the top. His faith, triumphant and
undimmed, was radiant with full assurance: 'Now I am near to
the getting of my crown, which shall be sure; for I bless the
Lord, and desire all of you to bless him, that he has brought
me here and made me triumph over devils and men and sin.
They shall wound me no more. I forgive all men the wrongs
they have done me, and pray the Lord may forgive all the
wrongs that any of the elect have done against him. I pray that
sufferers may be kept from sin and helped to know their
duty.' The napkin was tied about his face. He lifted it for a
moment, and called out: 'Farewell, all relations and friends in
Christ; farewell, all acquaintances and all earthly enjoyments; farewell, reading and preaching, praying and believing, wanderings, reproaches and sufferings. Welcome, joy
unspeakable and full of glory. Welcome, Father, Son and
Holy Ghost. Into thy hands I commit my spirit.' And, as he
prayed, with his hands lifted up to heaven, the executioner
did his office, and in a moment Cargill's work on earth was
done.

His dear friends, Walter Smith and James Boig, with
William Thomson and William Cuthill, all shared the same
scaffold. 'Mr Smith,' writes Patrick Walker, 'as he did cleave
to him in love and unity in life, so he died with his face upon
his breast . . . these five worthies hung all on one gibbet at the
Cross of Edinburgh, on that never-to-be-forgotten bloody
day 27th July 1681. The enemies got this great glut of blood
. . . innocent blood, precious blood, dear blood, blood that
cries both loud and long. How can or shall the tyranny of
shedding innocent blood be forgot?' It was indeed a scene
which impressed itself indelibly upon the minds of many who
witnessed it. For one spectator, a young man of nineteen, by
the name of James Renwick, it set the seal on his resolve to
identify himself completely with the suffering church and with
the cause for which Cargill and his friends had laid down their
lives. Two years later, at Darmead, Renwick, now an
ordained minister, took for the text of his first sermon Isaiah
26:20: 'Come my people, enter into thy chambers . . .' It was
the well-remembered text of Cargill's last sermon, and it was
James Renwick's way of showing to the world that he had

taken up the mantle that Cargill had so honourably laid down.

The rest of the sentence, in all its hideous details, was duly carried out. What became of his body is not known; it may, like so many other martyrs of the time, have been interred in the Greyfriars Churchyard, in that part of it then allotted to criminals but now hallowed as sacred ground. Or it may, according to a persistent local tradition, have been taken home to Rattray and there interred in the family tomb in the local churchyard. If it be so, he now rests among his own people, in a place of honour among his kinsfolk, his memory treasured and revered by the many descendants of his name in all the scattered parts of the globe where they have made their home.

For seven long years the persecution dragged on, reaching a climax in the two terror years of 1684 and 1685, when the 'suffering remnant' felt the full fury of the storm. At length in 1688 deliverance came — a deliverance so swift and comprehensive as for some to be scarcely believable. But deliverance it was, and with the deposition of the Stuart dynasty, by the common consent of the people, the persecution of twenty-eight years came to an end. The obnoxious laws were swept aside, episcopacy was abolished and Presbyterianism restored; the old acts asserting the spiritual independence of the church were revived. Here was the vindication of all that Cargill and others with him had contended for. For Cargill himself the final vindication was to come in the eighteenth act of the Parliament of 1690. In this great statute, all the fines and forfeitures imposed on those who had suffered in the persecution were rescinded and set aside. In the centre of the list of worthies stands the name of 'Mr Donald Cargill'. 'The forfeitures,' says the act, 'shall be void, and of no avail, force, strength, nor effect in all time coming, rescinding the same for ever . . . like as Their Majesties and three estates rehabilitate, reintegrate and restore the memory of those who are deceased, their heirs, successors and posterity.'[12] The shame of the public proclamations, the branding as a traitor, the condemnation as a criminal were for ever effaced from the record. To Donald Cargill there was no country on earth so dear as his native Scotland. It is fitting that his country's last public mention of him should be one of honour.

Epilogue

Any evaluation of Cargill's life must take as its starting-point his deep personal conviction of having been specially called by God to be a minister of the gospel and to glorify God's name on earth. His unshakeable assurance of this basic fact lay at the heart of all his public actions. He was not, as we have seen, by temperament a man of controversy or contention, and it is not difficult to envisage him, had his lot been cast in more peaceful times, choosing to minister contentedly to his own congregation without concerning himself about the public affairs of church and state. Such a life, indeed, he could have enjoyed, if he had, like many of his contemporaries, chosen to avail himself of the tempting offers held out by the authorities. But such was his conviction of his divine commission and of his accountability to the God who had called him that he could not remain impassive when his Master's interest was under threat. The temptation to be silent, to comply for the sake of peace, must often have been almost irresistible, and his sensitive spirit must often have shrunk from the sacrifices which a public testimony demanded of him. Yet throughout it all he persevered; he never deviated from his straight course; he never yielded nor compromised his testimony in the face of threats, persecutions or false friends.

It was this very quality of perseverance and resolution against almost overwhelming odds that made Cargill so much admired by so many of the others who suffered at that time.[1]

Probably there is no more moving tribute to him than that of James Stuart, a young man who was executed at the

Gallowlee of Edinburgh on 10 October 1681: 'I am sure that the now glorified martyr, Mr Donald Cargill, his name shall last from generation to generation; and he shall have cause to rejoice in his King, Head and Master, who is Jesus Christ, when those who condemned him shall not know where to flee for shelter. And what brethren (disaffected as they were) did cast upon him as a shame, was his glory and decorment. He was of a high heroic spirit, and was free of a base and simonian carriage. He was a man hated of his brethren; but the great Elijah in his time was so. Time and tongue would fail me to speak to his commendation. He was the man who carried the standard without the help of any visible; but he had the help and assistance of his Master, at whose command he was aye wandering here without residence, yet knew of one above, and had full assurance of his dwelling-place.'[2]

Cargill's influence in the great struggles of the time was an enriching and ennobling one. He never forgot, nor did he allow others to forget, that the great issues for which they were contending were spiritual issues and that the supreme aim they were striving for was to glorify God on earth. To all his work he brought this distinctive spiritual quality, and so real and vital was his own spiritual experience that his very presence, especially in his later years, diffused an aura of sanctity and graciousness which impressed many who came in contact with him. John Finlay, another of the martyrs, touches on this when he tells that one of the crimes alleged against him was that of being in company with Cargill, 'for which', he says, 'with my whole soul I desire to bless and magnify the riches of his grace, that ever he conferred such company upon such a sinful wretch'. And to Robert Hamilton, who knew Cargill well, is ascribed this eloquent tribute, surely one of the most gracious that could be paid to any man: 'As he was of a most holy, strict, tender and composed practice and conversation, so he was affectionate, affable and tenderhearted to all he judged had anything of the image of God in them: sober and temperate in his diet, saying commonly, it was well won that was won off the flesh; generous, liberal and most charitable to the poor, a great hater of covetousness, a frequent visitor of the sick, much alone, loving to be retired; but when about his Master's public work, laying hold of every

opportunity to edify; in converse still dropping what might
minister grace to the hearers; his very countenance was edifying to beholders, often sighing with deep groans; preaching in
season and out of season, upon all hazards, ever the same in
judgement and practice.'[3]

By persuasion, Cargill was a Protestant and a Presbyterian
in the true succession of the Scottish Reformers. But for him
Presbyterianism was not merely an ecclesiastical system, or
the developed product of a theological tradition: it expressed
the very truth of God, and the emphasis which it placed upon
the right of Christ to rule in his church was an integral part of
divine revelation. In his dying testimony he declared, 'I die a
Christian, a Protestant and a Presbyterian', the three great
principles which for him comprised the sum of divine truth.
Significantly, in his dying testimony Cargill did not once mention the Covenants. For one whose name is inextricably
linked with the Covenants and their testimony this may seem
strangely surprising, but Cargill, as always, was acting logi-
cally. He yielded to no one in his loyalty to the Covenants, but
his allegiance was to what they represented, not to what they
were in themselves. For him, the Covenants did not constitute, but rather expressed, those vital issues of divine truth for
which a public testimony must be made.

It was here that Cargill parted company with those like
Robert Hamilton who in later years saw the Covenants as an
indispensable part of the constitution of church and state. For
Cargill this could not be so, and one of his contemporaries,
Thomas Lining, was clear on this point when, writing in 1706,
he strongly implied that, had Cargill lived, he would have cast
in his lot with the Revolution Settlement. Says Lining, speaking of the persecution: 'There being then no settled church
judicatory according to Christ's institution, ministers and
people were obliged to withdraw from these courses which
they were convinced in their consciences to be sinful, seeing
they had no clear and sufficient method to testify their
abhorrence of the courses of defection of those times . . . but
this was without any design ever to own these things to be sufficient grounds of separation in a constitute church, or when
with personal safety application could be made to settled
church judicatories, who were not under the tyrannical influ-

ence of enemies of the work of God. It was upon this ground that the reverend and worthy Mr Donald Cargill, late minister of the Barony of Glasgow, and martyr for the truth, often declared that his soul hated separation, and obtested his hearers to pray for faithful ministers.' And Lining goes on to quote in this connection Cargill's sermon at Loudon Hill in May 1681 when he himself had been present.

Indeed, Cargill stands amply vindicated from the charge of schism. When he advocated separation, which he increasingly did towards the close of his ministry, it was always in the context of withdrawal from apostasy and defection; where there was faithfulness to God's Word and loyalty to his truth, separation was not only erroneous but positively sinful. In this regard Cargill was fully at one with the Scottish Reformers and their successors, who had looked on separation from the church as a singular evil, to be avoided if at all possible. This view had been strongly argued by Cargill's old teacher, Rutherford, and both he and James Durham, for whose opinion Cargill had a profound respect, had advocated that church unity should be preserved even where it meant accepting some imperfections in doctrine and practice.[4] At the same time, however, they had been careful to stress that fellowship could not be entered into where it would involve an individual in known sin, or in the approval of it in others. For Cargill, despite his hatred of separation, it is clear that union with the ministers who had accepted the Indulgence could not be contemplated without contracting a sense of personal guilt. But, as he made clear on at least one occasion, his separation from them was related directly to their tenure of their offices by virtue of the king's authority, not to what they were as ministers; and so there are grounds for believing that the inclusion of some of the complying ministers in the Revolution Settlement, when the rightful government of the church was eventually restored, would not have been an insuperable barrier to Cargill's acceptance of it. For him there was one central issue, to which all the others were subordinate. 'The cause of my suffering', he declared in his final testimony, 'is not acknowledging the present authority as it is established in the Supremacy and Explanatory Act. This is the magistracy that I have rejected, that was invested with Christ's power.'

Cargill's place in the history of his church and country is
secure. In the long history of the reformed church of
Scotland there have no doubt been others as faithful, others
as loyal, but there have been few called upon to display their
faithfulness and loyalty in times so testing and in circumstances so challenging. In the annals of the Scottish
church Cargill occupies a unique place.

Appendix 1
Cargill as a preacher

Born and bred as he was in the Scottish Presbyterian tradition, Cargill's preaching was thoroughly Calvinistic and Reformed. Underlying all his theology was a deep sense of the sovereignty of God. God was supremely sovereign, in his justice and in his mercy; he could exercise both as he would. For Cargill this was no capricious or arbitrary doctrine, but one which enhanced all the more the grace and mercy of God in electing to eternal life those who were worthy only of his wrath and condemnation. As early as his student days in St Andrews he is found expounding this theme with his customary clarity: 'There is a particular number of persons given of the Father to the Son to be saved. It is the Father that chooses, the Son suffers, the Holy Ghost sanctifies. There can be no reason given of this point, but only the free and rich grace of God, that some are put in the bargain and not all; this is free grace and the good pleasure of God.'

God's sovereign care over his elect was a theme on which he often dwelt, as in another sermon many years later when he pondered the mystery of God's redemptive purpose in Christ: 'Now must it be so? Must it be so that the Son of God must be put to these things? Was there a necessity for this? Can it be done no otherwise? No, there was no creature that could give merit to his suffering but he who was God indeed: the bearing of suffering was not enough, but the communicating of infinite merit and worth. That is the thing that looses the prisoners, that they were sufferings of infinite merit; and no creature, be what he will, could give infinite merit but his own Son. And it was by reason of that union, the hypostatical union, that this infinite merit was joined to the sufferings of Christ. It is our great shame and sin that we are not more exercised with our redemption, seeing it has been the thought of the infinite God from eternity, the work of the Son in time and it is the great work of the providence of God in the world, for there is more work bestowed upon the small number of the elect than there is upon all the world beside.'

This stupendous work could be traced to no other source than the love of God, a theme on which Cargill dwelt with awed admiration whenever he spoke of it: 'The love of God is so great a stream that it comes in and takes some away violently and yet willingly, against all the gates of brass and powers of devils . . . What was man, and the redemption of man, that brought Christ from heaven to earth, from dwelling in an infinite glory, to be an inhabitant of a tabernacle of clay? What means all this, for whom is it? For man, for poor man, unworthy man. How is it that such great things are done for a poor creature? It is love, and here all must rest, and all here is drowned.'

God's care of the believer in his daily battle against sin and temptation was another favourite theme of his preaching.This was merely a consequence of Christ's victory over the devil, or as Cargill liked to put it, 'the greatest person about the best of works, Christ destroying the devil and what he has done'.

For Cargill, the doctrine which he taught was not merely a system of theology, but a set of living realities to be put into daily practical experience. From Rutherford he had learned not only the principles of Reformed doctrine, but also the art of applying these principles in a devotional way to the everyday experience of the individual. Schooled as he was in the varied experiences of life, with his share of personal sorrow, he was well able to convey these truths to his hearers with sympathy and understanding. It was this identity of heart, preacher with hearer, that was the foundation of his popular appeal.

Above all, as has been seen, he cherished the highest possible regard for the office of the ministry. More than once he declared his belief that the ministers of Christ were the successors of the Old Testament prophets as the spokesmen of God. It was this exalted conception of his calling that lay behind his pronouncements on the public affairs of his time. Probably in no department of his ministry has Cargill been more misunderstood than in this. Indeed, it was a fashionable view among some of his contemporaries that Cargill was basically a devoted and honest-hearted minister who had unfortunately allowed himself to be drawn away by others into matters of public controversy which were outside his proper concern. However, Cargill was beholden to no one for his pronouncements on public matters; on the contrary, they were for him of the very essence of the ministerial office. Just as the Old Testament prophets had warned the Israelite kings of their apostasy, so it was the duty of the minister of Christ to warn the rulers of his own day of their departure from the ways of the Lord. This duty was incumbent upon the minister at all times, but particularly so in a time of national apostasy and decay. As the number of faithful witnesses declined, so the public duty of the minister — the watchman, the messenger of God — became all the more compelling. Cargill himself certainly became much more keenly conscious of this aspect of his ministry as the years passed. Hence the increasing insistence with which, in his closing years, he pressed this issue in his public ministry and preaching. The supreme example was, of course, his action at Torwood, in which he stood forth, with utter conviction, as the herald of divine judgement on an apostate king and rulers.

Cargill's personal feeling of identity with the prophets is clearly evidenced in his sermons. With the prophet Jeremiah he seems to have felt a particular affinity of spirit. The prophet, diffident and self-depreciating, sensitive to criticism and abuse, was yet charged to declare the mind of the

Lord to rulers and people, whether they would hear or whether they would forbear. So it was with Cargill. It was this unshakeable conviction of the divine commission which also lay at the root of his unyielding opposition to the Indulgence, the acceptance of which he saw as a betrayal of that very call to the ministry to which alone he owed obedience.

The imminence of coming judgement, of deprivation of spiritual mercies, was a theme which pressed upon him increasingly as his life neared its close. Gladly would he have kept silent about it, but he had an inner compulsion to speak that could not be stilled. 'We do confess', he remarked, 'that if we dared refuse God in any message, men that were tender would refuse this message, and would be ready to say God forbid; they had rather chosen exile or banishment when they consider that they are to be set to such a work. But it is that which is God's glory, so we must be silent sometimes though it be bitter. Curses and threatening must be denounced at God's command, as well as the message of mercy; in obedience to God we must denounce curses as well as promises; the herald must give obedience to the Master in the one as well as in the other.'

This great task, indeed, was too much for mortal man unaided by the power of God. And yet, in much weakness, it had to be performed. On the scaffold Cargill said, 'I go up this ladder with less fear and perturbation of mind than ever I entered the pulpit to preach.' It was not so much that he feared the face of man — though his natural diffidence never left him — as that he was afraid of not doing the work of God as he ought, of bringing dishonour on the name of the Master he served. This was a dread responsibility, but it was one that at the same time was accompanied with the highest honour. As the messenger of God, the declarer of his will, the minister had an authority that no earthly power could challenge or call into question.

Cargill made it a general rule not to deal in his ordinary preaching with matters which were not primarily of spiritual consequence. He well knew, and often warned against, the danger of displaying zeal in public matters without a corresponding spiritual concern, a 'zeal without tenderness', as he more than once expressed it. And so his main emphasis was ever on the things of the spirit: on God's glory above all things, on the welfare of the church, on man's relationship with God. 'I have been most in the main things,' he said in his last testimony, 'not that I thought the things concerning our times little, but I thought none could do anything to purpose in God's great and public matters, until they were right in their conditions.' This spiritual dimension was therefore the main emphasis in all his ordinary preaching. At times, however, particularly at public fasts, he would deal more explicitly with the affairs of the church and nation, more than once maintaining that the sad condition of both was due to the recognition of what he termed the 'malignant interest', or the interest of those who were opposed to the principles of the Reformation and Covenants. The most grievous sin, and the one from which all the others had sprung, was the acceptance of Charles II as king and the blind adherence of the church and nation to a cause which, from earlier manifestations of providence, was blighted with the divine disfavour. To this he had no hesitation in ascribing

the disastrous military defeat at Dunbar and later the defeat at Bothwell.
Both had been manifestations of God's judgement on national sins. There
could be no recovery for the nation, or for the church, until that interest was
disclaimed.

But he was always careful to distinguish between these public matters
and the spiritual needs of the individual. In a time of national and
ecclesiastical apostasy there was a remnant that continued faithful. It was to
this remnant that Cargill owed a particular duty and in whose fellowship he
found the greatest satisfaction. 'There is a small remnant in Scotland', he
wrote in his last testimony, 'that my soul has had its greatest comfort on
earth from.' And so, while his message to the church and nation was so
often one of judgement, his message to the individual, the member of the
remnant, was frequently one of consolation and peace.

Cargill's attitude to the Scriptures was always one of deepest reverence;
for him they were the infallible utterances of the Holy Spirit. 'The Holy
Ghost has that word,' was his usual expression when introducing a quotation from Scripture. His preaching style clearly reflected and expressed this
basic conviction. An example of a service he conducted during the most
active period of his ministry gives a typical illustration of his approach. He
had led in the singing of one of the most oft-sung psalms of the period, the
74th, 'O God, why hast thou cast us off?', after which he announced his text
in this way: 'For the Lord's sake, hear this word. You will find it written in
the ninth of Daniel, verse 13: "As it is written in the law of Moses, all this
evil is come upon us, yet made we not our prayer before the Lord our God."
Oh, that the very reading of these words might leave a conviction upon you!
Now God be with us through the word.' He frequently prefaced his sermons
with a solemn exhortation in this strain, sometimes also appealing for quiet,
a necessary precaution when speaking to a large open-air audience. Once
started he generally gave a brief introduction, then proceeded to divide his
subject into three or more heads. These he would again divide into a
number of sub-heads, following a strict and logical order of thought and
ending with a few words of application or 'use'. He kept closely, almost
rigidly, to his text throughout. He was not an exponent of the art of oratory,
and nowhere can his preaching be said to have reached any heights of
eloquence. Indeed, compared with the preaching of Richard Cameron, it
sometimes appears subdued, almost pedestrian, in tone. But what Cargill
may have lacked in oratorical skills was more than compensated by his
handling of his message and his manner of communicating it. His intense
earnestness and concern and the evidence he showed of a close communion
with God left on his hearers an impression that words alone could not convey. This, without doubt, was the secret of his magnetism as a preacher.

In his services Cargill used the metrical Psalms of David, almost certainly
in the 1650 version in use to this day, since it was then the only one
sanctioned for public worship by the General Assembly. He generally led
the singing himself, though in his later years, when he was suffering from
fatigue and the effects of constant travel, this duty was performed for him
by his young friend Walter Smith. He usually preached standing on a chair,
facing his audience with his Bible in his hand, speaking to them directly

without the aid of a pulpit or bookrest. He scorned the use of a 'tent' or shelter, even in the severest weather. In rain, hail or snow he preached in the open, bareheaded, anxious in all respects to accommodate himself to his hearers. In prayer he would hold both hands up to heaven, as if invoking a blessing, an attitude in which, his friends observed, he uttered his last words on the scaffold. His voice, after its temporary breakdown, was renowned for its clarity and resonance and enabled his audience, however large, to follow his preaching without difficulty.

Cargill had his mannerisms. The most notable of these was his frequent use of the expression: 'We shall add that one word,' or 'In effect, we shall say that one word', when he wanted to underline a point with particular emphasis. The use of this expression against him in mockery after his capture is evidence of how closely he had become identified with it. On occasion too he would use simple rhetorical questions to focus his hearers' attention. He would sometimes end his sermons with an almost laconic, 'But we shall leave it,' or 'We shall say no more,' perhaps reflecting an awareness of inattentiveness on his hearers' part or a diminishing sense of spiritual energy or concern on his own. Always self-effacing, he shunned using the first person singular in his preaching.

He did his utmost to convey his meaning to his audience and to make himself understood in their language. Skilled as he was in the classical tongues, he rarely used a Latin or Greek quotation. On the contrary, he had a liberal vocabulary of Scots vernacular expressions which he used frequently and to good purpose. He used few quotations from literature, though it is plain that he was well versed in the writings of the early church fathers and the works of the Reformers. His experience in law found frequent expression in references to legal practices and styles, which he used to illustrate his sermons. He also alluded on occasion to contemporary customs and popular pursuits. These were, of course, designed to bring home his meaning with greater clarity to his audience and were subservient to his main purpose.

Cargill's sermons

In common with those of the other field-preachers of his day, many of Cargill's lectures and sermons were taken down in a form of shorthand by his hearers and circulated from hand to hand. At least fifty of these survive, many of them only in a fragmentary state. It was not, of course, possible to have the sermons printed without incurring the risk of heavy penalties and there is no evidence that any of them were printed or published during Cargill's lifetime.

There seems to have been an intention shortly after his death to publish a volume of sermons by both himself and Richard Cameron, and the United Societies apparently entrusted Robert Hamilton, then acting as their agent in Holland, with the arrangements for this project. It is now clear that the brief biographical notes written by Hamilton which were incorporated in an abbreviated form in the *Cloud of Witnesses* (see Appendix II) were intended to form a preface or prologue to a volume of Cargill's sermons. Hamilton introduces his original manuscript with the words: 'Christian, consider these few labours of that renowned champion of Jesus Christ, which God in his infinite goodness hath put in the hearts of his people to collect for thy instruction.' He closes the preface by saying, 'Christian reader, I have shown thee some acts of providence in God's owning the author hereof, but it is but a few of many to invite thee to peruse the following labours for thy profit and edification in the way of holiness. But none can commend them unto thee as they will commend themselves, when seriously pondered and perused; so that I may not prove tedious to thee, I refer thee to the works themselves; the Lord bless them to thee.' For some reason however, now unknown, the sermons were never published. Michael Shields, in a postscript to a letter to Hamilton written in 1683, asked, 'Sir, friends in Glasgow desired me to write to you to send them word what is become of that book of Mr Donald Cargill's and Mr Richard Cameron's, if it be corrected and put to the press.' There is no record of Hamilton's reply.

The first of Cargill's sermons to be printed bore the title *A Lecture and Sermon Preached at Different Times* and appeared, with neither publisher's name nor date, shortly after his death in 1681. It contained an exposition of 2 Chronicles 19:1-2 and a sermon on Isaiah 10:3, neither of them with dates, but the sermon could well be that which he preached on 19 June 1681. The exposition, or lecture, appears to have been delivered some time earlier.

The Torwood excommunication is known to have been circulated widely and to have been posted up in some of the most prominent places in Edinburgh and other towns. It was not, however, published in full until 1741, though the action of the excommunication — excluding the exposition and discourse — appeared as early as 1714 as an appendix to the first edition of the *Cloud of Witnesses*. A sermon preached by Cargill on 17 November 1678 on the text 'Remember Lot's wife' (Luke 17:32) was published in 1744.

In 1779 John Howie of Lochgoin published four of Cargill's expositions and seven of his sermons, together with the excommunication, in his *Collection of Lectures and Sermons* drawn from the manuscript notes of hearers.[1] Howie's *Collection* was reprinted in 1880 by the Rev. James Kerr of Greenock under the title *Sermons in Time of Persecution in Scotland*. Some further expositions and sermons, copied from a collection of unpublished notes by Howie, were included in the Rev. W. H. Carslaw's biography of Cargill published in 1900. Notes of others, including several quoted in this volume, survive in manuscript form.

Notes of a sermon

This sermon, preserved in manuscript, was preached by Cargill before the St Andrews Presbytery on 29 March 1654, about a year before his ordination to the ministry. It is quite different in style from the popular discourses of his later years which have been published, and forms an interesting example of the analytical type of preaching which occupied the first part of the presbytery's regular 'exercise' (see chapter 1, note 10). It also provides clear evidence of Cargill's knowledge of contemporary theological controversy and acquaintance with the original languages.

John 17:11-12: *'And now I am no more in the world, but these are in the world, and I come to thee. Holy Father, keep through thine own name those whom thou hast given me, that they may be one, as we are. While I was with them in the world, I kept them in thy name: those that thou gavest me I have kept, and none of them is lost, but the son of perdition; that the scripture might be fulfilled.'*

Christ, speaking of his departing, subjoins a petition for supplying that want, and for beating down all perplexed thoughts. In the 11th verse we have:
1. A general petition put up for those that were given him.
2. The reasons of the petition, which are two.
Question. How is it he says 'now' — in the present time — 'I am no more in the world'?
Answer. The present time is put for the future by a hebraism, because of the near approaching of it; so Christ within a short time was to leave the world.
Q. How is Christ said to leave the world? Is he not God?
A. 1. Christ as God filleth all things and is bounded in no place and comes not under the laws of access and recess.
    2. Christ according to his bodily presence as man is not everywhere, for Christ as man comes under going or coming, and this meets with (i.e. confutes) the opinion of Ubiquitaries.
    3. Christ as a man has withdrawn his bodily presence from this earth fully and finally; fully, for he says 'I', and finally, which we understand till the day of judgement; and this meets with papists who maintain his bodily presence yet in the sacraments, neither is it to any purpose that they say he is not now present in such a way as before he was in the world.
    For the petition, there is in it:
1. The style, 'Holy Father', a prayer full of love and reverence, but especially we think that he eyes the righteousness of God in fulfilling his promises.
2. The prayer itself: 'keep' or 'preserve' them.
3. The efficient cause, 'through thy name', that is 'by thy power' (Proverbs 18:10).
Q. What union is this he prays for?
A. Christ prays both for unity betwixt him and believers, and for unity among themselves (John 15:5,12). Yet we think that unity among themselves especially is aimed at; Christ prays here for the confirmation of this union.
Q. How prays he that they may be one as he and the Father?
A. Arians argue from this place against the deity of Christ, saying that the Father and the Son are no other way one than believers among themselves, in affection and judgement. We say that the union betwixt Christ and believers is not only in judgement and affection (as Cartwright[2] says) but also a mystical union, whereby they are bone of his bone and flesh of his flesh. The word *kathos* here does not signify an identity, but only a

similitude, whereby is not held out the essence of the union but only a parity in the qualities of the union, as that it should be

1.　A spiritual one.
2.　A constant and perpetual one.
3.　A holy one, not as that union between men and their sinful ways, which is not holy.

Q.　Ought believers to aim at that perfection which is in God, one as he is one, and holy as he is holy?

A.　Believers ought to desire the things that are in God, as holiness and righteousness, but not in that perfection in which they are in God, for that were with Adam to desire to become gods and not creatures.

We come to the next verse, wherein Christ shows his faithfulness: he gives in his accounts. This we have in the circumstances of time, where

1.　Christ does not deny his care of them before he had taken on our nature.
2.　Nor does he deny his care that he has over them after he is glorified.
3.　Nor does he deny that the Father kept them, for he says 'through thy name', i.e. 'by thy power'.

This he says, that he might draw their eyes off his bodily presence, and that he might show the fountain of his keeping. Keeping is twice repeated, and the latter word in the original signifies:

1.　A watchful and painful keeping (Luke 2:8).
2.　A keeping like a treasure.
3.　A sure and secure keeping, as in prison.

All these are true of Christ. 'And none of them is lost' where he removes the scandal of the defection of many (John 6:66) and the scandal of Judas' defection.

Q.　How is it said that he has lost none but Judas?

A.　Lutherans make the particle *ei me* to denote an exception, to maintain the defection of the saints. Other writers make the particle to denote an opposition, as in Revelation 21:27; Galatians 2:16. And it seems to be taken so here, because Christ has said twice, 'I have lost none whom thou hast given me,' and then he names the son of perdition. Stapleton[3] answers otherwise, but Calvin answers this, for he says he is an 'improper' exception.

Q.　In what sense is Judas called 'the son of perdition'?

A.　We understand not only by it the lost man, but also the man appointed to destruction, and even Gerhard[4] concedes this.

Q.　How is it said, 'that the scripture might be fulfilled'?

A.　The particle *hina* denotes not the cause but the event; we think it signifies the end. And yet it will not follow that God is the author of Judas' sin, for sin falls not under God's efficiency, but his ordination.

Objection.　But then Judas was under the necessity of sinning, because there was a decree for it.

A.　There is a necessity of co-action, and that we deny; and secondly a hypothetical necessity, while some distinguish again between necessity of infallibility and necessity of immutability, the first in regard of God's prescience and the second in regard of his decree.

A lecture and sermon in the fields

The following are typical examples of Cargill's later preaching. The 'lecture', which was properly a sermon on an extended portion of Scripture, was delivered at Partick, Glasgow, on 3 November 1678. The date of the sermon is unknown, but it can probably be attributed to the same period. Both were first published in John Howie's *Collection of Lectures and Sermons* in 1779.

I. Lecture

2 Corinthians 5:4-11: *'For we that are in this tabernacle do groan, being burdened: not for that we would be unclothed, but clothed upon, that mortality might be swallowed up of life. Now he that hath wrought us for the selfsame thing is God, who also hath given unto us the earnest of the Spirit. Therefore we are always confident, knowing that, whilst we are at home in the body, we are absent from the Lord. (For we walk by faith, not by sight.) We are confident, I say, and willing rather to be absent from the body, and to be present with the Lord. Wherefore we labour, that, whether present or absent, we may be accepted of him. For we must all appear before the judgement seat of Christ; that every one may receive the things done in his body, according to that he hath done, whether it be good or bad. Knowing therefore the terror of the Lord, we persuade men; but we are made manifest unto God; and I trust also, are made manifest in your consciences.'*

We may say of these words, before we begin to speak upon them, the Lord make them like Christ's box of ointment, wherewith he was anointed unto his burial! We may say, oh how great alterations does grace make upon nature! It makes its greatest aversion its greatest desire. And what is nature's greatest aversion? Is it not death? Yet through grace it becomes the greatest and most solid desire of man. But this is not the first work of grace upon man's soul. There must be diverse works prior to this. The soul will not be made willing to step off the stage of time except it see what it is to step into. But there are several things in these words that hold out to us what precedes or begets this desire.

1. There is *preparation*. Now, in a word, a soul that has a right desire of death is a wrought soul (so to speak). And who has been the worker? The Spirit of God. 'Now he that hath wrought us for the selfsame thing is God.' Now the preparation is wrought in the soul, and the worker is God. And what has he been doing with it? Just like a piece of clay in the hand of the potter, he has been beating and working it and then forming it after his own image and likeness; and now it is thus a prepared and wrought soul. The worker is God. The thing he is working them to is his own image, and so the Lord is working an image to himself in every soul to which he has given a desire of death. Now we may say, 'What working is there yet amongst you?' Death is working with some, but we know not if life be working with it; and woe to that soul that finds not death and life working together.

2. As there is preparation, so there is *mortification*, which must be the second thing prior to this desire of death. We have now been for a long time withered, but now something of experience and something of religion lets us see the vanity of all temporary things, and we begin to esteem them as

little as they esteem us. A soul that esteems worldly things little must be a soul that is making for heaven. In a word, every man has waited upon a vain heart, and upon vain expectations. Now, this is here discovered to the apostle, and this discovery begets an aversion in him to them, and so he begins to turn himself another way. And how long will an immortal soul follow a vain and a foolish heart? We may say that there is a certain point of eminence, and till a soul arrive at that where it may get a view of the world's vanity, as the devil gave Christ of its glory (and that is mortification) — I say, until we come at that sight of the vanity of the world, that will beget an aversion and detestation of it in us, and until we have been on that mount, we never can set our hearts and affections upon heaven as we ought. You are not climbing up this mount yet, perhaps, but you must fall about it, and be dead unto sin, before you get a view that will mortify your hearts fully: 'For we walk by faith, not by sight.'

3.   There is a third thing, which is some *assurance of eternal life.* 'For we are confident, I say, and willing.' A soul will never loose the one foot until assured where to set down or fix the other. We will not say but that crosses and afflictions beget passionate wishes in many, but they will soon retract these. But the solid desire that the soul abides at is in consequence of the assurance of eternal life. In this case the soul desires to be transported. We may say that the assured Christian is as sorry to go back again as others are to go forward. And how is it that some are, as it were, dragged away to eternity, and others go off willingly and triumphantly? There is a dying man, but yet he is as a bridegroom going out of his chamber, as it were, to be espoused to the Queen of heaven. Assurance, we say, should then be had, and it is no wisdom to venture upon eternity, until we be in some measure sure about the things of eternity. We may say this one word, and we dare not come below it, that we should scarcely leap off the stage of time into eternity until once assured that we have our peace made up with God. But more particularly, we may observe these words.

First, there is a Christian affection, a great Christian affection shown to eternity, and the reason of it is given: 'And willing rather to be absent from the body, and to be present with the Lord.' He is a man subject and submissive to God, and he dare not well tell his mind until first he hear some intimation from him; and if once he hear God say it, he will run before, as you know it is said of Christ, that after he told his disciples that he was going up to Jerusalem, 'that he set his face steadfastly to go up to Jerusalem', and was the foremost, we may suppose, in all the company. You know, he was going up there never to return back to the world again.

Secondly, we must have resolution. And what is that? Why, it is just to carry well until we come to God, even labouring. And for what? For this: 'That, whether present or absent, we may be accepted of him' — that is, that when we come home to God we may get the welcome of 'good and faithful servant'. As long as we stay here, it is the Christian's resolution to carry well until he get there. And further, Paul gives the reasons of his resolution (1) in regard to himself; and (2) in respect of others.

1.   *In regard to himself:* 'For we must all appear before the judgement seat

of Christ.' He shall then take and examine all our works, like a schoolmaster who comes in at night and takes an account of all his scholars. 'Let me see', says he, 'how you have learned, how you have performed your task,' or like a mistress with her maid who says, 'How have you wrought today?' In a word, we must every one give an account to him of what we have done in the body. We may say that it will be a long account with many; but grace will make it short to some, and will end it all in a word: 'I freely forgive it all, yea, I have done it already.'

2. There is another reason, and it is *in respect of others*. 'Knowing, therefore, the terror of the Lord, we persuade men.' When we think upon this we would gladly have others with us, and we know not if they shall be discharged before God who have not been useful or helpful in bringing in others to him. But this we are sure of, that the more you can be instrumental to bring others to God, you shall be the more welcome to him. It is a wonder that any who have the least impression of the terrors of God upon them are not more earnest in their dealing with him on the behalf of others. But we shall speak a word further upon these words.

First, 'For we in this tabernacle do groan, being burdened.' Now, all groan, but they groan differently and on different accounts. All groan, both good and bad, but if your ears were at their heart you would hear a great variety of reasons. (1) Some groan; but why? Because the world is not more full and successful to them; (2) because it is not free of all affliction; and (3) because it is not of longer continuance; for ere ever they are aware of it age is upon them.

Firstly, we say that some groan, because the world is not more full, free and of longer continuance to them. Such folk evidence clearly that they have no right to anything, at least their heart believes it so. Again, we may say that there are some, on the other hand, who rejoice that the world is no fuller, freer, or of longer continuance to them. They say that all this is needful. And, indeed, if the world wanted its crosses it would be worse for us, and it is also well that it is of no longer continuance.

Secondly, we would say that, though they be groaning under various wants and on different accounts, yet there is another thing here. There are some put between two great straits, or as you use sometimes to say, 'between the devil and the deep sea'. They are both afraid to die, and they cannot live with pleasure, even as they would. They are afraid of dying, like children that are afraid to go in the dark, because they know not what may be there. We shall say this one word to you: either make more haste to be holy, or else pray for a long life. But what will long life do to you? It shall soon be expired.

Thirdly, here is another kind of groaning, and this is a great cause of it. The words seem emphatical, importing, as was said before, that we believe and rejoice, and we groan and mourn too and therefore there are these three things that make us do so.

1. The believer's crosses and trials make him mourn. And why so? Even because every cross has a temptation in it. Indeed, we said a word before which seems to contradict this, but they agree well together. Believers may be content with these crosses in the world, and yet may groan under them.

222 *No King but Christ*

They may groan when they find their sorrows and rejoice when they find
their profit therein; and so both joy and mourning may be contained therein
together.

2. They groan because of the bondage and thraldom they are under. And
what are they like? They lie low, and they are, as it were, under the devil's
foot, so to say. Oh, this thraldom of sin! When shall we see an end of it? We
think that every soul of you should be essaying to have this yoke broken in
pieces. Oh, when will it be taken off never to be put on again? And when
will it be said, 'Henceforth thou shalt be free from all temptations to sin,
and shalt be no longer in thraldom unto it'?

3. A third thing is 'hope deferred that makes the heart sick'. The great and
vast disproportion between what they are entitled to and their condition
makes them groan. What is their right? Why, for as low as I sit here, I have
a patent right in my bosom to a kingdom. It is well hid there, and if it is not
there it is not well. So I say there is a vast disproportion betwixt their rights
and their present condition. Why, they are under the feet of men, and the
vilest of men, under devils, and the malice of devils; but they never get all
their will about them, so that hope deferred makes the heart sick and makes
it groan. Oh, when shall we be fully freed from this?

A second thing that we may speak a word here to is, that this groaning is
the effect of sin. It began with the body, and it will end with the body; for
so long as the body continues here, sin and it will be together. Sin began
with the body in the womb. We never heard of a babe that leaped in the
womb for joy but one. Others may do it, but it is on another account. I say,
we never read of any but one who leaped upon this consideration, viz., that
of the hope that the soul had of its eternal freedom through its Mediator. So
I say, this may help to diminish your affections to the world. You must be
kept groaning. That is the first thing that makes us content to quit the body,
for we groan while we keep it. So choose whether ye will dwell with it, or
be divorced from it in your affections, or be content with these groanings ye
shall have while in the body. But we say, they are great fools who have great
expectations of freedom while in this tabernacle. You have been
disappointed, and yet you will set it up. But set it up when you will, you will
find it shaken, and sometimes the soul drooping and full of fears. But we
may say that it shall always groan while here, until it groan out its last; and
then it shall have its freedom: 'For we that are in this tabernacle do groan.'
It is not without cause that we groan. For we sit beside ill neighbours, and
we have great taxes laid upon us. We are like a people in slavery, whose
rents are all taken from them by reason of bondage, and burdens laid upon
them. So that there is cause of groaning; and this one thing, that there will
be still a burden on every soul so long as it is in this tabernacle. If there were
no more but this body of death it would be a great burden. It is true, it is not
become the burden of some; I may say, of many. But the worse is their case.

Thirdly, we come more particularly to show the cause.

First, *negatively*. 'Not that we would be unclothed, but clothed upon.'
Grace has brought all the terrors of death to this. It is but just like one
putting off a worn suit of clothes and putting on a suit of new apparel. O
death, who wast so dreadful, thou art now but like the putting off old rags

and on new apparel! Did you never see the fondness of a child in putting on new garments? Though there be no such fondness here, yet there is as great a resolution and desire in every true Christian to be thus clothed upon. So says the true Christian, 'I would see how it would fit me. I would gladly see how this clothing would fit me.' So first Paul lets you see negatively, 'Not that we should be unclothed,' that is, 'We have no pleasure in thinking that we shall be annihilated, or reduced to nought.' The passionate wishes of the worldly man look no further than 'Oh, if I were dead!' But if dead, what would then become of you? Before you wish for that, see better to it. Where there is not suitable preparation for death, life is better; but where there is preparation for it, say, not passionately, but calmly, 'Lord, send it when thou wilt,' or 'Let thy servant depart in peace, for mine eyes have seen thy salvation.' 'Not to be unclothed.' What is that? Not to be brought to nothing, but to have my body taken away.

But secondly, *positively*. 'I desire to be clothed upon.' I am like a man that has a rich marriage to consummate. I would have both my wedding and my wedding clothes on. And in effect death will both bring me to my marriage and the putting on of my rich suit of wedding garments. 'So that I desire', says the believer, 'to be clothed upon.' He would be braw,[5] and he cannot be braw enough, for his Bridegroom. But the bride, or believer, knows that the Bridegroom will prepare a suit for him. And in a word, some folk say of their clothes that they were never well since they put them on. But we are sure that we shall be for ever well after we have put this heavenly clothing on. The witness of the Spirit continues with them. They shall continue and last through all eternity so. Oh, happy soul that never rests till it come to look upon the terrors of death, like one just putting off his old clothes, and putting on a suit of new robes or apparel, to meet the blessed bridegroom of souls, 'that mortality might be swallowed up of life'! 'I would be through death', says the believer, 'and I must be through it. I would have mortality swallowed up of life, and I would die once and never die more. My dying shows me to be mortal, but I shall be immortal after that. I would have it over once for all.' Only these desires are with great submission. He submits to the disposal of God, that mortality might be swallowed up of life.

Now in the next verse here are sweet things: 'He that hath wrought us unto the selfsame thing is God, who hath also given unto us the earnest of the Spirit.' This shows that he makes no more haste than good-speed, as we sometimes say; for all desires without these things are foolish. They are sinful desires; till these experiences take place I am wrought to it and have the earnest of it. We shall not speak further on this preparation, having noticed somewhat anent it already; but we think that right preparation has
1. An interest in Christ.
2. Blessedness. 'Blessed is that servant that, when his master comes, shall find him so doing', that is, the great preparation. And the thing we should look well to is to have an interest in Christ and to be diligent in the work of mortification and holiness. 'He that hath wrought us unto this selfsame thing is God.' And there are these three things included in it.

First, it is God that has in effect wrought that in us.
Secondly, it is that same God that has wrought that fitness in us for that

kingdom and glorious inheritance above, 'with the saints in light and glory'.

And lastly, he has given the earnest of the Spirit, and that makes all sure. We have fitness and we have aptness and we have the earnest of the Spirit, and that ensures all to us.

II. Sermon

Hebrews 13:14: *'For here we have no continuing city, but we seek one to come.'*

In vain would we hope to bring men to a course of godliness, considering how averse the flesh is to it, and in vain would we deal with ourselves for that purpose, if great and real advantage lay not in taking that way. Whatever the flesh objects as to disadvantage, yet there is no real disadvantage in a religious life; yea, there is more advantage in this course than will make up for all other disadvantages. It were good that we were considering what advantages there are in this way and comparing our advantages with our disadvantages. It would gain our affections to it, considering that our Lord is calling us to leave all that which at last will prove our eternal ruin. As for anything lawful, he is not calling us to leave that; but we are not to idolize, or make a god, as it were, of it. Consider what he is calling us to pursue. It is that without which we cannot be eternally happy.

Now, this is the scope of the words. The apostle is here pressing that exhortation which he was giving in the thirteenth verse. Says he, 'Let us therefore go to him without the camp, bearing his reproach.' But this seems heavy, and therefore he puts in this reason in the text: 'For here we have no continuing city.' In these words, we have

Firstly the shortness of man's life signified. It is here compared to a city. In opposition to the present life, Paul sets forth the length of eternity: 'But we seek one to come.'

Secondly, there is the employment of those that leave it. How are they taken up? They are as travellers going from one place to another, until they at last come to their long abode, or resting-place, which is heaven.

Now the words hold forth these few things to us:

1. That man's continuance on earth and enjoyments of earthly things are but for a short time.

2. That the consideration of this short time on earth should take our hearts off from earthly things and set them upon Christ only.

3. That we must all flit and remove from this earth, for 'Here we have no continuing city.'

4. That all should be seeking after Christ and that city or eternal habitation of rest.

Now we shall speak to some of these.

I. The first thing which we proposed to speak to was that man has but a short time or lease on earth. The Spirit of God points it out by sundry expressions: 'Lord, make me know mine end, and the measure of my days.' And what is the answer? 'Behold, thou hast made my days as an hand breadth', yea shorter, 'and mine age is as nothing before thee.' Says Moses, when speaking of man's life, 'They are like a sleep; in the morning they are

like grass that groweth up, and in the evening it is cut down, and withereth.'
Our days are but as a thought; nay, the Holy Ghost points them out to be
shorter: 'For what is your life? It is even a vapour that appeareth a little, and
then vanisheth away.' It is rather a vapour than a reality. It is but a vapour
that continueth a little time. And does not experience prove all this? Are we
not here today and away tomorrow? The great thing we ought to consider
is that our time here is but short — a truth seldom minded and more seldom
laid to heart.

Use 1.   If our time here be short, it ought to be the better employed; it
should make us early up in the morning, and late up at night about our main
work. It becomes us,

1. To consider our ways and what belongs to our peace. It is a good advice
that Solomon gives us: 'Remember thy Creator in the days of thy youth,
before the evil days come'; and yet the most part of us, for all that is spoken
from the Word of the Lord concerning the shortness of man's life, think not
that our time is short, but long enough, and so remember not that the evil
days are coming upon us.

2.   We lie down, and know not if ever we shall rise up again. Should we not
then improve our time? For is there any person so certain of his life that he
can say, 'I shall live so long'? And is it not of God's good providence that it
is so short and so uncertain to us?

3.   Consider that it is not only short and uncertain, but also full of trouble
and misery. And is it not enough for every person? What is dying and a
decaying old age but labour and misery? And should not this be considered
and laid to heart, that our life is not only short and uncertain but full of
misery? And should not the time we now have be well employed on that
account?

4.   To incite you to employ your time, consider that the time is short and
the task is great. Are there not many strongholds of sin and corruption to
subdue and conquer? Has not man a little world to subdue in his own heart?
Now, lay these two together, that your time is short and your work great,
and this may make you employ and improve it to the best advantage.

5.   To provoke you to a right improving of time, consider further that
there is nothing of greater moment or concernment than eternity — an
eternity of happiness, or an eternity of misery. It were good for us that we
were considering this, and laying the preciousness of the soul in the balance
with all earthly things, that we might see which of them is of most value; for,
as our Lord says, 'What is a man profited, if he should gain the whole world,
and lose his own soul?'

6.   Consider that eternity is fast approaching and our Lord Jesus is coming
to judgement. His last words are 'Surely I come quickly'. And is Christ
hastening? Should not every believer then be hastening to meet him? If
believers loved Christ as well as he loves them, they would be more hasty
to meet him. It is a wonder to see what we are employed in, and yet never
employing our time aright.

Lastly, consider that the Bridegroom is coming, and the bride must be
prepared. It ought to be all our work or talk here to be ready to meet him,
that we may not be found unprepared. Oh, what a dreadful thing will it be

to be found unprepared when Christ comes — when the midnight cry is made: 'Behold the Bridegroom cometh, go ye out to meet him'!

Use 2. That we may further incite you to a right employing, or improving of time, consider the advantages that those who rightly employ their time have.

First, they have this advantage, that it keeps from many challenges of conscience that we otherwise might have. Oh, those who employ their time right have much peace! There are much comfort and good spoken to them. Indeed there are none that have such a peaceable outgate as that man who is still preparing and looking for it.

Secondly, it has this advantage, that it makes them have a clear and comfortable outgate, when they enter into eternity, when about to launch out of time. You have nothing in that case to do but to step into your Master's house. And oh, what sad thoughts they will have who have employed their time otherwise!

Thirdly, it has this advantage also, that all his refreshments are sweet who employs his time aright. His sleep is sweet, his waking is sweet and all is sweet. The wise man says that the 'rest of a labouring man is sweet', but especially when he has been about his master's work. Now we shall give you some directions how you may employ your time aright.

1.   You ought to divide your work into tasks, setting so many hours apart for hearing, so many for reading, praying, meditating, etc., and so many for your ordinary calling. It would be an excellent thing if we were tasking ourselves and saying, 'Such a thing we resolve to do, and such a thing we must do.' Oh, but this would make a Christian's work sweet to him!

2.   You should employ your time well. You must have much heavenly and sweet prayer. With the psalmist, 'Lord make me know mine end.' 'So teach us to number our days, that we may apply our hearts unto wisdom.' If this were our main care and principal petition, there would not be so much misspent time amongst us as there is.

3.   In the morning when we rise, we should be thinking upon our last end, and in the evening we should take an account how we have spent the day, and then be mourning over what we have done amiss therein.

Use 3. We should not be troubling our thoughts with vain prospects. Are there not many who have projected things for twenty years hence? And who knows if they shall live so long? But it were good for us that we were employing our time and casting off vain and foolish prospects. The apostle James speaks well to this: 'Go to, now, ye that say, today or tomorrow we will go to such a city, and continue there a year, whereas ye know not what shall be on the morrow.' If we would consider the shortness of our time we would think the care of every day enough for itself. But this is a burdening of ourselves with unnecessary cares, adding a load to a burden. Are not the cares of a day sufficient for itself? Why then do we care for tomorrow, or for many days hence? And further, you should consider that these unnecessary cares put the heart out of frame. They indispose the heart so that we cannot get our time so well spent as we ought. Nor do they only indispose for duty, but duties are jostled out; and these things that are at hand are put far off, and these things that are afar off are brought near. You know far off thoughts put death and eternity out of mind. And are there not many who when they put death, judgement and eternity far out of mind, are suddenly surprised by them. Now consider which of these are most necessary, and having found that which is most necessary, let your thoughts be employed about it.

Use 4. That the consideration of this shortness of our time should not only take off our hearts from earthly things, but it should even help to mitigate the cross and help to render it more easy, that we may suffer more contentedly. Our longest afflictions must be, as it were, but for a moment, since our time is but as a moment and shall shortly be at an end.

1. Consider, that even whilst we are eating, drinking, sleeping, etc., our time is fast elapsing, and all our crosses and afflictions ere long shall be ended. We speak this to believers; but for unbelievers, however bad their crosses may be, it were better for them that they were thus continued and lengthened out to them through all eternity. At death they emerge out of one woe only to enter into a greater woe and misery. But death to believers is an entrance into eternal happiness, and they ought to be more earnestly longing for it, as the hireling for the end of the day. It is strange that there is any intermission of afflictions in our moments of time, for a cross abides not always: there is still some intermission of it. Hence our life is compared to a weaver's shuttle: it slips through many threads in a little time and so steals away unperceived, or insensibly.

2. Consider that though you be under many crosses or afflictions, yet, if believers, you shall be freed from them all by Jesus Christ. Jesus Christ shall make up all your hardships. You shall shortly arrive at rest, and rest unto them that are weary — oh, how sweet is it! And a sweet rest it is for those who are seeking after him. But those who mind not Christ have nothing to do with this rest 'that remaineth for the people of God'. But, O believer, 'in thy Father's house are many mansions'! Thou mayst well be straitened here, but there are no straitening circumstances there.

II Is our life short? Then it becomes us to be moderate in all things, even in the use of all lawful enjoyments. The apostle inculcates this: 'The time is short: it remaineth that both they that have wives, be as they that have none; and they that weep, as though they weep not; and they that use this world, as not abusing it: for the fashion of this world passeth away.' It becomes us to be taking our hearts off from all earthly things and studying to be weaned from them, for what are they? They are as nothing. It is strange that we, who seek after other things, should be so taken up with such frivolous things. But those who weep for Christ's presence shall be made to rejoice. Now for directions how to get your hearts taken off from earthly things, take these two things.

1. Do not bestow too much of your time upon those things that are of a perishing nature. It is strange to see even believers so much taken up with the world and the cares of this life. This eats out the comfort of the soul, and where there is very much of this, there cannot be much prosperity in true godliness, and where there is much real godliness there cannot be much of this, these two being inconsistent with one another. We cannot serve God and mammon, for as the thoughts of the one rise up, the other goes down.

Is it not strange that we should be so much taken up with these things? The apostle gives it as a mark of those that perish: 'But they that will be rich fall into many temptations, and hurtful lusts, which drown men in destruction and perdition.'

2.   If thou wouldst have thy thoughts weaned from the world, as thou shouldst let it have little of thy time, so give it little of thy affections. If believers were doing this, they would be more cheerful; and he that is most cheerful in going about duty is most taken up with this city. 'But we seek for one to come', and consider what a stir it would make if Christ should come and take these things away and if our mountain were moved. Think what you would do if put to difficulties. Indeed it would be better if this world had none of our affections.

III.   This doctrine reproves those who cast away all thoughts of employing their time aright, and whose consciences tell them not of their misspending of time. It is the apostle's direction: 'See that ye walk not as fools, but as wise; redeeming the time, because the days are evil.' There are few of us, but what have our bygone time to take in again and redeem. In the short time we have to live, we ought to be as travellers who have sat their time till the day be far spent and are obliged to run more in one hour than in three before.

IV.   And from this we would pose you, 'Are you ready to meet Christ, and ready for eternity? Have you nothing to do but to come and meet him?' We say, 'Are you ready to step into eternity?' Well, if it be not so, you have need to be serious in time, for we are not sure of another day or another sermon. Consider eternity will come once, and if you spend not your time well it will be ill with you. Take the apostle's advice: 'Walk, while ye have the day.' Has God given you a day? Then you should be serious in it, for we wot not if we shall have another. And is it not a mercy that we are not lying in the bosom of the earth unprepared and unconverted? If you misspend this time, then wrath will come upon you. On the whole, these words are a direction to you, to consider the time is passing on, and ere long we must all away: 'For here we have no continuing city, but we seek one to come.'

Appendix II
Bibliographical notes

The first edition of the *Cloud of Witnesses,* published in 1714, contained some fragmentary notes of Cargill's life by Robert Hamilton, apparently drawn from personal recollection. It is evident from Hamilton's original manuscript, acquired by the National Library of Scotland in 1971, that these were substantially edited by the compilers before publication, and some details of particular incidents were omitted. Hamilton's notes were intended as a preface to a volume of Cargill's sermons (see Appendix I) though no reference is made in the *Cloud of Witnesses* to that intention.

Some further biographical material appeared in Robert Wodrow's *History of the Sufferings of the Church of Scotland,* published in 1721/2, drawn largely from the public records. A few additional reminiscences of Cargill were included in Wodrow's *Life of James Wodrow,* first published in 1828. The first and best-known biography of Cargill is Patrick Walker's *Some remarkable passages in the Life and Death of that singular exemplary holy in life, zealous and faithful to the death, Mr Daniel [sic] Cargill,* published in 1732. Walker had been a frequent hearer of Cargill after Cargill's return from England in April 1681, and his account gives a fairly full record of the last three months of his life. It is, however, virtually silent about Cargill's earlier years, for Walker was only a youth of fourteen or fifteen when he heard Cargill preach and his personal recollection of him does not appear to go back beyond the beginning of 1681. Walker's account has been several times reprinted, the latest being under the title *Six Saints of the Covenant,* edited by Dr David Hay Fleming, in 1901. John Howie's *Scots Worthies,* published in 1775, contained a biographical notice of Cargill based largely on Walker's narrative. In his *Collection of Lectures and Sermons,* published in 1779, Howie included some previously unpublished material from Hamilton's manuscript, which he later incorporated in his second edition of the *Scots Worthies* in 1781.

Of the three more modern 'Lives' those published by G. M. Bell in 1837 and by Rev. W. H. Carslaw in 1900 are largely résumés of the better known facts of Cargill's life, the latter including some extract notes of his sermons from a previously unpublished manuscript of John Howie. The brief biographical sketch published by Jean Watson in 1880 shows a sensitive appreciation of Cargill's work and witness and has some perceptive insights into his character.

Cargill has, of course, figured prominently in the standard works on the period such as Smellie's *Men of the Covenant,* J. King Hewison's *The Covenanters* and other similar works. More recent publications of this kind are *Light in the North* (J. D. Douglas, 1964), *Fair Sunshine* (J. Purves, 1968), *Torchbearers of the Truth* (A. S. Horne, 1968) and *The Two Kingdoms* (Mrs E. Whitley, 1977) — all of them to one degree or another in sympathy with Cargill's position. There is also a valuable unpublished thesis by Robert B. Tweed (Ph.D., Edinburgh, 1964) on Cargill's family background and other formative influences, drawing largely on material researched by Dr Featherston Cargill, a family genealogist.

Appendix III
Mementoes of Cargill

Cargill's Bible, his signature in the Matriculation Register at St Salvator's College and a copy of the Solemn League and Covenant signed twice by him are preserved in the library of the University of St Andrews. Some other original documents are preserved in Register House, Edinburgh. These include an acknowledgement of payment for the education of the six Beaton children, signed by Cargill and his wife, Margaret Brown, on 19 April 1656, a letter written to David Beaton of Bandone on 28 March 1657 and Cargill's signed confession before the Privy Council. The testimonial of the Glasgow Presbytery to Robert M'Ward, bearing Cargill's signature as Moderator, is preserved in the National Library of Scotland.

A cairn has been erected to Cargill's memory at Hatton, and there is a memorial tablet to him in Rattray Parish Church.[1] At Covington Mill a small monument marks the place of his capture by Irvine of Bonshaw in 1681.

A number of elegiac poems were written in Cargill's memory after his death. These are of very small value as poetry, but they do provide some idea of the honour in which his name was held, and they have about them a poignancy and pathos often absent from more refined verse. One early example, written in the form of an acrostic on his name, runs as follows:

> Did not this star in Scotland reign
> Once in our orb full bright?
> Now ceasèd from its old abode
> Ascended up on height.
> Lo, in this land this star did shine.
> Did not we his beams see?
> Comforted with his Master's love
> As faithful ones did see.
> Reigned in his time so faithfully
> God's people for to teach;
> In giving warning faithfully
> Lo he the truth did preach.

Another, of considerably more literary merit, was published in 1741:

> Most sweet and savoury is thy fame,
> And more renowned is thy name,
> Surely, than any can record,
> Thou highly favoured of the Lord!
> Exalted thou on earth didst live;
> Rich grace to thee the Lord did give.
> During the time thou dwelt'st below,
> On in a course to heaven didst go.
> Not casten down with doubts and fears,
> Assured of heaven near thirty years,
> Labour thou didst in Christ's vineyard;
> Diligent wast, no time thou spared.
> Christ's standard thou didst bear alone,
> After others from it were gone,
> Right zeal for truth was found in thee,
> Great sinners censur'dst faithfully.
> In holding truth didst constant prove,
> Laidst down thy life out of true love.

Typical of other early productions is the following:

> Oh, famous, famous, once he was
> Oh, now more famous is,
> For he God's truth in Scotland taught
> As is well known by his.
>
> For Iss'char like he did not crouch
> When storms they did arise,
> But Naphtal' like jeopard' himself
> Against God's enemies.
>
> Until the time his work he end'
> His Master did him keep,
> And then to seal the truths of God
> Led was like to a sheep.
>
> Unto the shambles he was brought
> Even in that bloody town,
> And thus the truths of God he sealed
> And so he got his crown.

Finally, a quaint little piece in irregular metre, apparently composed very shortly after his death:

> Oh, zealous, zealous in his day!
> His work, ye see, does say
> He did the truth declare
> To all that needy were,
> The truth he spake
> To Christ's poor sheep
> To feed
> In need
> As is well known
> By Christ alone.
> For he of nature meek
> Could not endure the beik[2]
> Until his charge he had resigned
> To God who had him sent.

Select bibliography

Bell, G.M., *The Life of the Rev. Donald Cargill*, 1837.

Carslaw, W.H., *Donald Cargill*, 1900.

Cloud of Witnesses, 1714.

Fleming, Dr David Hay, *Proceedings of Society of Antiquaries of Scotland*, 1910/11.

Howie, John, *Scots Worthies*, 1775: *A Collection of Lectures and Sermons*, 1779.

M'Millan, John, *A Collection of Letters*, 1764.

Tweed, Robert B., *Donald Cargill, Covenanter: A Background Study, with special reference to his family connections and other formative influences (unpublished) Ph.D., Edinburgh*, 1964.

Walker, P., *Some remarkable passages in the Life and Death of that singular exemplary holy in life and death, Mr Daniel Cargill*, 1732.

Watson, Jean, *Donald Cargill*, 1880.

Wodrow, R., *History of the Sufferings of the Church of Scotland*, 1721/2: *Life of James Wodrow*, 1828.

Notes

Chapter 1
1. *Register of presentations to benefices,* vol. 1, fol. 106; *Registrum secreti sigilli,* vol. VI, no. 2504.
2. *Admission of Notaries Public, Original Warrants,* no. 71.
3. The date of Cargill's birth has long been shrouded in doubt, and even now it is impossible to determine it with complete accuracy. It can be shown convincingly, however, that the traditional dates of 1610 and 1619 are both significantly wide of the mark, and that at the time of his death Cargill was a considerably younger man than is commonly thought. As Dr David Hay Fleming pointed out *(Six Saints of the Covenant,* vol. II pp. 199-203) the traditional dates are derived from the first and second editions of John Howie's *Scots Worthies,* the date appearing as 1619 in the first edition and 1610 in the second. The absence of any apparent reason for the difference led Dr Hay Fleming to suggest that a typographical error had crept into the text of the second edition, a supposition which seems to be confirmed by the damaged appearance of the '0' in '1610', and most subsequent writers have chosen to accept the later date. Howie himself had no first-hand knowledge of Cargill's background and, as Dr Hay Fleming suggested, he may well have based his date on Patrick Walker's statement that Cargill was 'past sixty years' at the time of his death in 1681. Walker had, of course, seen Cargill and heard him preach, and he seems to have been personally acquainted with one of his relatives in Edinburgh from whom he could have gathered some of the materials for his biography.

There are, however, obvious difficulties about the traditional date, which have been remarked upon by several writers. For one thing, Cargill is known to have entered St Andrews University in 1645, when on Howie's reckoning he would have been twenty-five or twenty-six years of age — unusually old for a first-year student. Again, Robert Hamilton, who knew him personally, records that 'After that he had perfected his philosophy course at the University of St Andrews, his father, a godly and religious gentleman, pressed much upon him to study divinity in order to fit him for the ministry' *(Cloud of Witnesses,* 1714, p. 261). It is difficult to imagine a man of twenty-nine or thirty years of age, as Cargill would then have been, being advised by his father on his life's vocation, let alone being unsure of it himself, and it is clear that some explanation must be found to account for the difficulty. There are other indications too which point to an earlier date than the traditional one. In a letter written in 1657 by James Sharp to Robert Douglas *(Register of Consultations of ministers of Edinburgh,* vol. II, p. 11), Cargill is referred to as a 'young expectant' at the time of his entry to the ministry some two to three years earlier, when according to the traditional date he would have been thirty-four or thirty-five years of age. Again, according to Patrick Walker's account, Cargill preserved his physical fitness until his latest years: he 'ran fast on foot' when escaping from his pursuers and, whatever truth there may be in the popular tradition of his leap over the Ericht, it is clear that the feats of physical endurance recorded of him in later life could hardly have been supported by a man as advanced in years as the traditional date would make him to be.

Clearly then there are strong indications that the tradition of a man 'past sixty' *(Six Saints of the Covenant,* vol. II, p.3) or even 'seventy' (James Dodds, *Fifty Years Struggle of the Scottish Covenanters,* p. 261) is far from correct. On the other hand the task of establishing the true date is no easy one. The Rattray Parish Register, potentially the most promising source of information, records the births of no fewer than four children by the name of Donald Cargill between 1610 and 1616, but it has been conclusively proved (Dr Hay Fleming, *Six Saints of the Covenant,* vol. II, pp. 199-203) that none of these is the subject of this biography. The register ends in December 1621, following which there is a thirty-year gap, so that no further definite information can be gathered from that source.

The register does, however, provide one clue to the solution of the problem. As sons of Donald Cargill, the local reader and notary, John Cargill and his brother Lawrence were often called upon to act as witnesses to baptisms, and their names appear regularly in the register together with that of their father. In the earlier entries John is referred to merely as 'eldest son of Donald Cargill of Kirktoun of Rattray', his father's domicile. In March 1614, however, he is mentioned for the first time as 'portioner of Haltoun of Rattray', showing that he had then acquired part of the estate of Haltoun (Hatton) in his own right. The reason for this becomes clear a little later, when the register refers to his marriage. Clearly then John Cargill had bought his portion of Hatton as a future home for himself and his wife and as a base from which to carry on his business.

John's brother Lawrence, on the other hand, is never associated with a domicile of his own, but continues to be referred to merely as 'son of Donald Cargill of Kirktoun of Rattray' up to the close of the register in 1621. The presumption is therefore that at that time he was still unmarried, a supposition which is confirmed by the absence from the register of any reference to his marriage. Had it taken place during the register's currency it would almost certainly have been recorded, since the register seems to have been kept by old Donald Cargill himself and it records in detail the marriages of the other members of his family and the births of their children.

So Lawrence Cargill was unmarried and his son Donald not yet born at the end of 1621. This negative evidence, important as it is, does not, of course, go far enough, and the gap in the register after that date makes it necessary to seek evidence from other sources. Two of these are particularly important and go a long way towards solving the problem. In the *Register of the Great Seal* (vol. IX, no. 193) there is a confirmation of a Charter dated at Alyth on 10 February 1630, which itself confirms an earlier contract made at Kirktoun of Rattray on 26 and 30 May 1626, by which Lawrence Cargill, 'sometime of Kirktoun' bought from William Chalmer the estate and lands of Nether Cloquhat. Lawrence is mentioned in another source *(Laing Charters,* no. 1981) as being resident in Nether Cloquhat in November 1626. The parallel with his brother John is apparent: Lawrence can be assumed to have bought this estate as a preliminary to his own marriage, which on that basis would have taken place some time in the summer of 1626. His son Donald, who is known from other sources to have been the eldest member of the family (cf. *Perthshire Sasines,* 1 August 1665) could therefore have been born no earlier than the spring of 1627 and perhaps as late as 1628. This would make him sixteen or seventeen years old on his entry to university in 1645, and twenty-five or twenty-six at the commencement of his ministry eight years later, conclusions which agree much more readily with the contemporary evidence mentioned earlier.

One possible difficulty, however, remains. On the basis of his birth in 1627 Cargill would have been no more than fifty-four at the time of his death in 1681, whereas Patrick Walker, who both saw and heard him, refers to him several times as an 'old man'. The difficulty is, however, probably more apparent than real. At the time of which he wrote Walker himself was no more than fourteen or fifteen years old and to the eye of youth a man past fifty could well have appeared 'old'. More probably, however, Walker's recollection is true enough from the point of view of visual observation, for his memory of people and events, even many years afterwards, was often surprisingly accurate. On that basis his account can be taken as a touching testimony to the effect of Cargill's trials and privations in later years upon his personal appearance, which led his contemporaries and even those closest to him to take him to be considerably older than he actually was.

4.   The whole question of Cargill's family background and relations was investigated earlier this century with great thoroughness by Dr Featherston Cargill (1870-1959), a family genealogist. Dr Cargill's findings are reflected in an unpublished thesis by Robert B. Tweed (Ph.D, Edinburgh, 1964) on Cargill's family connections and other formative influences, which forms the basis of the first part of this chapter.

5.   The available evidence suggests strongly that Cargill was surrounded from his earliest days by influences sympathetic to the reformed faith and Presbyterian tradition, and that in all probability he grew up in the company of contemporaries who shared the same kind of upbringing. On his father's side this influence was derived, of course, from his grandfather, who had been nurtured in the Reformation period and was old enough to have remembered Knox. Donald would have been too young to remember his father's brother John, who died when he would have been about five

years old, but there is strong evidence to suggest that he formed a
particularly close friendship with John's son, also called Donald, who was
ten years his senior. John's son obviously shared the same home
background and later became an elder in Rattray Kirk. A fellow-elder of
the same period was George Drummond, Donald's uncle by marriage, who
had married Lawrence Cargill's sister Grissell. Drummond's
granddaughter Marjory subsequently married Thomas Whitson, a local
notary and close friend of the Cargill family, who later himself became an
elder in Rattray. Whitson appears to have been a close friend of Cargill in
later years, and their names appear frequently as joint signatories in bonds
and other legal documents.

On his mother's side Donald Cargill had the advantage of similar family
influences. Two of his first cousins were prominent supporters of the
Presbyterian position. John Robertson, a grandson by marriage of James
Blair, the eldest member of his mother's family, was a contemporary in age
and a fellow-student at St Andrews. He became minister of Meigle in
Perthshire in 1650 and was ejected for nonconformity in 1662. Thomas
Lundie, who was minister of Rattray Church from 1637 until his deposition
for nonconformity in 1664, was a son of Jean Blair, Cargill's mother's sister;
and Patrick Blair, another cousin on his mother's side, with whom Cargill
appears to have lodged during his stay in Aberdeen, seems to have shared
the same sympathies. From his earliest days therefore and during important
stages of his development, Donald Cargill was surrounded by influences
strongly favouring the reformed position. That these influences helped to
mould his character and outlook there can be no doubt, and in his earlier
years they would certainly have provided strong reinforcement for the
home teaching he received from his father. Lundie in particular, as his
parish minister, may well have exercised the most powerful external
influence, though since Donald was absent from home from about the age
of ten or eleven it is to Aberdeen and St Andrews, rather than to his home
in Rattray, that we must look for the influences which were most decisive
in shaping the future course of his career.

6.   There was a large collateral branch of the Cargill family in Aberdeen,
though Donald Cargill does not seem to have had any association with it
during his stay. The family of Thomas Cargill, merchant, had achieved
particular eminence: one son, David, had been a burgess of the city and had
held the offices of Dean of Guild and Burgh Treasurer; a second, James,
had been a Doctor of Medicine and left a generous bequest to the Grammar
School; and a third, Thomas, had been headmaster of the Grammar School
from 1580 to 1602.

7.   Cargill's name is preserved in the *Matriculation Register of St Salvator's
College* for 1645. As was customary, he signed his name in its Latinized
form 'Donaldus Cargill'.

8.   It has been suggested that the wife of Thomas Lundie, Anna Somervill,
had family connections in the Bothwell area (cf. *Register of Deeds,
MacKenzie's Office,* vol. XIV, p. 93).

9.   To the end of his life Rutherford maintained his testimony against civil
interference in church government. 'We acknowledge all due obedience in

the Lord to the king's majesty; but we disown that ecclesiastical supremacy in and over the church which some ascribe to him: that power of commanding external worship, not appointed in the Word, and laying bonds upon the consciences of men, where Christ has made them free . . . Christ is a free independent Sovereign, King and Lawgiver. The Father has appointed him his own King in Mount Sion, and he cannot endure that the powers of the world should encroach upon his royal prerogative, and prescribe laws to him . . . The lordly and spiritual government over the church is given unto Christ, and none else. He is the sole ecclesiastic Lawgiver' (S. Rutherford, *Testimony to the Covenanted Work of Reformation*, 1726).

10. In Hew Scott's *Fasti Ecclesiae Scoticanae* (vol. III, p. 392) Cargill is said to have been 'licensed by Presbytery of St Andrews, 13 April 1653'. This statement is, however, without support in contemporary sources and appears to be based on a misunderstanding or misreading of the record.

The relevant entry in the *St Andrews Presbytery Register* is: 'April 13 1653. The doctrine John 15 vv. 13-14 delivered by Mr Patrick Scougall censured and approven, follows Mr Andrew Honeyman to make and Mr Donald Cargill to add.' The reference here is to the 'exercise', or period of devotions, with which each meeting of the presbytery began, and in which all the ministers took part by rotation. The common practice was for a book of Scripture to be worked through — in this case the Gospel of John — with two or three verses being considered at each meeting. The exercise generally consisted of two parts: the first, the 'making', also known as the 'delivery of the doctrine', consisting of an analysis and interpretation of the text, and the second, the 'adding', developing and applying its doctrine in a series of devotional 'uses'. In the St Andrews Presbytery it was customary for three ministers to take part in each exercise, so that one of the duties was gone through twice.

Several of the exercises performed by ministers in the presbytery have been preserved, including a few by Cargill. The register records three further occasions on which he took part in the exercise, on 1 and 15 March 1654, when he gave the 'addition', and on 29 March when he 'delivered the doctrine'. On the last two of these occasions his work was 'censured and approven' by the presbytery.

Since the register suggests that only ministers already licensed, whether holding settled charges or not, took part in the regular exercise, it is clear that Cargill was licensed before 13 April 1653 when he conducted the exercise for the first time; and since the register nowhere records his trials for licence, which it certainly would have done had he been licensed by the presbytery, it is equally clear that he had undergone these elsewhere.

The probability is therefore that on completing his divinity course in 1652 Cargill applied for, and obtained, licence from his 'home' presbytery of Dunkeld, though since the records of the Dunkeld Presbytery for this period have not survived this cannot now be proved conclusively.

There is also the interesting possibility that the Dunkeld Presbytery from whom Cargill received licence was not the regular presbytery of that name but the separate 'Protester' Presbytery which functioned from 1651 until about 1660 (cf. *Fasti,* vol. IV, p. 140). This supposition gains added credence from the fact that one of the members of the separatist presbytery was Cargill's own parish minister and first cousin, Thomas Lundie, who had undoubtedly had an important influence on his early development. A counter-argument to this theory is that the St Andrews Presbytery, where Rutherford was in a Protester minority of one, would hardly have accepted into its fellowship a licentiate with credentials of this sort. There is, however, some evidence that the presbytery did indeed have some doubts about Cargill's qualifications, for when they were approached by the Cupar Presbytery to release him to preach at Strathmiglo their approval was given subject to 'his testimonial being clear'. If this is to be taken, as the context suggests, as a reference to the testimonial Cargill had brought with him from his licensing presbytery, the supposition that he had been licensed by the Protester presbytery is further strengthened.

Curiously enough, the two men with whom Cargill shared his first exercise in the St Andrews Presbytery later became bishops in the post-Restoration church, Scougall at Aberdeen and Honeyman in Orkney.

11. The record of Cargill's call to Strathmiglo, and the controversy which surrounded it, is preserved in the extant minutes of the Cupar Presbytery. In 1733 the Rev. George Logan, minister of Trinity College Church, Edinburgh, used the record of the call to support his case in a controversy then being waged about the method of electing ministers to vacant charges (*An Account of the Method of Electing a Minister to the Parish of Strathmiglo,* pp. 8-9; cf. also Warrick, *Moderators of the Church of Scotland from 1690 to 1740,* p. 370).

12. The character of the opposition to Cargill may be judged from the fact that one of the three objectors to his settlement was William Barclay, former minister of Falkland, who had been deposed in 1645 for his support of Montrose. Barclay was readmitted to his charge under the new episcopal order in 1663 and appears to have been a close friend and confidant of James Sharp. Sharp himself denied a charge by James Guthrie that Cargill's settlement had been opposed on the ground of the Protester/Resolutioner controversies (*Register of Consultations of Ministers of Edinburgh,* vol. II, p. 11) but his denial was made in qualified terms and there seems no reason to doubt Guthrie's version of the facts. Curiously enough, it was almost certainly Barclay whom Richard Cameron later assisted when he acted as 'schoolmaster and precentor to the curate in Falkland', as Patrick Walker records (*Six Saints of the Covenant,* vol. I, p. 218).

13. The Barony parish had been formed some eighty years earlier from the rural or landward part of the parish of Glasgow, and its congregation met at this time in the crypt of the cathedral or high kirk. The accommodation in the crypt was none of the best and preaching in it must have been something of an ordeal: 'Being of an arched roof, which is low, and supported by a great number of massy pillars, it is exceedingly dark, dirty and incommodious' (*Statistical Account of Scotland,* 1794, vol. III, p. 120). A separate church was not provided for the parish until the end of the eighteenth century; the present building, the third to house the congregation, dates from 1889.

14. The entry in the presbytery register for 21 February 1655 is in these terms: 'A testimonial being desired for Mr Donald Cargill's exercising here and preaching in these bounds, and his conversation while he remained here, referred to the next day.' On 21 March occurs the final brief record: 'Mr Donald Cargill's testimonial delayed.' The terms of the entry for 21 February, with its lack of any reference to his licensing, corroborate the impression of a temporary association with the presbytery rather than a relationship of any standing.

15. *Cloud of Witnesses,* 1714, p. 262. The month of Cargill's ordination — but not the date — is preserved in Robert Hamilton's original manuscript notes (see Appendix II). Neither the records of the Barony Kirk session nor the Glasgow Presbytery during the period of Cargill's ministry have survived, but certain of the Glasgow Synod records for 1654-55 are preserved among the *Wodrow MSS.* Cargill's name first appears, as a member of the Glasgow Presbytery, in the Roll of Synod for 15-17 May 1655.

Chapter 2

1. In a document dated at Blebo on 19 April 1656 Cargill and Lady Blebo acknowledged receipt of the sum of 1,400 merks from Robert Beaton for the education and maintenance of the six Beaton children from Whitsunday 1655 to Whitsunday 1656 *(Blebo Writs,* 2.43). The names of the children were Andrew, John, David, Margaret, Mary and Elizabeth.

2. The date of Cargill's marriage, together with other family details mentioned in this chapter, is preserved in a document in the *Blebo Writs* (1.52).

3. 'When it happens that the marriage has been dissolved within a year and a day, and without a living child, the relationship is not by the law regarded as of a character so permanent that the *jus relictae,* or the *jus mariti,* are to have effect... The husband yields up the possession of his wife's heritage, and is bound to restore to the representatives of the wife all the wife's moveable funds which he has received on occasion of the marriage, whether by the mere operation of law or by convention and marriage contract' (Bell, *Commentaries on the Law of Scotland,* vol. I, p.679).

4. As part of her marriage settlement with Andrew Beaton, Lady Blebo was entitled to an annuity of 14 chalders of grain and 1,000 merks yearly from the Blebo estate. Her personal assets at the time of her death amounted only to £133 6s. 8d., the value of 32 bolls of grain in the granary at Blebo. She was, however, owed a further £1,165 6s. 8d. by five of the Blebo tenants in respect of outstanding rent payments in feu-duty and produce for the years 1655 and 1656 *(Register of Confirmed Testaments,* Glasgow, 28 March 1657).

5. The merk was equivalent to two-thirds of a Scots pound, and since a Scots pound was worth only one-twelfth of the English pound 1,300 merks represented about £72 sterling.

6. *Register of Deeds, MacKenzie's Office,* vol. 11, p. 507: *Charters and other Documents relating to the City of Glasgow,* vol. II, pp. 322-3. The

contract is dated 20 September 1658. Under an agreement with the commissioners of the former Duke of Lennox, the Council were obliged to pay the Barony minister's stipend for so long as he continued to hold the charge. There is little doubt that the reason for their difficulty in Cargill's case was the failure on the part of the Barony landowners to make timely payment of the 'teinds' due by them to the Council for the maintenance of the Barony ministry. The Council's negotiations with Cargill appear to have started very soon after his settlement in the parish in 1655, and by the following year they had apparently agreed in principle to pay him the equivalent of 8 chalders of grain (128 bolls) yearly. It was a further two years, however, before the arrangement was put on a formal basis. The finally agreed figure represented the equivalent value of 8 chalders at 10 merks the boll, plus an additional 20 merks over and above. Characteristically, Cargill had a clause inserted in the contract that the agreement should not prejudice his successors in office from seeking a larger stipend.

Chapter 3
1.   The early writers on the persecution can scarcely find words strong enough to express their abhorrence of Sharp. To John Howie he was 'that arch-traitor to the Lord and his Christ', and to Patrick Walker 'that monster of wickedness'. Even the more restrained Wodrow calls him an 'infamous and time-serving person' and 'a cunning apostate'.

It may be remarked here, however, that while agreeing in their detestation of Sharp and the policy he represented, the early writers are at variance on other matters. Robert Wodrow was critical of the editors of the *Cloud of Witnesses* for publishing some testimonies which he considered to be extreme and of 'no great service to the interests of religion and the kingdom of Christ' (*History*, III, p. 226). Patrick Walker, on the other hand, criticized the *Cloud* for omitting the testimony of Alexander Russel, which the editors had left out because certain things in it were 'not very conveniently expressed' (*Six Saints of the Covenant*, 1901, vol. I, pp. 330-1). Walker strongly censured Wodrow for giving what he considered to be a distorted and prejudiced account of Cameron, Cargill and Renwick and for unduly favouring the ministers who accepted the Indulgence (*Ibid.*, p. 294 *et seq.*). Wodrow, in his turn, thought Walker's *Life of Peden* to contain 'a heap of singular things... rude and undigested... not in my opinion agreeable to the spirit of Christianity' (*Wodrow Correspondence*, p. 230). And John Howie, who drew extensively on Walker's narrative, did not hesitate to criticize him for portraying Robert Hamilton as an extremist (*Scots Worthies*, 1775, p. 601 note).

Chapter 4
1.   For most of his exile M'Ward was closely associated with the Scottish Church in Rotterdam. In January 1676, when the church was raised to the status of a collegiate charge, he was formally settled as joint minister of the congregation. He was obliged, however, to resign this office in February 1677 when, under pressure from the British Government, the Dutch

authorities ordered him and two of his fellow-exiles, John Brown and James Wallace, to withdraw from the country temporarily. He returned after an absence of little over a year, Robert Fleming having meantime been appointed minister in his place. In his remaining years M'Ward was much preoccupied with the controversy over the Indulgence, on which he felt very deeply; his views on this subject, in opposition to the case advanced by Fleming for union with the complying ministers, were published long after his death under the title *Earnest Contendings* (1723). His closing years were clouded by internal dissension in the Rotterdam congregation which originated during the temporary stay of the fugitives from Bothwell (see chapter 9). M'Ward died in Rotterdam on 26 May 1681.

2.   Opinion has been divided on whether this incident took place on the first anniversary of the Restoration (1661) or the second (1662). The two early sources (Patrick Walker and Robert Hamilton) are unspecific on the subject. The evidence, however, points strongly to 1662, for if Cargill had preached his sermon on the first anniversary in 1661 it is surprising that the Council's proclamation against him was so long delayed; and since the act ordaining the 'solemn anniversary thanksgiving' was published only on 13 May his failure to observe the occasion could well have been overlooked on the grounds of ignorance. In 1662 29 May fell on a Thursday, and there is strong evidence to suggest that Thursday was Cargill's normal preaching day (compare his rebuke by the woman in James Durham's house). The fact that Cargill was moderator of the Glasgow Presbytery at the beginning of 1662, when the testimonial to M'Ward was drawn up, seems to settle the matter conclusively.

3.   According to Patrick Walker, Cargill went on to say, 'Whoever of the Lord's people are this day rejoicing, their joy will be like the crackling of thorns under a pot; it will soon be turned to mourning. He [i.e., the king] will be the woefullest sight that ever the poor Church of Scotland saw. Woe, woe, woe to him! His name shall stink while the world stands for treachery, tyranny and lechery.' Walker asserts that he 'had this account from several old Christians who were his hearers that day'. Notwithstanding this, however, there must be serious doubts about the accuracy of Walker's account. It is hardly likely, for one thing, that Cargill would go out of his way on this occasion to make an outspoken personal attack on the king, and the vigour of his language as reported by Walker is uncharacteristic of his public utterances. It is surprising too that if Cargill did speak in such terms the consequences for him were not much more serious than in fact they were. M'Ward had been banished the kingdom the previous year for a much milder offence and had narrowly escaped execution. On the other hand, it is not beyond belief that Cargill did deliver himself at some stage of such opinions as Walker records, since the expression 'His name shall stink while the world stands,' is later recorded as being applied by him to John Gibb. The likelihood is therefore that the words reported, or terms similar to them, were used by Cargill among a group of friends — as was his denunciation of Gibb — to depict his forebodings of the evils about to befall the church and his view of the king as the author of them.

4.   On 24 October 1662 the Town Council ordered payment of the out-

standing balance (650 merks) of Cargill's stipend for the year 1661, 'notwithstanding any ordinance of before in the contrair' (*Extracts from the Records of the Burgh of Glasgow*, 1630-1662, p. 494).

Chapter 5

1. *Perthshire Register of Sasines*, 1 August 1665.
2. *Perthshire Register of Sasines*, 18 December 1665.
3. *Perthshire Register of Sasines*, 29 June 1670.
4. *Perthshire Register of Sasines*, 22 November 1671 and 27 June 1678.
5. *Perthshire Register of Sasines*, 26 October 1670.
6. *Rattray Parish Register*, 5 August 1666.
7. *Register of Deeds, MacKenzie's Office*, 10 June 1672, 26 June 1673 and 20 May 1675; *Durie's Office*, 1 December 1670 and 29 September 1719; *Perthshire Hornings*, 27 May 1672; *Perthshire Inhibitions*, 2 July 1670; *Perthshire Sasines*, 26 October 1670 and 10 January 1672.
8. *Perthshire Hornings*, 27 May 1672; *Perthshire Inhibitions*, 7 January 1676 and 31 May 1678.
9. A further act of generosity on Cargill's part was to be seen in 1673, when he granted his brother James, now forced through financial stress to give up his occupancy of Bonnytown, a permanent tenancy of part of the Hatton estate for the relatively modest sum of 1800 merks. There is some evidence to suggest that Cargill's tenants at Hatton were not regular in their payments, and that this was partly responsible for his later financial troubles. At least two of the debts were still outstanding at the time of his death in 1681.
10. The issue of the proclamation at Forfar, rather than at Perth, seems to suggest that Cargill was mainly based in Angus during his years of banishment. See also chapter 15, note 4.
11. It is likely that one of those who interposed on his behalf was David Beaton of Bandone, with whom Cargill seems to have enjoyed good relations despite the earlier disagreement with his father over Lady Blebo's estate. Among his own relatives support may have come from John Blair, his mother's brother, who was a Justice of the Peace for the county of Perth, and possibly also from George Drummond, a Bailie and later Lord Provost of Edinburgh, who was a brother-in-law of Cargill's cousin Donald.

Chapter 6

1. The eloquence of Blackader's description (*Memoirs*, 1826, pp. 182-9) has often been remarked upon (cf. Herkless, *Richard Cameron*, pp. 66-8; Smellie, *Men of the Covenant*, 1905 ed., pp. 179-81). It is not, however, original, despite the quotation marks misleadingly used by his editor Andrew Crichton (cf. *The Bass Rock*, 1848, p. 335, note). Blackader's own description, preserved in the *Wodrow MSS*, is considerably less polished, though graphic.

Blackader does not give the date of the East Nisbet communion, but in Robert Garnock's narrative (*Scots Worthies*, 1781 ed., p. 439) it is given as 20-22 April 1677. The year, however, is an insertion by the editor, John Howie, and is certainly incorrect. (It appeared in square brackets in the original editions, but these have unfortunately been omitted by subsequent editors.) In 1677 the dates quoted fell on a Friday/Sunday and not on a Saturday/Monday which was the period of the communion season. These dates did, however, fall on a Saturday/Monday in 1678, and the general context of Garnock's narrative (and of Blackader's) suggests strongly that this is the correct date. This is confirmed by the narrative of Mrs Goodal, who recalled that the East Nisbet communion was 'in the year 1678, in the spring of the year' (*Wodrow Soc., Select Biographies,* vol. II, p. 484). There is also a letter of 7 May 1678 from the Earl of Murray to The Duke of Lauderdale, in reply to one from Lauderdale of 30 April, (*Lauderdale Papers,* III, p. 88) which refers to a recent notable conventicle kept by John Welsh at 'Chirnside Moor in the Merse', Chirnside being in the close vicinity of East Nisbet.

According to Blackader, the Irongray communion took place in 'June 1678' (*Memoirs,* original MS, not in published version). A despatch from a government correspondent in Dumfries, dated 1 June, states, 'A very great conventicle is to be within 5 miles of this tomorrow, and the sacrament to be given by Mr Welsh. 'Tis thought there will be above 7 or 8000 people at it' (*Calendar of State Papers,* 1678, p. 201). Welsh was the principal celebrant at Irongray and, since Irongray is some five miles from Dumfries, the evidence that this was indeed the notable Irongray communion is fairly conclusive. This certainly agrees with the sequence of other events recorded by Blackader at around the same period.

The date of the last and largest of the field communions of the time — that at Maybole in Carrick on 4 August 1678 — is well authenticated by a variety of sources (cf. *Register of the Privy Council,* Third Series, vol. 5, p. 495; John Howie, *A Collection of Lectures and Sermons,* 1779, p. 603 note).

Chapter 7
1.   A document in the *Wodrow MSS,* dated 22 August 1678, asserts that Cameron had been licensed five months earlier, i.e. in March of that year. If, as seems probable, he was licensed at the same time as Thomas Hog, the date of his licensing can be fixed as 7 March (see note 5).
2.   Patrick Walker credits two other young probationers, John Welwood and John Kid, with having preached separation from the complying ministers before Cameron (*Six Saints of the Covenant,* vol. I, pp. 333-4). Kid, who was among those executed after Bothwell, testified against the Indulgence in his dying speech (*Naphtali,* 1680, Part II, p. 39) though he was careful to add that this was 'without any offence given to the many godly and learned that are of another judgement'. Welwood, who died early in 1679, is said by Alexander Shields to have been 'among the first witnesses against that defection' (*Hind Let Loose,* 1687, p. 122). From his surviving letters Welwood is known to have been a close friend and correspondent of Cameron and could well have had an important influence on his early development.
3.   The other ministers, besides Welsh, were Archibald Riddell, Patrick Warner, Andrew Morton and George Barclay. Cameron preached from

Psalm 85:8: 'He will speak peace unto his people, and to his saints: but let them not turn again to folly.'

4.   Hamilton was a nephew by marriage of Bishop Burnet, to whom his activities seem to have been a source of some embarrassment: 'The person that led them had been bred by me, while I lived at Glasgow, being the younger son of Sir Thomas Hamilton that had married my sister, but by a former wife: he was then a lively hopeful young man, but getting into that company, and into their notions, he became a crackbrained enthusiast' (*History of His Own Time*, 1724, vol. I, p. 471).

5.   Hog was a son of Thomas Hog, minister of Larbert, who had been ejected from his charge in 1662 and was on the list of ministers named in the letters of intercommuning. He was licensed on 7 March 1678, probably at the same time as Richard Cameron (see note 1). A complaint was made against Hog, along with Cameron and Kid, to the meeting of ministers at Edinburgh in August 1678 to which Cameron was later summoned. In or about March 1679 he went over to Holland, where he seems to have received ordination at the hands of M'Ward and Brown. He was himself present at the ordination of Cameron and may have returned to Scotland with him later that year. He did not, however, take any further part in field-preaching and later chose to settle permanently in Holland, where he was successively minister of the Scottish churches at Delft, Campvere and Rotterdam. He died in Rotterdam in 1723, at the age of sixty-eight. The character of Hog's early preaching drew forth the commendation of Robert Hamilton, though in later years Hamilton was to claim that Hog's early zeal against the Indulgence had been a pretence, and he charged him and others with having attempted to prevent the ordination of James Renwick (*Faithful Contendings Displayed*, p. 214). He also levelled charges of a more personal nature against Hog and some of his former associates, alleging among other things that they had carried liquor to field-meetings (*Ibid*, p. 198). This, says Hamilton, 'was very heavy to some, particularly to Mr Cameron, Mr Cargill and Henry Hall, I shall name no more'. By a typical piece of distortion the latter charge was foisted upon Cameron and Cargill themselves by Mark Napier in his *Memorials of Claverhouse* (vol. II, p. 243). The grounds of Hamilton's accusations remain somewhat obscure. Patrick Walker, who was a shrewd judge of men, seems to have known Hog personally (*Six Saints of the Covenant*, vol. I, p. 236) and has nothing to say against him.

Chapter 8

1.   Phinehas was a grandson of Aaron, the brother of Moses, who averted the plague from the children of Israel by executing summary justice upon an Israelite prince and a woman of Midian whom he had brought into the camp (Numbers 25:6-9). He is commended in Scripture for his deed: 'Then stood up Phinehas, and executed judgement: and so the plague was stayed. And that was counted unto him for righteousness unto all generations for evermore' (Psalm 106:30-31).

   Jael was the wife of Heber the Kenite, who killed Sisera, captain of the host of Canaan, by driving a nail through his temples when he sought refuge in her tent from the pursuing Israelites (Judges 4:17-22). She too is commended: 'Blessed among women shall Jael the wife of Heber the Kenite be, blessed shall she be above women in the tent' (Judges 5:24).

2.   The version of the declaration given by Wodrow (*History,* III, pp. 66-7) is a more extended and developed one than that published in the contemporary *London Gazette* (9-12 June 1679) and concurrently in the *True Account of the Rising of the Rebels in the West of Scotland* (London, 1679). In particular, Wodrow's version includes a reference to the Indulgence which is not to be found in either of the contemporary versions. Since the latter agree in all but a few minor details with the copy later published by the United Societies (*Informatory Vindication,* 1687, pp. 116-8) there is no reason to regard them as other than authentic. Wodrow's surmise that the reference to the Indulgence is an evidence of Hamilton's desire to 'form their public appearances very soon against other Presbyterians, and the indulged in particular' is therefore without foundation.

3.   Hamilton, who was in command, had ordered that no quarter be given. By his own account, written in 1685, he seems to have personally put to death at least one of the enemy to whom some of his men wanted to offer quarter. He also appears to have ordered the execution of five more who were given quarter without his knowledge, but his commands, if given, were not carried out (*Faithful Contendings Displayed,* 1780, p. 201). To judge from a copy of Hamilton's letter in the *Laing Manuscripts,* the version published in the *Faithful Contendings,* edited by John Howie, is a considerable abridgement of the original, which gives a fuller and more positive account of Hamilton's actions in the latter incident. According to this version Hamilton wrote, 'There were five more that without my knowledge got quarter, who were brought to me after we were a mile from the place, as having got quarter, whom notwithstanding I desired might have been sent the same way that their neighbours were, and its not being done I reckoned ever amongst our first stepping aside.' The published version omits mention of Hamilton's desire that the men be 'sent the same way as their neighbours were' and relates the 'stepping aside' to the giving of quarter rather than to the failure to carry out execution (cf. also Dr David Hay Fleming, *Six Saints of the Covenant,* 1901, pp. 215-6). Apart from placing Hamilton's conduct in a sharper light the omitted words suggest strongly that more than one man was involved in the earlier incident, a fact which does not emerge clearly in the published version. The latter, incidentally, is the version quoted by Sir Walter Scott in *Old Mortality* (Nelson edition, p. 512).

4.   Hamilton later found himself having to justify his action against charges of compromise of principle. In his account of the incident, written in 1685, he records that the supplication was brought to him for signature on the morning of the 22nd — the day of the battle — when he was busily engaged in organizing the army. 'In the very midst of all these confusions came Mr William Blackader to me with a paper in one hand and pen and ink in the other, and told me he came from Mr Cargill with this supplication to Monmouth, and who begged me in all haste to send it over to him. I asked

him in haste if it was Mr Cargill's work, he said yes. Whereupon I did subscribe it without reading it' (*Faithful Contendings Displayed*, 1780, p. 195). The original document, bearing the subscription 'R Hamiltoune in naim of the Covenanted army now in armes', is preserved in the British Library (*Add. Mss.* 23244, fol. 14).

5.   One of the grounds for Cargill's later excommunication of Monmouth (see Chapter 11) was his 'refusing, that morning at Bothwell Bridge, a cessation of arms, for hearing and redressing their injuries, wrongs and oppressions'.

6.   It may be noted here that some of the 'traditional' incidents which have come to be associated with Drumclog and Bothwell Bridge may be traced to a so-called 'account' of both these events said to have been written by 'the Laird of Torfoot, an officer in the Presbyterian army', which first appeared in an American newspaper in the early nineteenth century. The 'account' does not itself seem to have been intended as a factual record of the events, but merely an idealistic reconstruction of them. Its high-flown and somewhat melodramatic style certainly bears out this impression.

7.   'I told Mr Cargill, he rendered himself odious by his naughty principles. He was very much offended with me' (Narrative of James Ure of Shargarton, in *M'Crie's Memoirs of Veitch and Brysson*, 1825, p. 471).

8.   That M'Ward's invitation was a general one to all the fugitives from Bothwell seems to be confirmed by James Russel, who with several others, including Hall, Hackston and Balfour, was with Hamilton at this time. Russel records that on Tuesday, 29 July, 'There came a woman out of Edinburgh seeking them, and with letters to Mr Hamilton that resolved them all what to do' (*Russel's Account, Appendix to Kirkton's History*, p. 477). According to Russel's account, Hamilton and Hall then separated from the rest of the party, presumably to go to Edinburgh to meet Cargill. The rest stayed together for some weeks until eventually Hackston and Balfour left for Holland on 5 September, with Russel and the others following on 18 October. Meanwhile, Hamilton reached Edinburgh probably about the beginning of August and, presumably accompanied by Cargill and Hall, left for Holland some days later. Patrick Walker records that Cargill's departure took place immediately after the execution of John Kid and John King, which occurred on 14 August.

9.   Patrick Walker (c. 1666-1745) was Cargill's first biographer. He seems to have been a chapman or travelling bookseller, and to have resided in his latter years at Bristo Port in Edinburgh, where he brought out a series of lives of the foremost of the field-preachers. Walker himself had been a victim of the persecution and had suffered torture at the hands of the Privy Council; he had been imprisoned in Dunottar Castle and had narrowly escaped transportation. As a young boy of fourteen or fifteen he had heard Cargill preach some of his last sermons, and the impression had remained with him for the rest of his life. He writes of all the field-preachers with esteem, but when he writes of Cargill he does so with a particular affection and tenderness; his account of Cargill's last sermon at Dunsyre is a moving tribute, rich in its eloquence and poignant in its memories. Walker seems to have been at one time in danger of being ensnared by the Gibbites, and it

is to Cargill that he ascribes his deliverance, 'which', he says, 'has endeared his name to me, upon this and other accounts, above all other ministers'. Though writing over fifty years afterwards, when well into his sixties, Walker records Cargill's sermons with a vividness of detail which shows the deep impression they made upon his mind, and his highly individual style, while lacking in literary grace, has about it a freshness and vitality which make his recollections live before the eye. He has an attention to detail that is particularly striking. 'I well remember, it was a cold easterly wet fog,' he says of the occasion of Cargill's encounter with John Gibb; and, 'He came and stood upon a chair, and had nothing to rest upon, with his Bible betwixt his hands,' describing Cargill's sermon on the same occasion. Walker was closely associated with the work of the United Societies, which were formed under Michael Shields after Cargill's death, and he was a frequent companion of James Renwick. He did not, however, follow Robert Hamilton in standing out against the Revolution Settlement, but chose rather to side with Alexander Shields, Thomas Lining and the others who, after initial opposition to the settlement, accepted it. He had little time for the Protesters, whom he dubs 'Hamiltonians' after Robert Hamilton. In taking this stance Walker was only following the course, according to Lining, that Cargill himself would have taken had he lived (*Preface to Shields' Essay on Church Communion*, 1706).

Chapter 9

1. Professor Herkless disputes this view, on the ground that the record of the Dunscore meeting shows plainly that Cameron gave no such promise on that occasion (*Richard Cameron*, 1896, p. 75). Patrick Walker, however, from whom the account is taken, is careful to say that Cameron's promise was secured from him not by the Dunscore ministers but by 'others who would not sit with them upon that design, who pretended to be as much against the indulged men as he was' (*Six Saints of the Covenant*, vol. I, p. 221).
2. Professor Herkless has shown (*Richard Cameron*, 1896, p. 79) that Cameron went over to Holland about the beginning of May 1679 and was there at the time of Bothwell Bridge. He was still in Holland at the end of July, for the records of the Scottish Church, Rotterdam, show him as a witness to a baptism there on the 30th of that month. He was certainly back in Scotland by 30 October, as he wrote to M'Ward from Edinburgh on that date, and since he refers to having written earlier to M'Ward from Newcastle, and to a subsequent visit to Annandale and Nithsdale, it is likely that he had left Holland at least two months previously. Cameron's ordination certainly took place no later than September, for John Brown, who was present, died in that month; and since it is reasonable to assume that M'Ward and Brown would have needed some time to assess Cameron's character and suitability for the ministry, it seems likely that the ordination took place in July or perhaps early August. Cargill is nowhere recorded as having been present, and it seems probable therefore that he did not arrive in Holland until after Cameron had gone. This supposition agrees with the evidence presented elsewhere about the probable date of Cargill's departure for Holland (see Chapter 8, note 8).

3.   During the time of his self-imposed exile in Holland Hamilton acted as commissioner for the United Societies, formed after Cargill's death, and in this capacity he travelled widely on the Continent. He is credited with having secured the ordination by the Dutch church of James Renwick and later of Thomas Lining. At the Revolution he returned to Scotland, and at about the same time he fell heir to the family estate of Preston on the death of his brother William. Since, however, his entry to the estate would have involved an acknowledgement of the 'uncovenanted' rule of William and Mary, he refused to accept possession of his inheritance, or to be involved with it in any way. Over the next few years he continued to stand out firmly against the Revolution Settlement, and he was involved, with some others, in publishing a declaration of protest at Sanquhar in 1692, on which account he was arrested and imprisoned. After being kept in custody for some eight months he was released, the authorities having apparently decided that his activities, though troublesome, presented no threat to the public peace. He persisted in his separatist position, supported by a small band of sympathizers, until his death in 1701.

A few weeks before he died he penned a 'last testimony' in which he wrote, 'As for my own case, I bless my God, it is many years since my interest in him was secured; and under all my afflictions from all airts, he has been a present help in time of my greatest need. I have been a man of reproach, a man of contention; but praise to him, it was not for my own things, but for the things of my Lord Jesus Christ. Whatever were my infirmities, yet his glory, and the rising and flourishing of his kingdom, was still the mark I laboured to shoot at; nor is it now my design to vindicate myself from the many calumnies that have been cast upon my name, for which his slain witnesses shall be vindicated, his own glory and buried truths raised up, in that day when he will assuredly take away the reproach of his servants, and will raise and beautify the names of his living and dead witnesses. Only this I must add, though I cannot but say that reproaches have broken my heart; yet in what I have met with, before and at the time of Bothwell, and also since, I had often more difficulty to carry humbly under the glory of his cross than to bear the burden of it" (*The Christian's Conduct,* 1762, pp. 59-60).

4.   The original communion cups of the Scottish Church, almost certainly those used by Cargill in dispensing the sacrament, are still preserved, having (together with the church records) providentially survived the destruction of the old church by enemy action in May 1940.

5.   In a letter to the church at home in late 1679 or early 1680 M'Ward wrote, 'I was so confounded with these cause-destroying excesses that I was thereby, as I suppose you have heard, brought to the gates of death, and as I told them then, so it has proved too true since, and will prove more true every day, that if the principle whereby they defend their practice were owned, it would not only infer the dissolution of the united visible church, but also of all Christian society.' Despite John M'Main's view (*Earnest Contendings,* 1723, pp. 380-4), who would have it that M'Ward was referring to Gibb and Russel, it is clear that the reference is to Hamilton, who himself admits, in a letter dated 15 August 1682, that his fellowship

with M'Ward, which had previously been close, ended with the arrival of Fleming. Says Hamilton: 'Mr M'Ward continued extraordinary kind until Mr Fleming came over, and then we differing in judgement he became greatly against me, to the making of me so far as possible odious in the whole provinces' (Letter to William Brackel, in *Laing Mss.* no. 344, fol. 53).

6.   Cargill never expressed any public criticism of Fleming. He did, however, reflect rather severely on one occasion on the title of Fleming's celebrated book *The Fulfilling of the Scripture* which at that time enjoyed a wide currency. Preaching from Daniel 9:13, 'As it is written in the law of Moses, all this evil is come upon us', he remarked, 'You have heard of a book called *The Fulfilling of the Scripture* — men would beware of giving great titles to books.'

7.   It may be noted here that the term 'Cameronian', often loosely applied to the adherents of Cameron and Cargill, was originally coined about 1678 or 1679 to describe, disparagingly, those who shared Cameron's views on the supremacy and Indulgence (cf. *The Nonconformist's Vindication,* 1700, p. 16; *A True and Impartial Relation of Bothwell Bridge,* 1797, p. 16). It did not, however, gain much currency until after the Revolution of 1688, when it was used to denote those elements of the United Societies which did not join the Revolution Settlement (cf. *Six Saints of the Covenant,* vol. I. p. 251). The term was never owned by those to whom it was applied, and it is uniformly described in their literature as a 'by-name' or 'nick-name' (cf. *A Short Memorial of Sufferings and Grievances,* 1690, title page). To the same effect are some remarks by John M'Main (*Earnest Contendings,* 1723, p. 376) when in taking Wodrow severely to task for using the term in his *History* he asserts, 'He calumniates and fixes upon these faithful witnesses of Jesus Christ that stigma, or name of reproach, wherewith their enemies had branded them, calling them after a man, and falsely alleging that they termed themselves so, and labours to make his readers, in this and future generations, believe the calumny thus confirmed, that they were not Presbyterians. But he cannot produce one instance among all the cloud of witnesses, whom he so reproaches, evincing that ever any of them did so term themselves.'

8.   Douglas, who does not seem to have held a settled charge, had been active as a field-preacher for some years and took a prominent part in some of the most notable events of the period. At first he seems to have disapproved of Cameron's forthrightness against the Indulgence, and he sat with Welsh, Semple and others as a member of the field presbytery which on two occasions at the end of 1678 sought to restrain Cameron's activities. Later, however, he appears to have had a change of heart, and during the early months of 1679 he is found closely associated with Cameron and Hamilton. He was directly concerned, with Hamilton and David Hackston, in drawing up and publishing the Rutherglen Declaration and he was the preacher at Drumclog when the meeting was surprised by Claverhouse. He was also prominent in Hamilton's party at Bothwell. As a result of these activities he was proclaimed a rebel and had a price of 3,000 merks put on his head. After Bothwell he went over to Holland, and settled with some of

the other exiles at Utrecht. While there he became involved in the disagreements that had broken out in the Scots congregation at Rotterdam, and his acceptance of an invitation to preach for Robert Fleming, at Robert M'Ward's insistence, led to a breach with several of his fellow-exiles and to his eventual separation from them for the remainder of his stay in Holland.

Early in 1680 Douglas returned to Scotland and joined himself for a time with Cameron and Cargill. Perhaps recalling his former opposition to Cameron, he seems to have inclined particularly to his side, and he even went so far as to sign the Bond of Mutual Defence which Cameron and his supporters drew up shortly before Ayrsmoss. But the disagreements in Holland were revived by some of the returning exiles, among whom was James Boig (*Six Saints of the Covenant*, vol. I. p. 284), and shortly after the emitting of the Sanquhar Declaration Douglas was summoned before a meeting at Carluke Moor where he was asked to give public satisfaction for his alleged offence. On his refusal to do so he was by his own account 'silenced and necessitated to depart', whereupon he withdrew to England and took no further part in Scottish church affairs until after the Revolution.

In 1682 the United Societies, now without a minister, invited him to return to Scotland to preach to them, but he was not satisfied that the feeling against him had changed and so declined the offer. The societies considered this reply 'not very satisfying' and did not press their invitation further at that time (*Faithful Contendings Displayed*, 1780, p. 30). A similar initiative some years later proved equally unsuccessful (*Ibid.*, p. 145). Douglas's reply is interesting as showing the position which he, Smith and M'Ward took up in the controversy, and which doubtless Cargill would have shared: 'My friends may know that I am where I was in the day when the Lord shined upon us at Drumclog, both as to principles and practice: but to insist upon that which may be forborne without sin renders us incapable to act . . . I am not for a sinful union with the indulged, nor for a sinful union with those that are for a sinful union with the indulged, and because of this my ministry has been rejected in many places by many persons before and since Bothwell Bridge; neither am I for a sinful separation from them that are not for a sinful union with the indulged, and because of this my ministry has been rejected these two years past and more by some.' Eventually, in 1690, Douglas returned to Scotland and was settled as minister of Wamphray in Dumfriesshire, where he died in 1695.

Chapter 10
1. The circumstances of the discovery of the paper are obscure. According to popular belief, as expressed in the testimonies in the *Cloud of Witnesses* and elsewhere, it was discovered on Hall; but government sources generally speak of it as having been found on Cargill. The latter cannot, of course, be literally correct, since Cargill did not fall into the government's hands, but it is more likely to be nearer the truth. The probability is that in his haste to escape Cargill was forced to abandon his horse, leaving the paper in his saddle-bag, where it was subsequently discovered with some other books and papers. This is borne out by the

account of the incident given in the *London Gazette* of 5-8 July, which
speaks of the paper as having been found in a 'port-mantle' (i.e. a travelling
or saddle-bag used when riding). An extract from a contemporary diary
quoted by Dr Hay Fleming gives a similar account, adding for good
measure that Cargill made his escape on Middleton's horse (*Six Saints of the
Covenant,* vol. II, p. 206).

2.   Wodrow's version of the paper (*History,* III, pp. 207-211) is
considerably more extended than the contemporary copy published by the
government (*A True and Exact Copy of a Treasonable and Bloody Paper,*
1680) and, like his version of the Rutherglen Declaration, has apparently
been expanded and developed to express in a more coherent form the
principles of its authors. Of the eight articles given by Wodrow, compared
with seven in the published paper, two are new, while one is a combination
of two of the articles in the original. The expanded version was apparently
in existence as early as 1684, for both John Richmond and James Nisbet,
who were executed in that year, bore witness in their last testimonies to the
'eight articles called the New Covenant'. A clue to an even earlier origin is
to be found in the testimony of William Thomson, who suffered along with
Cargill himself in July 1681. Says Thomson: 'I adhere to the Rutherglen
Testimony, to the paper commonly called Mr Donald Cargill's Covenant,
of the date June 1680; I say, I adhere to the original copies of these papers,
as they were corrected and revised by the authors' (*Cloud of Witnesses,*
1714, p. 116). It is by no means certain, however, that all the additional
material was the work of the original authors. In his *Martyr Graves of
Scotland* (p. 347) John H. Thomson well observes that the additional eighth
article, which is much more intransigent than any of the original seven, is
'the worst expressed in the whole document, and is by no means a fair
specimen of the vigorous writing in the paragraphs that precede'.

    Though summarized in Alexander Shields' *Hind Let Loose* (1687 ed. pp.
133-7) the paper was never published in full by the United Societies, who
did not own it as one of their formal declarations. Shields himself was
critical of some aspects of it, believing that its judgements on ministers
came 'too near separation', while its advocacy of a republican form of
government was 'not the expedient duty of the present day' (Letter of 22
November 1680, quoted in Wodrow, *History* III, pp. 209-12). In the
societies generally it was tacitly accepted that the paper had been mainly
drafted by Cargill, though care was taken not to associate him with its
opinions. As a rule it was only the extreme separatists such as Patrick Grant
who ascribed it to him unreservedly (cf. *The Nonconformist's Vindication,*
1700, p. 28) and then only to invoke support for their belief in the
assumption of magisterial authority, a principle which the societies had
expressly repudiated in their *Informatory Vindication.*

3.   Peden, one of the most noted ministers of the time, and a strong
individualist, could not bring himself to condemn the ministers who had
accepted the Indulgence, nor to preach separation from them. On this
account some members of the United Societies scrupled to join with him in
fellowship, and one of their number found himself in trouble with his
fellow-members for having had Peden baptize one of his children. Cargill,

apparently, felt no such scruples. In a letter to Patrick Walker, written after
the publication of Walker's *Life of Peden,* Alexander Gordon of Earlston
recalled that 'The last time that he saw Mr Peden was with Mr Donald
Cargill, when they continued a long time comparing notes: seeing with one
eye, and thinking with one mind, and speaking with one breath, of all things
past, present and what was to befall this church and nation' (*Six Saints of the
Covenant,* vol. I, p. 137).

4.   'We said, before their excommunication we would not have been so
clear to cast them off' (Testimony of Isobel Alison, *Cloud of Witnesses,*
1714, p. 81). Both Isobel Alison and her fellow-sufferer, Marion Harvie,
were frequent hearers and companions of Cargill (see chapter 12, note 3).

5.   The single exception was the memorable sermon preached by John
Livingstone at Kirk O'Shotts on the Monday of a communion in June 1630,
which is said to have resulted in the conversion or confirmation of no fewer
than five hundred of his hearers.

6.   The bond bears twenty-six signatures (*A True and Impartial Account of
the Examinations and Confessions of Several Execrable Conspirators,* 1681,
pp. 11-12), Cameron's name appearing second after that of Thomas
Douglas (see chapter 9, note 8). The other signatures include those of
Cameron's brother Michael, who died with him at Ayrsmoss, and of John
Malcolm, John Wilson, John Potter, David Farrie and James Stuart, all of
whom were later to die on the scaffold. According to John Potter's
examination at his trial, the bond was drawn up 'on a moor near Galloway'
some time in the summer of 1680.

7.   Patrick Walker was at pains to contradict a report, current at the time,
that Cameron's party were divided among themselves (*Six Saints of the
Covenant,* vol. I. p. 231). However, to judge from one of Hackston's letters
from prison, reproduced in the *Cloud of Witnesses* (1714 ed., p. 28), this
report may not have been without foundation. Says Hackston: 'I cannot
deny, but it was over the belly of conscience that I joined with some of our
party; for some of them had not their garments clean of the late defections,
and there was too much of pride amongst us. Oh that all would take
warning, by my reproof, not to venture to follow any man over conscience!
There were choice godly men among us, but one Achan will make Israel to
fall.'

The reference here is clearly to the situation before Ayrsmoss, and not
before Bothwell, as the editor of the 1871 edition of the *Cloud* makes out.
By the 'late defections' Hackston, who was a close associate of Robert
Hamilton, undoubtedly means the contentions in the Rotterdam Church
over recognition of the ministry of Robert Fleming, in which Thomas
Douglas, who was with Cameron's party for a time, bore a prominent part
(see chapter 9, note 8). It may be significant that Hackston's signature does
not appear in the bond signed by Cameron and the others, which bears
Douglas's name at its head.

Chapter 11

1.   The horrific details of Hackston's execution (*Cloud of Witnesses,* 1714,
preface, p. xiii; *Six Saints of the Covenant,* vol. I, p.233) have been often

enough recited. It is a sufficient commentary on the episcopal clergy of the day that Paterson, Bishop of Edinburgh, was a member of the committee of the Council which recommended the precise manner of his death (*Register of the Privy Council*, Third Series, vol. VI, pp. 507, 511).

2. Robert M'Ward's view that all subjects should pray for the conversion and salvation of their magistrates, even though these had become open tyrants and persecutors, has more than once been quoted (cf. D. Hay Fleming, *Six Saints of the Covenant*, vol. II, p. 186 note; J. D. Douglas, *Light in the North*, 1964, p. 164 note). This is based on a passage in M'Ward's *The Banders Disbanded*, published in 1681, in the course of which he gives an admirably succinct account of Presbyterian principles as applied to the respective duties of king and subjects. M'Ward's words are, however, worth quoting in full: 'We cheerfully acknowledge that it is the duty both of ministers and people and of every subject to pray for magistrates (whether supreme or subordinate) and all whom the Lord hath set in authority over us; and that not only so long as they continue to rule for the Lord or good of the land, but even when they become open tyrants, persecutors etc. and continue such. I say, we ought to pray for the conversion and salvation even of such, except the Lord should either expressly discharge the same, or by some infallible demonstration declare that he has rejected them (which I humbly think we cannot be infallibly ascertained of, especially as to particular persons, without divine revelation), or else give such clear and sensible significations of his refusing to hear any prayers for them and of his displeasure thereat, that we dare not adventure to put up such suits without fearing to offend him and provoke his discountenance in other things that we find clearness and freedom to pray for, or the like' (*The Banders Disbanded*, 1681, pp. 48-9). There are strong grounds for believing that M'Ward had been convinced of the latter view in the case of the king and government, just as the Torwood excommunication was the expression of Cargill's own conviction of it.

3. In the *Proceedings of the Society of Antiquaries of Scotland*, 1910/11, pp. 246-8, there is a copy of a letter found by Dr David Hay Fleming in a manuscript volume of letters and testimonies which had been sent to him for examination. The letter bears the name of neither writer nor recipient, but it is juxtaposed with two other letters, similarly anonymous, but known from other sources to be definitely by Cargill. The letter bears a marked resemblance to Cargill's style, and though it has not been authenticated from any other source there must be a very strong presumption that it is his. Who the recipient was cannot be known for certain, but the letter contains a strong hint as to his identity. The writer tells his friend: 'I think you can hardly mistake God or grudge with dispensations. He sent you already to prison to begin it, and you ought to think that he has sent you again to prison to increase if not to perfect it.' There is only one of those who suffered at this time known to have been twice in prison — John Malcolm. In his testimony he records that he was at Bothwell Bridge, that he was captured and was among the prisoners in the Greyfriars Churchyard and that he was subsequently put on board ship for the plantations. He had escaped when the ship was wrecked on the Orkneys and eventually made

his way home. He joined Cameron's party shortly before Ayrsmoss and was captured and brought to Edinburgh. It was apparently during this second imprisonment that he received this letter, written perhaps shortly before Cargill's joint letter to himself and Archibald Alison.

The letter itself bears ample testimony to the spiritual qualities of its author, as he ponders the ways of God towards his people: 'If my soul could be assistant to you in your suffering, it would; and though kindness to sufferers be our duty, yet it is sometimes their prejudice, for as men bestow he holds in, knowing we cannot bear both. Turn to him where you shall have it better, sweeter and surer. Let it be your comfort that, though all should stand aloof, he is near who is infinite in love, compassion, power and tenderness. But think not to find out his goodness so much by the way he takes, as by the end he aims at and the work he effectuates. His way is short when his end is good: his way is banishments, prisons, scaffolds, and his end purifying, perfecting, glorifying.'

The writer goes on to refer to 'the late papers and actions' — no doubt the Queensferry paper and Sanquhar Declaration — and to advise his friend that though they 'were not publicly concluded and consented to, yet search them, and so far as you find in them truth, give your testimony to them, for I am mistaken if the truths of God and the ease of your conscience be not in them'. There was certainly much in both papers of which Cargill would have approved, but it is difficult not to see in the words 'so far as you find in them truth' a hint of the reservations which, on other evidence, he is known to have felt.

4.   The Solemn League and Covenant was publicly burnt in London on 22 May 1661 (Wodrow, *History*, I, p. 243) though the action was not repeated in Edinburgh until 1682 (*Ibid.*, III, pp. 362-3).

5.   'Your Grace was forgotten by him in the forenoon, but uncanonically he brought you up in the afternoon, and after a scurrilous apology for his omission, he proceeded with his blunt thunder against you . . . P.S. Your Grace will see the learning of the curser, while he calls St Ambrose Bishop of Lyons' (Letter of Bishop of Edinburgh to Duke of Lauderdale, 18 September 1680: *Lauderdale Papers*, III, p. 209).

6.   Thus Alexander Smellie: 'In the clear dry light of prudence and sagacity we may decide that Cargill did a rash thing' (*Men of the Covenant*, 1905, p. 280). Similarly Marcus Loane: 'This went beyond the point of all that was wise or prudent' (*Sons of the Covenant*, 1963, p. 39).

7.   'To discipline must all estates within this realm be subject, if they offend, as well the rulers as they that are ruled' (*First Book of Discipline*, in Laing's *Works of Knox*, vol. II, p. 233). Similarly in the *Order of Excommunication* of 1569: 'All crimes that by the law of God deserve death, deserve also excommunication from the society of Christ's church, whether the offender be papist or Protestant, for it is no reason that under pretence of diversity of religion open impiety should be suffered in the visible body of Christ Jesus' (*Ibid.*, vol. VI, p. 449).

8.   'We confess and acknowledge empires, kingdoms, dominions and cities to be distincted and ordained by God; the powers and authority in the same, be it of emperors in their empires, of kings in their realms, dukes and

princes in their dominions, and of other magistrates in their cities, to be God's holy ordinance, ordained for manifestation of his own glory, and for the singular profit and commodity of mankind . . . not only they are appointed for civil policy, but also for maintenance of the true religion, and for suppressing of idolatry and superstition whatsoever' (*Scots Confession,* 1937 ed., pp. 93-5).

9.   *The Form of Prayers and Ministration of the Sacraments etc.,* in Laing's *Works of Knox,* vol. IV, p. 205.

10.   Cf. *The Second Book of Discipline,* chapter I, passim (*Book of the Universal Kirk,* Bannatyne Club ed., vol. II, pp. 488-90).

Chapter 12

1.   The account of Cargill's field-meeting in Fife is given by William Row, minister of Ceres, in his supplement to the *Life of Robert Blair* (Wodrow Society, 1848, pp. 279-81). Row, a minister who had accepted the Indulgence, was no friend of Cargill, and his account bears evidence of his prejudices. In particular, his assertion that some of Cargill's audience had been forced at gunpoint to hear him is not substantiated by any other contemporary evidence. There is no reason to doubt that some of Cargill's followers were armed, in legitimate self-defence, but that they used their weapons to coerce others into hearing him cannot be proved from the facts. Such conduct, needless to say, would have been wholly contrary to Cargill's own principles and to his declared views on several occasions.

2.   These remain unpublished. Manuscript copies are in the *Wodrow* collection.

3.   The indomitable courage of these two young women is worthy of better remembrance. Isobel Alison is said to have lived very privately at Perth. Marion Harvie, who was only twenty years of age, was a servant girl from Bo'ness. In witnessing before their accusers both gave fearless testimonies for the truths in which they believed. Marion's testimony in particular is a very human document, showing remarkable strength of character. 'They say I would murder,' she exclaimed. 'I could never take the life of a chicken, but my heart shrinked.' Bravely she told her judges: 'I love my life as well as any of you do, but will not redeem it upon sinful terms, for Christ says he that seeks to save his life shall lose it.' Her last brief testimony was: 'At fourteen or fifteen I was a hearer of the curates and the indulged, and while I was a hearer of these I was a blasphemer and Sabbath-breaker, and a chapter of the Bible was a burden to me; but since I first heard this persecuted gospel I durst not blaspheme nor break the Sabbath, and the Bible became my delight.' Even when led out to die her courage did not fail her. Paterson, the Bishop of Edinburgh, determined to overcome her resolution by one means or another, ordered one of his curates to pray, saying, 'Marion, you said you would never hear a curate, now you shall be forced to hear one.' But the indomitable servant girl was not to be beaten. 'Come, Isobel,' she called to her companion, 'let's sing the 23rd Psalm', and so the curate's prayer was effectively silenced. It was an action that, in the words of the old record, 'extremely confounded the persecutors'.

4.   Robert Wodrow says of Skene: 'It was said, a person who was very

warm, and had great weight with him, charged him to stand to his confession before the Council, and not retract, and urged peculiar arguments, otherwise he might have been brought to some condescensions' (*History*, III, p. 228). Wodrow does not identify the 'person' concerned, but he is referring to a lady known as 'Mistress Muir', who had been the means of Cargill's and Boig's escape when Skene and their other companions were apprehended. According to a report current at the time, she and Skene had formed a romantic attachment; and when Skene was in prison she had sent him a message urging him to stand to his confession and so to 'die in her love'. As Wodrow says, the truth of this cannot be avouched. 'Mistress Muir' later fell a prey to the Gibbites, but was reclaimed by Cargill's efforts and subsequently married John Flint, who became minister at Lasswade and later at the New North Church, Edinburgh, after the Revolution.

5. Carstairs was examined by a Committee of the Privy Council on 19 November, after some letters had been found which appeared to compromise his position. According to a contemporary account he 'with a great deal of emphasis disclaimed the follies and principles of these madmen [i.e. Skene and his fellows]. He said he could not express his indignation at and abomination of their madnesses with vehemency enough. He acknowledged the king to be the fountain of honour; he owned his authority, councils and other judicatories; he said he loved his person, he honoured and prayed for him.' The result of this declaration of loyalty, not surprisingly, was that 'He [Carstairs] was set at liberty, with the applause, love and respect of all.' Cargill had another opinion of Carstairs' conduct. In his letter to Skene he refers to him as 'that unsavoury salt that lately appeared, acknowledged them, and was ashamed of this testimony, and in so doing gave the first vote to your condemnation and proclaimed a lawfulness to the rest of assizers and murderers to follow in their condemnation'. Carstairs was a regular correspondent of Robert M'Ward, though latterly, when M'Ward and Brown espoused the principle of separation from complying ministers and expressed their support for Cameron, he made clear his dissent. Carstairs' son, William, was later a prominent figure in the post-Revolution church and a valued counsellor of William III.

6. This letter was first published in the *Proceedings of the Society of Antiquaries of Scotland*, 1910/11, pp. 248-9. In the published version only the name of the recipients, Stewart and Potter, is given. There is, however, another copy of the letter in the *Wodrow Manuscripts*, where it is definitely ascribed to Cargill (though in that copy, curiously, the name of the recipients is lacking). The letter's style bears such strong similarity to Cargill's that there seems no reason to doubt its authenticity.

7. Robert Wodrow says, 'I do not find by any papers in the process that Mr Skene, Stewart and Potter assert it was their duty to kill the king' (*History*, III, p. 231). Wodrow, however, does not seem to have had access to their answers before the Council, which were later published by the government (*A True and Impartial Account of the Examinations and Confessions of Several Execrable Conspirators*, 1681). The account of

Skene's examination, signed by himself, records 'that he thinks that the king being now excommunicate, and there being now a lawful declared war against him upon the account of the breach of the Covenant, that it is lawful to kill him'. This was a specific charge in Skene's indictment before the High Court. Stewart, when put to the same question before the Council, declined to give a direct reply, as did Potter. Under torture, however, Stewart admitted that he had heard talk of a plan to kill some noted persecutors, among them a member of the guard called Kennoway, who had been responsible for several arrests, and the curates of Bo'ness and Carriden, who had been the main accessories to the assault on Cargill and Hall at Queensferry. A similar fate, he said, awaited any of the bishops and judges, if there was opportunity. Stewart attributed these designs to two of his acquaintances from Bo'ness, John Murray and William Cuthill, who had told him that 'It was their design to kill all that were against them who came in their way, and that Mr Donald Cargill in his preachings advised them to these murdering designs.' It must be remembered that these statements were extracted from Stewart under very considerable duress and they should obviously be treated with extreme reserve. Of the two men to whom he referred, John Murray was condemned to death in March 1681 but was reprieved on acknowledging the king's authority and disclaiming Cargill's principles; William Cuthill was tried and executed along with Cargill in the following July. In his last testimony Cuthill admitted that 'being hard questioned' he had given his opinion that it was lawful to kill the king. The account of his examination bears that 'Being interrogate, if it be lawful to kill the king, answers, the king has broken the Covenant, and presses others to do so by his forces, and therefore he thinks he deserves to die.' Cuthill also appears to have held views on matters such as the payment of dues and customs, and the use of the names of months and days of the week, which were later espoused by James Russel and the other separatists from the United Societies (see chapter 13, note 1).

8. *Calendar of State Papers*, 1680-1, pp. 141-2. Three other field preachers, including Thomas Douglas (see chapter 9, note 8) were included in the summons.

Chapter 13

1. The view that the common names of the days and months, being derived from pagan deities, were not worthy to be used by Christians, was not confined to Gibb and his followers. As contemporary records show, it was one of the chief points of difference between James Russel and the United Societies in the years following Cargill's death. Russel's friend and associate, Patrick Grant, maintained that his and Russel's views on the subject had been shared by William Cuthill, who died along with Cargill, and that Cuthill had asserted them in the portion of his last testimony which was suppressed by the editors of the *Cloud of Witnesses* (1714 ed., p. 118). Grant also claimed that in his letter to Gibb's followers in the Correction House Cargill himself had expressed approval of these views, but there is nothing in Cargill's letter to lend support to this. Nevertheless it is clear that some who attended on Cargill's ministry and held him in the highest respect

adopted the practice at about this time. A manuscript copy of Cargill's sermon at Dovan Common on 26 June, obviously recorded by a friendly hand, is dated 'the 26th day of the sixth month'. A letter from Patrick Forman, who with four others was put to death at the Gallowlee in Edinburgh in October 1681, is dated 'the 16th of this ninth month' and his testimony 'the 8th day of the tenth month'. The practice did not, however, become general, and was not adopted by James Renwick nor the other members of the United Societies.

2.   There is no doubt that Cargill's character has suffered from his being represented, falsely, as a partaker in the errors of Gibb. As W.G. Blaikie well observes (*Preachers of Scotland*, p. 169), much of the blame in this respect attaches to Bishop Burnet, who attributes to the 'Cargillites', as he calls them, the excesses of Gibb and his followers (*History of His Own Time*, 1724, pp. 511-2).

Chapter 14

1.   'This last summer, 1681, was a very dry summer and hot: the corns were very short through drought, the grass much withered universally, the brooks and streams dried up' (Robert Law, *Memorialls*, 1818, p. 216). Fountainhall records that there was 'scarce any rain from March to near the end of June' (*Historical Observes*, p. 42). On 16 June the Privy Council ordained a fast to be kept for, among other things, 'God's anger and displeasure in inflicting a long, scorching and threatening drought, whereby the fruits of the ground, the necessary provision for the life of man and beast, are in danger to be burnt up and consumed' (*Register of the Privy Council*, Third Series, vol. VII, p. 132).

2.   So Cargill's sermon was interpreted by Patrick Walker, who was a bitter critic of Robert Hamilton and his fellow-dissenters at the Revolution and after, and by Thomas Lining (*Preface to Shields' Essay on Church Communion*, 1706: see also Epilogue).

3.   This incident is recorded in *The Judgment and Justice of God Exemplified*, 1782, p. 34 note, which formed an appendix to the second edition of John Howie's *Scots Worthies*. The omission of the appendix by some subsequent editors has meant that the record of the incident has unfortunately been lost from later editions.

4.   The date of M'Ward's death is given as 26 May, and that of his funeral as 30 May, in a letter written by Alexander Shields from Utrecht on 4 June (*Laing MSS*, no. 350, fol. 25). This contradicts the date of December 1681 quoted in Steven's *History of the Scottish Church, Rotterdam* (p. 336, note). M'Ward's death was lamented in elegiac verse by the young soldier-poet William Cleland, who had fought at Bothwell and Drumclog, and was to die heroically in the defence of Dunkeld against the Highland Jacobites in 1689. Cleland's tribute includes the following lines:

> Though he triumphs, yet we may mourn and weep,
> Since in such cloudy days is fall'n asleep
> So great a seer, such a shining light,
> Whereby our day is almost turn'd to night;

> For truth a champion both by tongue and pen,
> Regardless of the wrath and rage of men.
> What pen can write, or what tongue can express,
> His choicest parts, his worth, his usefulness?

5. This occasion produced a somewhat novel incident when Cargill, who had just been speaking of the devil's activity in turning men's thoughts away from the things of God, noticed that some of his audience were smoking their tobacco pipes. He stopped short and said, 'Now we must leave it, for we find you beginning to weary: you are fallen to tobacco; we are persuaded that the devil is at that thing that you use, that it should keep you from God, and keep you from your duty.' That tobacco smoking was general at this time, even among the field-preachers themselves, is indisputable: both Welsh and Blackader appear to have indulged the habit (*Memoirs of Blackader,* 1826, p. 117 note), as did John Livingstone, the noted preacher of earlier days (*Wodrow Soc., Select Biographies,* vol. I. p. 193). James Renwick made it plain that he was not opposed to tobacco as such, but only to its immoderate use and particularly its use during public worship (*Sermons,* 1776, p. 246). It is the latter practice, of course, which Cargill condemned on this occasion; rather surprisingly, it seems to have been not uncommon about this time.

6. This record of Cargill's last sermon is taken from the version published by John Howie, who transferred the fragmentary notes of hearers into a more readable and coherent form (see Appendix I — Cargill's sermons). From an old manuscript record of Cargill's last sermon, perhaps one of those used by Howie, one can still read Cargill's final appeal in what were probably his actual words. The conversational, almost homely, style is noteworthy: '. . . hide thyself as it were for a little. This is it then: hide you, enter in. Hiding and entering make all one thing. It's this now, make all sure with God, hide you. Where will you hide you? There is no place to hide you but in him. There is no other hiding-place: that word in the 32nd of Isaiah: "A man shall be a hiding place, and a covert from the wind and the rain, and a shadow of a great rock in a weary land, and a river of waters in a dry place." We would say that one word: there are chambers of defences, and well are they furnished, and we would lay it on you, that you would be serious for yourselves, that you may enter into them and make all sure. Shut the door behind you, and God will never bid you go out again, till the dove come back to the ark with the olive leaf in her mouth.'

Chapter 15

1. According to Patrick Walker, Cargill's capture took place on the morning immediately after his last sermon at Dunsyre, i.e. Monday, 11 July. This is, however, at variance with three other contemporary sources and the balance of view is therefore against Walker on this occasion. Fountainhall (*Historical Observes,* p. 44) states clearly that the capture took place on the 13th (i.e. the Wednesday following) as does Robert Law (*Memorialls,* p. 197). The Duke of Hamilton, writing to the Duke of Queensberry on the 13th, says 'Cargill and two more preachers, one Smith and Broun [i.e. Boig] were taken last night at Covington Mill by a party of

Captain Stuart's dragoons whose Lieutenant was just now with me' (*Buccleuch MSS, Hist. Mss. Commission,* 1897, p. 240). Hamilton's account can be reconciled with the others by taking 'last night' to mean the early hours of the 13th, and this view is strengthened by Walker's statement that the capture took place some time after Cargill and his friends had retired for the night. In order to account for Cargill's movements between 10 July, when he preached his last sermon, and the night of the 12th/13th, when he was captured, it is necessary to assume either that he spent the nights of the Sunday and Monday elsewhere and travelled to Covington on the night of the Tuesday, or that he arrived in Covington on the night of the Sunday and remained there for a further two days and nights. Admittedly, either is possible, but the first accords more closely with the contemporary evidence, slight as it is, and particularly with Walter Smith's testimony, quoted below. Despite Walker's inaccuracy in the date, there seems no reason to doubt his account of the circumstantial details of the capture, nor of Bonshaw's involvement in it, which is amply attested by Privy Council records. His implication that Bonshaw had been informed of Cargill's likely whereabouts and was actively searching for him is not, however, borne out by the other evidence, which suggests strongly that Cargill's capture was entirely fortuitous. Robert Law is alone in recording that Bonshaw and his men, in their search that morning, 'were in seeking of a countryman who had killed one of their number', but his statement, though uncorroborated, has a strong ring of truth. Cargill himself records in his last testimony, 'I had a sweet calmness of spirit and great submission as to my taking, the providence of God was so eminent in it' (*Cloud of Witnesses,* 1714, p. 2). Walter Smith's testimony is still more explicit: 'We were singularly delivered by providence into the adversaries' hand and, from what I could learn, were betrayed by none, nor were any accessory to our taking more than we ourselves, and particularly let none blame the lady of St John's Kirk in this' (*Ibid.,* p. 19).

2. This is obviously a mistake. The Bishop of Edinburgh's letter to Lauderdale, dated from Edinburgh on 18 September (a Saturday) mentions the excommunication as having taken place 'last Lord's day', i.e. Sunday, 12 September (*Lauderdale Papers,* III, p. 209).

3. The two Hendersons, Andrew and Alexander, were wanted for their part in the killing of Sharp.

4. The reference to Angus seems to confirm the surmise that during his years of banishment Cargill had made his headquarters there rather than in Rattray (see Chapter 5, note 10).

5. This is presumably the basis of Fountainhall's assertion that Cargill gave 'shifting answers' when questioned by the Council, and later that he 'behaved most timorously to save his life (if it could have been converted to banishment) and minched [i.e. played down] their principles, and begged for a longer time, that he might be judged in Parliament: but finding there was no remedy, he put on more stayedness and resolution after his sentence' (*Historical Observes,* p. 44). There is no support either in the official records or any other source for Fountainhall's remarks about Cargill's behaviour. Patrick Walker records that an old minister who was

present at the trial had often stated 'that he admired the composedness and confidence of Mr Cargill'. A contemporary dispatch dated from London on 23 July states: 'The ministers mentioned in my last taken in Scotland are brought prisoners to Edinburgh and have been examined before the Council, before whom they behaved with great boldness and resolution, rather justifying the action they are charged with than otherwise' (*Calendar of State Papers*, 1680-1, p. 371).

6.   Boig had apparently sided with Robert Hamilton in the disagreement with M'Ward over Robert Fleming (*Six Saints of the Covenant*, vol. I, pp. 280-5). His relations with Smith and Thomas Douglas, both of whom had supported M'Ward, cooled as a result, and according to Patrick Walker, the continuance of the controversy after their return from Holland led directly to Douglas's withdrawal to England (see chapter 9, note 8). It would seem that Cargill, by his close association with Smith, had also fallen out of favour with Boig, though Hamilton himself, who was foremost in the controversy, never expressed any criticism of Cargill on this issue. Despite the reconciliation Smith felt keenly the slight done to him by the withdrawal of Hamilton and the others from his fellowship and he made particular reference to it in his last testimony: 'I was withdrawn from by some, as having given offence to them by my protesting against their way in a particular, wherein I am sure as to the manner they were wrong: and though they had been right, it was not a ground to have made such a separation from me, much less from these who joined with me' (*Cloud of Witnesses*, 1714, p. 19).

7.   According to Patrick Walker, when the clerk of court was reading the indictment and had reached the words 'having cast off all fear of God', which were common form in criminal charges, Cargill caused him to stop and pointing to Mackenzie said, 'The man that has caused that paper to be drawn in that form has done it contrary to the light of his own conscience, for he knows that I have been a fearer of God from my infancy; but I say the man that took the Holy Bible in his hand and said that it would never be well with the land until that book was destroyed, with many other wicked expressions and actions in his life — I say he is the man that has cast off all fear of God.' Walker was quoting this incident from the recollection of 'an old reverend minister in the north of Scotland' who, he says, was witness to it. The official record, as is to be expected, is silent about the incident, but Fountainhall (*Historical Notices*, vol. I. p. 310) has a passage which may support its accuracy. At the subsequent meeting of Parliament, he records, 'There was an accusation surmised against the king's advocate, for saying at the trial of Mr Donald Cargill on the 26 of July last, that the permitting the common people to read the Scriptures did more evil than good, which was a blasphemous popish error.' The issue of the complaint against Mackenzie is not recorded.

8.   Considerable uncertainty surrounds this incident. It is not mentioned anywhere in the official records, and the only evidence of it is derived from Patrick Walker's narrative (*Six Saints of the Covenant*, vol. II, p. 58). Since, however, the Privy Council Register does not give anything like a full account of the Council's proceedings, but only their main acts and

resolutions, the absence of a record of the incident from the register is not proof that it did not take place. Indeed, the record of Cargill's two examinations before the Council is not included in the register at all but is preserved in the records of the Justiciary Court.

Walker says that the motion was brought ostensibly out of consideration for Cargill's age and because 'he had done all the ill he would do'. He also asserts that the movers were strongly influenced by the fulfilment of Cargill's prediction against Rothes, now approaching death. If such a motion was made it was obviously brought after sentence on Cargill had been passed, and so must either have been debated fairly late on the 26th (the day of the trial) or at the latest on the morning of the 27th (the day fixed for the execution). The Privy Council register does record a meeting at Holyroodhouse on the 26th, though without mentioning the incident.

According to Walker, the motion was defeated by the contrary vote of the Earl of Argyll, who remarked, 'Let him go to the gallows, and die like a traitor.' This, in Walker's words, 'cast the votes upon him to die'. The register shows that Argyll was present at the meeting on 26 July, but as an ordinary member of the Council. He was not in a position therefore to exercise a casting or deciding vote, as Walker's words have sometimes been taken to mean. The probability is rather that, if such a vote took place, it was defeated by a simple majority — perhaps of one — with Argyll, contrary to expectation, joining those voting against. Argyll had earlier shown some reluctance to follow the Council in some of their more extreme acts of repression and this could well explain why his action on this occasion was singled out for comment.

Argyll himself was soon to fall out of favour with the government he had so long supported. Shortly afterwards he declined to take the oath required by the Test Act passed by the ensuing Parliament and was tried and convicted for treason. He escaped from imprisonment the following December and made his way to England. Walker tells how he was conducted by a friend, William Veitch, to the home of a Mr and Mrs Bittlestone near Newcastle, where several refugees from Scotland had previously found shelter. From the sequel, it seems very probable that this was the very house where Cargill himself had lodged during his stay in England at the beginning of the year. Argyll's hosts, who were unaware of his identity, had heard of his escape from prison. Both Veitch and Bittlestone expressed their satisfaction at the news, but Mrs Bittlestone was less enthusiastic. Argyll, she pointed out, had been a member of the Privy Council for the past eighteen years, 'where many a wicked thing has been acted and done; but above all, it was his wicked vote that took away the life of our worthy dear friend, singular Mr Cargill; and I am sure his blood may lie heavy on him now'. Argyll 'made no reply'.

Argyll had good cause to remember his landlady's remark. His notorious vote was almost certainly a major factor against him in recruiting support for his later rebellion against the government in 1685 and, again according to Walker, it lay heavy upon his conscience to the end. Remarking one day on the failure of his enterprise he said, 'But all that does not trouble me so much, as that unhappy wicked vote I gave against that good man and minister, Mr Cargill; and now I am persuaded I'll die a violent death in that same spot where he died.' Argyll was duly executed at the Mercat Cross of Edinburgh on 30 June 1685. 'Some say', adds Walker, 'that he spoke of that vote to some friends that morning before he died, that above all things in his life, that lay heaviest upon him.'

Walker, as is his wont, asserts that the truth of his account can be attested by several still alive when he wrote, from whom he appears to have heard it at first hand. Certainly the circumstantial evidence which he presents seems strong and is not lightly to be discarded. The balance of view therefore is that some such motion as Walker records was brought forward in the Council; that it was defeated by a narrow margin; and that Argyll, for reasons which he afterwards regretted, was among those who opposed it. Beyond that it would be fruitless to speculate, though the subject could well repay continuing research.

9. There is an obvious inconsistency between the '*near* thirty years' of this statement and Cargill's assertion in his last speech that 'These thirty years *and more* I have been at peace with God, and was never shaken loose of it.' The latter version is without doubt the correct one, for clearly Cargill had undergone his momentous spiritual experience some considerable time before July 1651, when he was within a year of completing his divinity training. The discrepancy can doubtless be accounted for by the straitened circumstances in which Cargill was obliged to prepare his final testimony. Curiously, however, the two accounts of his experience preserved by Robert Wodrow, the historian, are similarly inconsistent and imprecise. In the one (*Life of James Wodrow*, pp. 160-2) Cargill is said to have told Wodrow's father, again in July 1681, that his experience took place 'about twenty-five years ago'. In the other, however (*Analecta*, vol. I, p. 69) Wodrow recalls his father as having told him that it was 'a long time, some twenty or thirty years before his [Cargill's] death, or more, he does not mind'.

10. According to Gabriel Semple, who was brought into the Canongate Tolbooth on the day that Cargill was executed, Cargill had time for one final act of charity before his death. In his unpublished memoirs Semple records: 'Mr Cargill, a worthy minister, was hanged that day, and the goodman of the Tolbooth offered me his gown he left there for the prisoners; this I refused, being unwilling to carry upon my body the remembrance of the death of that worthy man, the impression whereof was sufficiently upon my mind without that object.'

11. The Bible is preserved in the library of the University of St Andrews. Its authenticity has been confirmed by Dr Featherston Cargill, the family genealogist, who presented it to the university in 1930.

12. The rescinding of Cargill's forfeiture was successfully pleaded fifty years later by his grandnephew Lawrence, of Barnsley in Yorkshire, as a reason for restoring the estate of Hatton to the Cargill family.

Epilogue

1. It is interesting to note the respect in which Cargill's memory was held, even by such men as James Russel and Patrick Grant, who quarrelled

violently with the United Societies in the years after Cargill's death. In a paper which Russel and Grant drew up in 1684, in which they vehemently attacked the societies in general and Robert Hamilton in particular, they referred to Cargill as 'that shining light, and faithful servant of Jesus Christ, and never-to-be-forgotten martyr'. This was despite the fact, as alleged by the societies in their answer to the paper, that in a conference with Russel some years earlier Cargill had expressed his condemnation of Russel's 'great and sinful presumption' in publishing opinions on the rights of the civil magistrate which were contrary to the teaching of the Westminster Confession. The reference is no doubt to the paper which Russel affixed to the church door of Kettle in Fife on 3 April 1681, in which he renounced allegiance to the king on the grounds of his tyranny and breach of the Covenants.

2.   Testimony of James Stuart, *Cloud of Witnesses*, 1714, p. 146.

3.   *Cloud of Witnesses*, 1714, pp. 260-1. Hamilton's tribute has often been quoted. Like Blackader's description, however, (chapter 6, note 1), it is not original, but has been substantially edited by the compilers before publication (see also Appendix II). The extent of the editing may be gauged from a comparison with Hamilton's original manuscript, in which the same passage runs less elegantly as follows: 'First, he was of a holy and pious practice, kind-affectioned and tender-hearted towards all he judged godly; second, sober in diet, for instance being asked by one why he made so little use of the creature it was answered, "These several years I never rose from meat but could have eaten as much as when I sat down." He said it is well won that is won off the flesh. Third, charitable to the poor and hater of covetousness: a frequent visitor of the sick, still loving to be retired, but when he was about his Master's work, in which he was diligent, still watching for an opportunity to edify, always dropping that which might minister grace to the hearers, with a convincing countenance, almost continually sighing with deep sighs; being interrogate "Why sigh you so far?" he answered, "My sighing comes before I eat." [The reference here is to Job 3:24.] Fourthly he continued preaching in season (as is known to you all) and out of season without alteration in his practice both while he was in his kirk and when he was outed.' Hamilton adds a passage not included by the editors of the *Cloud:* 'Fifthly, he embracing the ministry which was [blank] of March 1655 to the day that he was crowned with martyrdom at the Cross of Edr. the 27 of July 1681 that he was still the same and so finished his course with joy to the conviction of the enemies themselves and the comfort, consolation and confirmation of the Lord's people over all their sorrows for his absence and removal of such a shining light as he was.'

4.   Cf. James Walker, *The Theology and Theologians of Scotland*, 1888, pp. 99-101. Durham puts the point forcefully: 'It is the duty of all Christians, especially of ministers of the gospel, to endeavour the preserving of unity, and the preventing of division . . . never did men run to quench fire in a city, lest all should be destroyed, with more diligence than men ought to bestir themselves to quench this in the church; never did mariners use more speed to stop a leak in a ship, lest all should be drowned, than ministers especially, and all Christian men, should haste to stop this

beginning of the breaking-in of these waters of strife, lest thereby the whole church be overwhelmed . . . what length may warrantably be gone, even to the utmost border of duty, men ought to go for this end; so that nothing ought to be a stop or march in condescension, but this, "I cannot do this and sin against God"; otherwise one ought to be all things to others' (*A Treatise Concerning Scandal,* 1680 ed., pp. 288, 298).

Appendix I

1. Howie has been criticized, unfairly, for presuming to put the sermons of the field-preachers into a more modern dress (cf. Herkless, *Richard Cameron,* 1896, p. 109; Thomson, *Cloud of Witnesses,* 1871 ed. p. 496). But Howie was no mere antiquarian: great as was his interest in the past, his aim was to preserve the spirit, rather than the letter, of his worthies' sermons. A comparison between Howie's revisions and the originals shows that in no case has he significantly altered the substance of the message. Often the changes are minor and involve the substitution of English words for the more homely Scots expressions of the original. Howie was conscious that the sophisticated taste of his age would look askance at productions couched in the popular dialect, and he was motivated as much by a desire to preserve his worthies' reputation as by the need to make their sermons intelligible to his contemporaries.

2. Thomas Cartwright (1535-1603), English Puritan divine.

3. Thomas Stapleton (1535-98), English Catholic controversialist.

4. Johann Gerhard (1582-1637), German Lutheran theologian.

5. One of the few original Scots expressions remaining in Howie's edited version. The meaning here is 'smart', 'presentable'.

Appendix III

1. The cairn was erected by public subscription in the mid-1950s, and was unveiled on 28 September 1958. Its inscription ('Donald Cargill, Covenanter, Born Here c. 1610, Martyred 1681') reflects the local tradition connecting Hatton with Cargill's birthplace, but as has been shown (chapter 1, note 3) both this and the date are certainly incorrect. The memorial tablet, which is set into the west wall of the church, was dedicated on 23 July 1922. It bears the tasteful inscription: 'To the glory of God, and in memory of Donald Cargill, of Hatton of Rattray, minister of the Barony Church, Glasgow, a steadfast Covenanter and fearless and faithful preacher of the Gospel, who serenely suffered martyrdom at the Cross of Edinburgh on the 27th day of July, 1681. Matt. xxiv., 12-13.' The Scripture quotation is choice and provides a fitting epitaph: 'And because iniquity shall abound, the love of many shall wax cold. But he that shall endure to the end, the same shall be saved.'

2. Possibly a Scots term meaning a nest of hornets.

Index